Learning Web Application Development

Semmy Purewal

Beijing · Cambridge · Farnham · Köln · Sebastopol · Tokyo

Learning Web Application Development

by Semmy Purewal

Copyright © 2014 Semmy Purewal. All rights reserved.

Printed in the United States of America.

Published by O'Reilly Media, Inc., 1005 Gravenstein Highway North, Sebastopol, CA 95472.

O'Reilly books may be purchased for educational, business, or sales promotional use. Online editions are also available for most titles (*http://safaribooksonline.com*). For more information, contact our corporate/institutional sales department: 800-998-9938 or *corporate@oreilly.com*.

Editors: Simon St. Laurent and Meghan Blanchette	**Indexer:** Judy McConville
Production Editor: Kara Ebrahim	**Cover Designer:** Randy Comer
Copyeditor: Kim Cofer	**Interior Designer:** David Futato
Proofreader: Kiel Van Horn	**Illustrator:** Rebecca Demarest

February 2014:   First Edition

Revision History for the First Edition:

2014-02-10:   First release

2014-08-01:   Second release

See *http://oreilly.com/catalog/errata.csp?isbn=9781449370190* for release details.

ISBN: 978-1-449-37019-0

[LSI]

To my parents.

Thanks for all of your support and encouragement over the years!

Table of Contents

Preface

In early 2008, after about six years of grad school and teaching part-time, I found myself hoping to land a job as a full-time computer science professor. It didn't take me long to realize that professor jobs are really hard to come by, and obtaining a good one has almost as much to do with luck as it has to do with anything else. So I did what any self-respecting academic does when faced with a scary academic job market: I decided to make myself employable by learning how to develop web applications.

This may sound a little strange. After all, I had been studying computer science for about nine years at that point, and had been teaching students how to develop software for about six years. Shouldn't I have *already known* how to build web applications? It turns out that there's a pretty large gap between practical, everyday software engineering and programming as taught by computer science departments at colleges and universities. In fact, my knowledge of web development was limited to HTML and a little CSS that I had taught myself at the time.

Fortunately, I had several friends who were actively working in the web development world, and most of them seemed to be talking about a (relatively) new framework called Ruby on Rails. It seemed like a good place to focus my efforts. So I purchased several books on the topic and started reading online tutorials to get up to speed.

And after a couple months of really trying to get it, I nearly gave up.

Why? Because most of the books and tutorials started out with the assumption that I had already been developing web apps for years! And even though I had a pretty solid background in computer programming, I found all of the material extremely terse and difficult to follow. For example, it turns out you can take an awful lot of computer science classes without ever coming across the Model-View-Controller design pattern, and some of the books assumed you understood that in the first chapter!

Nevertheless, I managed to learn enough about web app development to get a few consulting gigs to support me until I managed to land a professor job. And through that, I realized I enjoyed the practical aspects of the field so much that I continued consulting outside of teaching.

After a few years of doing both, I was offered the opportunity to teach my first class in Web Application Development at the University of North Carolina at Asheville. My initial inclination was to *start* with Ruby on Rails, but when I started reading the latest books and tutorials, I realized that they hadn't improved much over the years. This isn't to say that they aren't good resources for people who already have a background in the basics, it's just that they didn't seem suitable for the students I was teaching.

Sadly, but not surprisingly, the academic books on web development are far worse! Many of them contain outdated concepts and idioms, and don't cover the topics in a way that make platforms like Ruby on Rails more accessible. I even reviewed one book that was updated in 2011 and still used table-based layouts and the <font> tag!

I didn't have much of a choice but to develop my course from scratch, creating all the material myself. I had done a little work in some consulting gigs with Node.js (server-side JavaScript) at the time, so I thought it would be interesting to try to teach a course that covered the same language on the client and server. Furthermore, I made it my goal to give the students enough background to launch into the self-study of Ruby on Rails if they decided to continue.

This book consists largely of the material that I created while I was teaching this course at UNCA. It shows how to build a basic database-backed web application from scratch using JavaScript. This includes a basic web-development workflow (using a text editor and version control), the basics of client-side technologies (HTML, CSS, jQuery, Java-Script), the basics of server-side technologies (Node.js, HTTP, Databases), the basics of cloud deployment (Cloud Foundry), and some essential good code practices (functions, MVC, DRY). Along the way we'll get to explore some of the fundamentals of the Java-Script language, how to program using arrays and objects, and the mental models that come along with this type of software development.

Technology Choices

For version control, I picked Git, because—well—it's Git and it's awesome. Plus, it gave my students the opportunity to learn to use GitHub, which is becoming immensely popular. Although I don't cover GitHub in this book, it's pretty easy to pick up once you get the hang of Git.

I decided to use jQuery on the client because it's still relatively popular and I enjoy working with it. I didn't use any other frameworks on the client, although I do mention Twitter Bootstrap and Zurb Foundation in Chapter 3. I chose to stay away from modern client-side frameworks like Backbone or Ember, because I think they are confusing for people who are just starting out. Like Rails, however, you should be able to easily dive into them after reading this book.

On the server-side, I chose Express because it's (relatively) lightweight and unopinionated. I decided against covering client- and server-side templating, because I think it's essential to learn to do things by hand first.

I decided against relational databases because it seemed like I couldn't give a meaningful overview of the topic in the time I allotted to that aspect of the course. Instead, I chose MongoDB because it is widely used in the Node.js community and uses JavaScript as a query language. I also just happen to really like Redis so I provided coverage of that as well.

I selected Cloud Foundry as the deployment platform because it was the only one of the three that I considered (including Heroku and Nodejitsu) that offered a free trial and didn't require a credit card to set up external services. That said, the differences between the platforms aren't huge, and going from one to another shouldn't be too hard.

Is This Book for You?

This book is not designed to make you a "ninja" or a "rock star" or even a particularly good computer programmer. It won't prepare you for immediate employment, nor can I promise that it will show you "the right way" to do things.

On the other hand, it will give you a solid foundation in the essential topics that you'll need in order to understand how the pieces of a modern web app fit together, and it will provide a launching point to further study on the topic. If you work your way through this book, you'll know everything that I wish I had known when I was first starting out with Rails.

You'll get the most out of this book if you have a little experience programming and no previous experience with web development. At minimum, you probably should have seen basic programming constructs like if-else statements, loops, variables, and data types. That said, I won't assume that you have any experience with object-oriented programming, nor any particular programming language. You can obtain the necessary background by following tutorials on Khan Academy (*https://www.khanacade my.org/*) or Code Academy (*http://www.codecademy.com/*), or by taking a programming course at your local community college.

In addition to being used for self-study, I hope that this book can serve as a textbook for community classes in web application development, or perhaps a one-semester (14-week) college-level course.

Learning with This Book

Developing web applications is definitely a skill that you'll need to learn by doing. With that in mind, I've written this book to be read actively. What this means is that you'll get the most out of it if you're sitting at a computer while reading it, and if you actually type in all the examples.

Of course, this particular approach is fraught with peril—there is a danger that the code examples will not work if you don't type them exactly as they appear. To alleviate that risk, I've created a GitHub repository with all of the examples in this book in working order. You can view them on the Web at *http://www.github.com/semmypurewal/Learning WebAppDev*. Because the full examples live there, I try to avoid redundantly including full code listings throughout.

In addition, I leave big portions of the projects open-ended. When I do that, it's because I want you to try to finish them on your own. I encourage you to do that before looking at the full examples I've posted online. Every chapter concludes with a set of practice problems and pointers to more information, so I encourage you to complete those as well.

Teaching with This Book

When I teach this material in a 14-week class, I usually spend about 2–3 weeks on the material in the first three chapters, and 3–4 weeks on the material in the last three. That means I spend the majority of the time on the middle three chapters, which cover Java-Script programming, jQuery, AJAX, and Node.js. The students that I teach seem to struggle the most with arrays and objects, so I spend extra time on those because I think they are so essential to computer programming in general.

I definitely cover things in a more *computer-sciency* way than most books on this topic, so it might be a good fit for a course in computer science programs. Specifically, I cover mental models such as trees and hierarchical systems, and I try to emphasize functional programming approaches where they make sense (although I try not to draw attention to this in the narrative). If you find yourself teaching in a computer science program, you might choose to focus more clearly on these aspects of the material.

I currently have no plans to post solutions to the practice problems (although that may change if I get a lot of requests), so you can feel comfortable assigning them as homework and out-of-class projects.

Where to Go for Help

As mentioned before, there is a GitHub repository (*http://www.github.com/semmypur ewal/LearningWebAppDev*) with all of the code samples contained in this book. In addition, you can check out *http://learningwebappdev.com* for errata and other updates as they are necessary.

I also try to stay pretty accessible and would be glad to help if you need it. Feel free to tweet at me (*@semmypurewal*) with quick questions/comments, or email me any time (*me@semmy.me*) with longer questions. I also encourage you to use the "issues" feature of our GitHub repository to ask questions. I'll do my best to respond as quickly as I can.

General Comments on Code

I've done my best to stay idiomatic and clear wherever possible. That said, those two goals are sometimes in conflict with each other. Therefore, there are times when I didn't do things "the right way" for pedagogical reasons. I hope that those places are self-evident to experienced developers, and that they don't cause any grief for novice developers in the long run.

All of the code should work fine in modern web browsers, and I've tested everything in Chrome. Obviously, I can't guarantee things will work in older versions of Internet Explorer. Please let me know if you find any browser compatibility issues in the Internet Explorer 10+ or modern versions of any other browser.

For the most part, I've followed idiomatic JavaScript, but there are a few places I've strayed. For example, I preferred double quotes instead of single quotes for strings, primarily because I've been working under the assumption that students may be coming from a Java/C++ background. I choose to use quotes around property names in object literals so that JSON doesn't look too different from JavaScript objects. I also use $ as the first character in variables that are pointing to jQuery objects. I find that it maintains clarity and makes the code a little more readable for novices.

Conventions Used in This Book

The following typographical conventions are used in this book:

Italic

Indicates new terms, URLs, email addresses, filenames, and file extensions.

`Constant width`

Used for program listings, as well as within paragraphs to refer to program elements such as variable or function names, databases, data types, environment variables, statements, and keywords.

`Constant width bold`

Shows commands or other text that should be typed literally by the user.

`Constant width italic`

Shows text that should be replaced with user-supplied values or by values determined by context.

This element signifies a tip or suggestion.

 This element signifies a general note.

 This element indicates a warning or caution.

Using Code Examples

Supplemental material (code examples, exercises, etc.) is available for download at *http://www.github.com/semmypurewal/LearningWebAppDev*.

This book is here to help you get your job done. In general, if example code is offered with this book, you may use it in your programs and documentation. You do not need to contact us for permission unless you're reproducing a significant portion of the code. For example, writing a program that uses several chunks of code from this book does not require permission. Selling or distributing a CD-ROM of examples from O'Reilly books does require permission. Answering a question by citing this book and quoting example code does not require permission. Incorporating a significant amount of example code from this book into your product's documentation does require permission.

We appreciate, but do not require, attribution. An attribution usually includes the title, author, publisher, and ISBN. For example: "*Learning Web App Development* by Semmy Purewal (O'Reilly). Copyright 2014 Semmy Purewal, 978-1-449-37019-0."

If you feel your use of code examples falls outside fair use or the permission given above, feel free to contact us at *permissions@oreilly.com*.

Safari® Books Online

 *Safari Books Online* is an on-demand digital library that delivers expert content in both book and video form from the world's leading authors in technology and business.

Technology professionals, software developers, web designers, and business and creative professionals use Safari Books Online as their primary resource for research, problem solving, learning, and certification training.

Safari Books Online offers a range of product mixes and pricing programs for organizations, government agencies, and individuals. Subscribers have access to thousands of books, training videos, and prepublication manuscripts in one fully searchable database from publishers like O'Reilly Media, Prentice Hall Professional, Addison-Wesley Professional, Microsoft Press, Sams, Que, Peachpit Press, Focal Press, Cisco Press, John Wiley & Sons, Syngress, Morgan Kaufmann, IBM Redbooks, Packt, Adobe Press, FT Press, Apress, Manning, New Riders, McGraw-Hill, Jones & Bartlett, Course Technology, and dozens more. For more information about Safari Books Online, please visit us online.

How to Contact Us

Please address comments and questions concerning this book to the publisher:

O'Reilly Media, Inc.
1005 Gravenstein Highway North
Sebastopol, CA 95472
800-998-9938 (in the United States or Canada)
707-829-0515 (international or local)
707-829-0104 (fax)

We have a web page for this book, where we list errata, examples, and any additional information. You can access this page at *http://oreil.ly/learning-web-app*.

To comment or ask technical questions about this book, send email to *bookquestions@oreilly.com*.

For more information about our books, courses, conferences, and news, see our website at *http://www.oreilly.com*.

Find us on Facebook: *http://facebook.com/oreilly*

Follow us on Twitter: *http://twitter.com/oreillymedia*

Watch us on YouTube: *http://www.youtube.com/oreillymedia*

Acknowledgments

Thanks to the nice folks in the Computer Science department at UNC Asheville for letting me teach this class twice. And, of course, thanks to the students who took the class for being patient with me as this material evolved.

Thanks to my editor Meg Blanchette for doing her best to keep me on track and—of course—her constant patience with missed deadlines. I'm going to miss our weekly email exchanges!

Thanks to Simon St. Laurent for offering lots of advice early on and helping me get the idea approved by O'Reilly.

Sylvan Kavanaugh and Mark Philips both did a very careful reading of every chapter and gave lots of very helpful feedback along the way. Emily Watson read the first four chapters and gave lots of thoughtful suggestions for improvements. Mike Wilson read the last four chapters and gave invaluable technical advice. I owe you all a debt of gratitude and hope I can repay the favor one day.

Bob Benites, Will Blasko, David Brown, Rebekah David, Andrea Fey, Eric Haughee, Bruce Hauman, John Maxwell, Susan Reiser, Ben Rosen, and Val Scarlata read various revisions of the material and provided helpful suggestions. I sincerely appreciate the time and effort they put in. You rock!

Despite the all-around-excellence of the reviewers and friends who looked at the material, it's nearly impossible to write a book like this without some technical errors, typos, and bad practices slipping through the cracks. I take full responsibility for all of them.

Errata Reporters

Several readers were kind enough to report errors in the first printing of the book. Thanks to all of the people who took the time to do so: Olusola Akapo, Micheal Beatty, David Boles, Matthew Brockway, Dan Candela, Gilbert Desport, Douglas Eichelberger, Stephen Fickas, James FitzGibbon, Michael Hennessy, Ken Hommel, Nick Litwin, Daniel Overton, Michael Rasmussen, and Marco Vaccari.

The Workflow

Creating web applications is a complicated task involving lots of moving parts and interacting components. In order to learn how to do it, we have to break down these parts into manageable chunks and try to understand how they all fit together. Surprisingly, it turns out that the component we interact with most often doesn't even involve code!

In this chapter, we'll explore the web application development workflow, which is the process that we use to build our applications. In doing so, we'll learn the basics of some of the tools that make it a manageable and (mostly) painless process.

These tools include a text editor, a version control system, and a web browser. We won't study any of these in depth, but we'll learn enough to get us started with client-side web programming. In Chapter 2, we'll actually see this workflow in action as we're studying HTML.

If you're familiar with these tools, you may want to scan the summary and the exercises at the end of the chapter and then move on.

Text Editors

The tool that you'll interact with most often is your text editor. This essential, and sometimes overlooked, piece of technology is really the most important tool in your toolbox, because it is the program that you use to interact with your code. Because your code forms the concrete building blocks of your application, it's really important that creating and modifying it is as easy as possible. In addition, you'll usually be editing several files simultaneously, so it's important that your text editor provide the ability to quickly navigate your filesystem.

In the past, you may have spent a good deal of time writing papers or editing text documents with programs like Microsoft Word or Google Docs. These are not the types of editors that we're talking about. These editors focus more on formatting text than making it easy to edit text. The text editor that we'll use has very few features that allow us to format text, but has an abundance of features that help us efficiently manipulate it.

At the other end of the spectrum are Integrated Development Environments (IDEs) like Eclipse, Visual Studio, and XCode. These products usually have features that make it easy to manipulate code, but also have features that are important in enterprise software development. We won't have the occasion to use any of those features in this book, so we're going to keep it simple.

So what kinds of text editors should we explore? Two primary categories of text editors are commonly used in modern web application development. The first are Graphical User Interface (GUI) editors. Because I'm assuming that you have some background in programming and computing, you've most likely experienced a Desktop GUI environment. Therefore, these editors should be relatively comfortable for you. They respond well to the mouse as an input device and they have familiar menus that allow you to interact with your filesystem as you would any other program. Examples of GUI text editors include TextMate, Sublime Text, and Coda.

The other category of text editors are terminal editors. These editors were designed before GUIs or mice even existed, so learning them can be challenging for people who are used to interacting with a computer via a GUI and a mouse. On the other hand, these editors can be much more efficient if you're willing to take the time to learn one of them. The most commonly used editors that fall into this category are Emacs (shown in Figure 1-1) and Vim (shown in Figure 1-2).

In this book, we'll focus on using a GUI text editor called Sublime Text, but I encourage everyone to get some experience in either Emacs or Vim. If you continue on your web application development journey, it's highly likely you'll meet another developer who uses one of these editors.

Installing Sublime Text

Sublime Text (or Sublime, for short) is a popular text editor with several features that make it great for web development. In addition, it has the advantage that it's cross-platform, which means it should work roughly the same whether you're using Windows, Linux, or Mac OS. It's not free, but you can download an evaluation copy for free and use it for as long as you like. If you do like the editor and find that you're using it a lot, I encourage you to purchase a license.

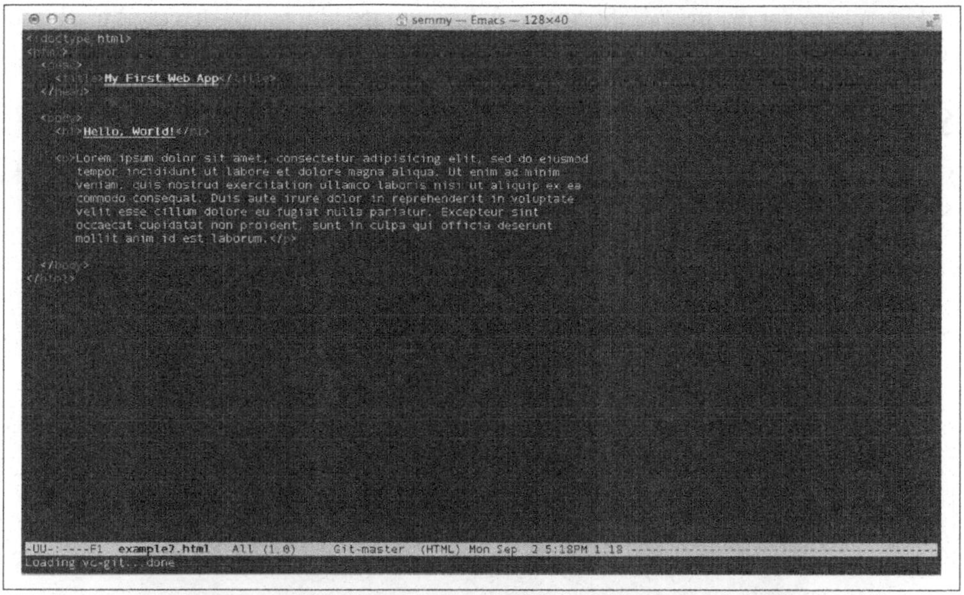

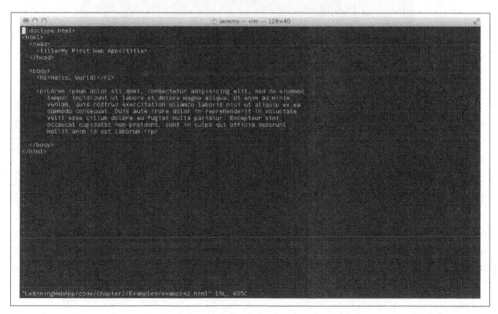

Figure 1-1. An HTML document opened in Emacs

Figure 1-2. An HTML document opened in Vim

To install Sublime, visit *http://www.sublimetext.com* and click the Download link at the top. There you'll find installers for all major platforms. Even though Sublime Text 3 is in beta testing (at the time of this writing), I encourage you to give it a try. I used it for all the examples and screenshots in this book.

Sublime Text Basics

Once you have Sublime installed and run it, you'll be presented with a screen that looks something like Figure 1-3.

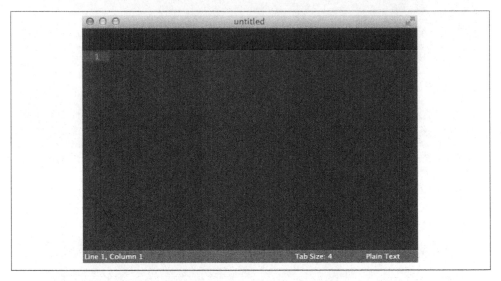

Figure 1-3. Sublime Text, after being opened for the first time

The first thing you'll want to do is create a new file. Do that by going to the File menu and clicking New. You can also do that by typing Ctrl-N in Windows and Linux or using Command-N in Mac OS. Now type `Hello World!` into the editor. The editor will look similar to Figure 1-4.

You can change the appearance of the Sublime environment by going to the Sublime Text menu and following Preferences → Color Scheme. Try out a few different color schemes and find one that is comfortable for your eyes. It's probably a good idea to spend some time exploring the theme options because you'll spend a lot of time looking at your text editor. Note that you can also change the font size from the Font submenu under Preferences to make the text more readable.

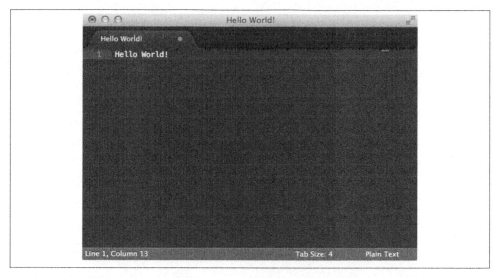

Figure 1-4. Sublime after a new file is opened and Hello World! is typed into the file

You probably noticed that Sublime changed the tab name from "untitled" to "Hello World!" as you typed. When you actually save, the default filename will be the text that appears in the tab name, but you'll probably want to change it so that it doesn't include any spaces. Once saved with a different name, the tab at the top will change to the actual filename. Notice that when you subsequently make any changes you'll see the X on the right side of the tab change to a green circle—this means you have unsaved changes.

After you've changed your theme and saved your file as *hello*, the editor will look similar to Figure 1-5.

 Because we'll be working from the command line, it's a good idea to avoid spaces or special characters in filenames. We'll occasionally save files using the underscore (_) character instead of a space, but try not to use any other nonnumeric or nonalphabetic characters.

We'll spend a lot of time editing code in Sublime, so we'll obviously want to make sure we're saving our changes from time to time. Because I expect that everyone has a little experience with code, I'll assume that you've seen the edit-save-edit process before. On the other hand, there's a related essential process that many new programmers don't have experience with, and that's called version control.

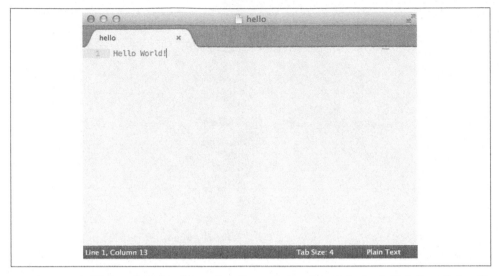

Figure 1-5. Sublime after the theme has been changed to Solarized (light) and the file has been saved as hello

Version Control

Imagine that you're writing a long piece of fiction with a word processor. You're periodically saving your work to avert disaster. But all of the sudden you reach a very important plot point in your story and you realize that there is a significant part of your protagonist's backstory that is missing. You decide to fill in some details, way back near the beginning of your story. So you go back to the beginning, but realize that there are two possibilities for the character. Because you don't have your story completely outlined, you decide to draft both possibilities to see where they go. So you copy your file into two places and save one as a file called *StoryA* and one as a file called *StoryB*. You draft out the two options of your story in each file.

Believe it or not, this happens with computer programs far more often than it happens with novels. In fact, as you continue on you'll find that a good portion of your coding time is spent doing something that is referred to as *exploratory coding*. This means that you're just trying to figure out what you have to do to make a particular feature work the way it's supposed to before you actually start coding it. Sometimes, the exploratory coding phase can spawn changes that span multiple lines in various code files of your application. Even beginning programmers will realize this sooner rather than later, and they will often implement a solution similar to the one just described. For example, beginners might copy their current code directory to another directory, change the name slightly, and continue on. If they realize that they've made a mistake, they can always revert back to the previous copy.

This is a rudimentary approach to *version control*. Version control is a process that allows you to keep labeled checkpoints in your code so you can always refer back to them (or even revert back to them) if it becomes necessary. In addition to that, version control is an essential tool for collaborating with other developers. We won't emphasize that as often in this book, but it's a good idea to keep it in mind.

Many professional version control tools are available and they all have their own set of features and nuances. Some common examples include Subversion, Mercurial, Perforce, and CVS. In the web development community, however, the most popular version control system is called Git.

Installing Git

Git has straightforward installers in both Mac OS and Windows. For Windows, we'll use the msysgit project, which is available on GitHub (*http://msysgit.github.io/*) as shown in Figure 1-6. The installers are still available on Google Code and are linked from the GitHub page. Once you download the installer, double-click it and follow the instructions to get Git on your system.

Figure 1-6. The msysgit home page

For Mac OS, I prefer using the Git OS X installer (*http://code.google.com/p/git-osx-installer*) shown in Figure 1-7. You simply download the prepackaged disk image, mount it, and then double-click the installer. At the time of this writing, the installer says that it is for Mac OS Snow Leopard (10.5), but it worked fine for me on my Mountain Lion (10.8) system.

Figure 1-7. The Git for OS X home page

If you're using Linux, you can install Git through your package management system.

Unix Command-Line Basics

There are graphical user interfaces to Git, but it's much more efficient to learn to use it through the command line. Before you learn to do that, however, you'll have to learn to navigate your filesystem using some basic Unix commands.

Like I mentioned before, I am assuming you have a background in computing and programming so you've most likely interacted with a desktop GUI environment. This means that you've had to use the desktop environment to explore the files and folders stored on your machine. You typically do this through a filesystem navigator such as Finder for Mac OS or Windows Explorer in Windows.

Navigating your computer's filesystem from the command line is almost the same as navigating it using your system's file browser. There are still files, and those files are organized into folders, but we refer to folders as *directories*. You can easily accomplish all the same tasks that you can accomplish in the file browser: you can move into a directory or out of a directory, see the files that are contained in a directory, and even open and edit files if you're familiar with Emacs or Vim. The only difference is that there is no continuous visual feedback from the GUI, nor are you able to interact via a mouse.

If you're in Windows, you'll do the following in the *Git Bash* prompt that you installed with the msysgit project described in the previous section. Git Bash is a program that simulates a Unix terminal in Windows and gives you access to Git commands. To fire up the Git Bash prompt, you'll navigate there via your Start menu. If you're running Mac OS, you'll use the Terminal program, which you can find in the *Utilities* directory of your *Applications* folder. If you're using Linux, it depends a bit on the particular flavor you're using, but there is usually an easily available Terminal program in your applications. The default Mac OS terminal window is shown in Figure 1-8.

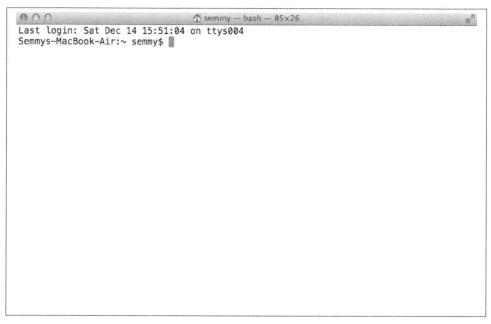

Figure 1-8. A default terminal window in Mac OS

Once you open the terminal, you'll be greeted with a command prompt. It may look different depending on whether you're using Windows or Mac OS, but it usually contains some information about your working environment. For instance, it may include your current directory, or maybe your username. In Mac OS, mine looks like this:

```
Last login: Tue May 14 15:23:59 on ttys002
hostname $ _
```

Where am I?

An important thing to keep in mind is that whenever you are at a terminal prompt, you are always in a directory. The first question you should ask yourself when presented with a command-line interface is "Which directory am I in?" There are two ways to answer this question from the command line. The first way is to use the pwd command, which stands for *print working directory*. The output will look something like this:

```
hostname $ pwd
/Users/semmy
```

Although I do use pwd on occasion, I definitely prefer to use the command ls, which roughly translates to *list the contents of the current directory*. This gives me more visual cues about where I am. In Mac OS, the output of ls looks something like this:

```
hostname $ ls
Desktop     Downloads  Movies  Pictures
Documents   Library    Music
```

So ls is similar to opening a Finder or Explorer window in your home folder. The result of this command clues me in that I'm in my home directory because I see all of its subdirectories printed to the screen. If I don't recognize the subdirectories contained in the directory, I'll use pwd to get more information.

Changing directories

The next thing that you'll want to do is navigate to a different directory than the one you're currently in. If you're in a GUI file browser, you can do this by simply double-clicking the current directory.

It's not any harder from the command line; you just have to remember the name of the command. It's cd, which stands for *change directory*. So if you want to go into your *Documents* folder, you simply type:

```
hostname $ cd Documents
```

And now if you want to get some visual feedback on where you are, you can use ls:

```
hostname $ ls
Projects
```

This tells you that there's one subdirectory in your *Documents* directory, and that subdirectory is called *Projects*. Note that you may not have a *Projects* directory in your *Documents* directory unless you've previously created one. You may also see other files or directories listed if you've used your *Documents* directory to store other things in the past. Now that you've changed directories, running pwd will tell you your new location:

```
hostname $ pwd
/Users/semmy/Documents
```

What happens if you want to go back to your home directory? In the GUI file browser, there is typically a back button that allows you to move to a new directory. In the terminal there is no such button. But you can still use the cd command with a minor change: use two periods (..) instead of a directory name to move back one directory:

```
hostname $ cd ..
hostname $ pwd
/Users/semmy
hostname $ ls
```

```
Desktop     Downloads  Movies   Pictures
Documents   Library    Music
```

Creating directories

Finally, you'll want to make a directory to store all of your projects for this book. To do this, you'll use the mkdir command, which stands for *make directory*:

```
hostname $ ls
Desktop     Downloads  Movies   Pictures
Documents   Library    Music
hostname $ mkdir Projects
hostname $ ls
Desktop     Downloads  Movies   Pictures
Documents   Library    Music    Projects
hostname $ cd Projects
hostname $ ls
hostname $ pwd
/Users/semmy/Projects
```

In this interaction with the terminal, you first look at the contents of your home directory to make sure you know where you are with the ls command. After that, you use mkdir to create the *Projects* directory. Then you use ls to confirm that the directory has been created. Next, you use cd to enter the *Projects* directory, and then ls to list the contents. Note that the directory is currently empty, so ls has no output. Last, but not least, you use pwd to confirm that you are actually in the *Projects* directory.

These four basic Unix commands are enough to get you started, but you'll learn more as we move forward. I've included a handy table at the end of this chapter that describes and summarizes them. It's a good idea to try to memorize them.

Filesystems and trees

Web development (and programming in general) is a very abstract art form. This roughly means that to do it effectively and efficiently, you'll need to improve your abstract thinking skills. A big part of thinking abstractly is being able to quickly attach mental models to new ideas and structures. And one of the best mental models that can be applied in a wide variety of situations is a tree diagram.

A tree diagram is simply a way of visualizing any kind of hierarchical structure. And because the Unix filesystem is a hierarchical structure, it's a good idea to start practicing our mental visualizations on it. For example, consider a directory called *Home* that contains three other directories: *Documents*, *Pictures*, and *Music*. Inside the *Pictures* directory are five images. Inside the *Documents* directory is another directory called *Projects*.

A tree diagram for this structure might look something like Figure 1-9.

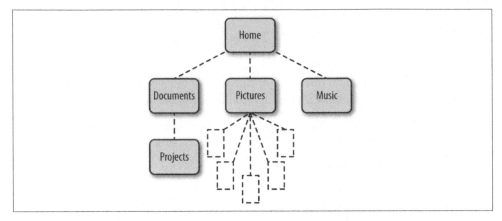

Figure 1-9. A tree diagram representing a file hierarchy

It's a good idea to keep this mental model in your head while you're navigating the filesystem. In fact, I would recommend adding an asterisk (or something similar) that denotes your current directory and have that move as you're moving through the filesystem.

More generally speaking, if you try to attach a tree diagram to any hierarchical structure you'll most likely find that it's easier to understand and analyze. Because a large part of being an effective programmer comes from the programmer's ability to quickly build mental models, it's a good idea to practice attaching these tree diagrams to real-world hierarchical systems whenever they make sense. We'll do that in a few instances throughout the rest of the book.

Git Basics

Now that we can navigate the command line, we're ready to learn how to keep our project under version control with Git.

Configuring Git for the first time

Like I mentioned before, Git is actually designed for large-scale collaboration among many programmers. Even though we're going to use it for our personal projects, it will need to be configured so that it can track our changes with some identifying information, specifically our name and email address. Open your terminal and type the following commands (changing my name and email address to yours, of course):

```
hostname $ git config --global user.name "Semmy Purewal"
hostname $ git config --global user.email "semmy@semmy.me"
```

We'll only need to do this once on our system! In other words, we don't need to do this every time we want to create a project that we're tracking with Git.

Now we're ready to start tracking a project with Git. We'll begin by navigating to our *Projects* folder if we're not already there:

```
hostname $ pwd
/Users/semmy
hostname $ cd Projects
hostname $ pwd
/Users/semmy/Projects
```

Next we'll create a directory called *Chapter1*, and we'll list the contents of the directory to confirm that it's there. Then we'll enter the directory:

```
hostname $ mkdir Chapter1
hostname $ ls
Chapter1
hostname $ cd Chapter1
hostname $ pwd
/Users/semmy/Projects/Chapter1
```

Initializing a Git repository

Now we can put the *Chapter1* directory under version control by initializing a Git repository with the `git init` command. Git will respond by telling us that it created an empty repository:

```
hostname $ pwd
/Users/semmy/Projects/Chapter1
hostname $ git init
Initialized empty Git repository in /Users/semmy/Projects/Chapter1/.git/
```

Now try typing the `ls` command again to see the files that Git has created in the directory, and you'll find there's still nothing there! That's not completely true—the *.git* directory is there, but we can't see it because files prepended by a dot (.) are considered hidden files. To solve this, we can use `ls` with the `-a` (all) flag turned on by typing the following:

```
hostname $ ls -a
.    ..    .git
```

This lists all of the directory contents, including the files prepended with a dot. You'll even see the current directory listed (which is a single dot) and the parent directory (which is the two dots).

If you're interested, you can list the contents of the *.git* directory and you'll see the filesystem that Git prepares for you:

```
hostname $ ls .git
HEAD        config        hooks    objects
branches    description   info     refs
```

We won't have the occasion to do anything in this directory, so we can safely ignore it for now. But we will have the opportunity to interact with hidden files again, so it's helpful to remember the `-a` flag on the `ls` command.

Determining the status of our repository

Let's open Sublime Text (if it's still open from the previous section, close it and reopen it). Next, open the directory that we've put under version control. To do this, we simply select the directory in Sublime's Open dialog box instead of a specific file. When you open an entire directory, a file navigation pane will open on the left side of the editor window—it should look similar to Figure 1-10.

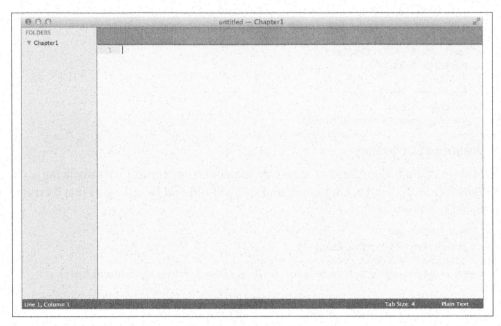

Figure 1-10. Sublime with the Chapter1 directory opened

To create a new file in the *Chapter1* directory, right-click (or Command-click on Mac OS) *Chapter1* in the file navigation pane and select New File from the context menu. This will open a new file as before, but when you save it, by default it will use the *Chapter1* directory. Let's save it as *index.html*.

Once it has been named, double-click it and add the line "Hello World!" to the top of the file, as shown in Figure 1-11.

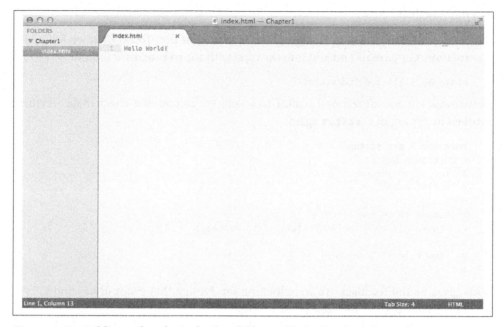

Figure 1-11. Sublime after the index.html file is added, edited, and saved

Let's see what has happened with our Git repo. Return to your terminal window and confirm you're in the correct directory:

```
hostname $ pwd
/Users/semmy/Projects/Chapter1
hostname $ ls
index.html
```

Now type **git status** and you'll see a response that looks something like this:

```
hostname $ git status
# On branch master
#
# Initial commit
#
# Untracked files:
#   (use "git add <file>..." to include in what will be committed)
#
#   index.html
```

There's a lot of information here. We're most interested in the section labeled Untracked files. Those are the files that are in our working directory, but are not currently under version control.

Notice that our *index.html* file is there, ready to be committed to our Git repository.

Our first commits!

We're interested in tracking changes in our *index.html* file. To do that, we follow the instructions Git gave us and add it to the repo with the `git add` command:

```
hostname $ git add index.html
```

Notice that Git doesn't respond at all. That's okay. We can double-check that everything worked by typing **git status** again:

```
hostname $ git status
# On branch master
#
# Initial commit
#
# Changes to be committed:
#   (use "git rm --cached <file>..." to unstage)
#
#	new file:	index.html
#
```

This gives us the feedback we were looking for. Notice that *index.html* is now listed under the `Changes to be committed` heading.

Once we've added the new files to the repository, we would like to commit the initial state of the repository. To do this, we use the `git commit` command along with the `-m` flag and a meaningful message about what has changed since the last commit. Our initial commit often looks something like this:

```
hostname $ git commit -m "Initial commit"
[master (root-commit) 147deb5] Initial commit
 1 file changed, 1 insertion(+)
 create mode 100644 index.html
```

This creates a snapshot of our project in time. We can always revert back to it later if something goes wrong down the road. If we now type `git status`, we'll see that *index.html* no longer appears because it is being tracked and no changes have been made. When we have no changes since our last commit, we say we have a "clean working directory":

```
hostname $ git status
# On branch master
nothing to commit (working directory clean)
```

 It's easy to forget to include the `-m` and a commit message when committing. If that happens, however, you'll most likely find yourself inside the Vim text editor (which is typically the default system editor). If that happens you can get out of it by hitting a colon (`:`) and then typing q! and pressing Enter to exit.

Next, let's modify *index.html* with a minor change. We'll add a second line that says "Goodbye World!" Go ahead and do that and save the file using the appropriate keyboard shortcut. Now let's see how `git status` responds to this change:

```
hostname $ git status
# On branch master
# Changes not staged for commit:
#   (use "git add <file>..." to update what will be committed)
#   (use "git checkout -- <file>..." to discard changes in working directory)
#
#   modified:   index.html
#
no changes added to commit (use "git add" and/or "git commit -a")
```

Notice that Git tells us that *index.html* has been modified, but that it's not staged for the next commit. To add our modifications to the repository, we have to first `git add` the modified file and then we have to `git commit` our changes. We may want to verify the add has correctly happened by typing **git status** before the commit. This interaction might look something like this:

```
hostname $ git add index.html
hostname $ git status
# On branch master
# Changes to be committed:
#   (use "git reset HEAD <file>..." to unstage)
#
#   modified:   index.html
#
hostname $ git commit -m "Add second line to index.html"
[master 1c808e2] Add second line to index.html
 1 file changed, 1 insertion(+)
```

Viewing the history of our repo

So now we've made two commits to our project and we can revert to those snapshots at any time. In "More Practice and Further Reading" on page 21, I'll link to a reference that will show you how to revert to a previous commit and start coding from there. But for now, there's one other command that may come in useful. We can look at our commit history by using `git log`:

```
hostname $ git log
commit 1c808e2752d824d815929cb7c170a04267416c04
Author: Semmy Purewal <semmy@semmy.me>
Date:   Thu May 23 10:36:47 2013 -0400

    Add second line to index.html

commit 147deb5dbb3c935525f351a1154b35cb5b2af824
Author: Semmy Purewal <semmy@semmy.me>
Date:   Thu May 23 10:35:43 2013 -0400
```

```
Initial commit
```

Like the four Unix commands that we learned in the previous section, it's really important to memorize these four Git commands. A handy chart in "Summary" on page 20 covers these commands.

Saving versus committing

In case it's confusing, I want to take a moment to clearly differentiate between saving a file (through your text editor) and actually committing a change. When you save a file, you actually overwrite the file on your computer's disk. That means that unless your text editor offers you some sort of built-in revision history, you can no longer access the old version of the file.

Committing to a Git repository allows you to keep track of all the changes you made since the last time you committed the file. This means that you can always go back to a previous version of the file if you find that you've made an unrecoverable mistake in your file's current state.

At this point, it probably looks as though Git stores your code as a linear sequence of commits. That makes sense right now because you've learned a subset of Git that allows you to create a repository of where every commit follows exactly one other commit. We refer to the first commit as a *parent* commit and the second commit as a *child* commit. A Git repository with four commits looks similar to Figure 1-12.

It's worth noting, however, that a commit is a series of instructions for taking your project to the next version. In other words, a Git commit doesn't actually store the entire contents of your repository in the way that you would if you were to copy a directory to another directory. Instead, it only stores what needs to be changed: for example, a commit might store information like "add a line with *Goodbye World*" instead of storing the entire file. So it's better to imagine a Git repository as a sequence of instructions. That's why we write our commit messages in the *present imperative* tense—you can think of a commit as a series of instructions for taking your project from one state to the next.

Why does all this matter? Actually, a Git repository may have a much more complex structure. A commit may have more than one child, and—in fact—more than one parent. Figure 1-13 shows an example of a more complex Git repository where both of those are true.

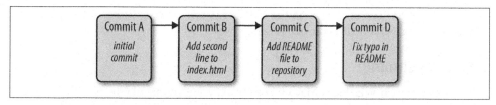

Figure 1-12. A Git repository with four commits

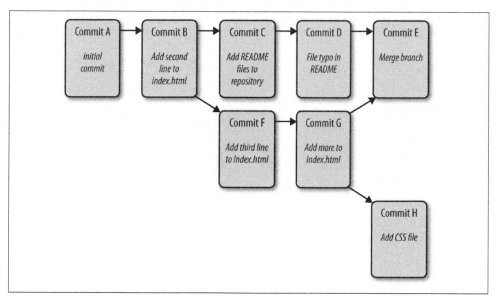

Figure 1-13. A more complex Git repository

Right now, we don't know any Git commands that will allow us to create a structure like this, but if you continue on in your web app development journey, you'll have to learn them eventually. The point is that this should motivate you to start picturing your Git repo in a more visual way so that when things *do* get complex, you don't get overwhelmed.

Browsers

The last tool that we'll interact with regularly is the web browser. Because we're learning to build applications that run in the web browser, it's essential that we learn how to effectively use our browser as a developer tool, and not just as a window into the Internet.

There are several excellent web browsers including Firefox, Safari, and Chrome. I would recommend becoming proficient in using the developer tools available in all of these browsers. But to keep everyone on the same page and to keep things simple, we'll use Google Chrome as our browser of choice.

Installing Chrome

Whether you're on Windows, Mac OS, or Linux, you can install Google Chrome easily by going to the Google Chrome web page (*http://www.google.com/chrome*). The installation process will, of course, vary, but the instructions are very clear. Once you install Chrome and run it for the first time, it should look something like Figure 1-14.

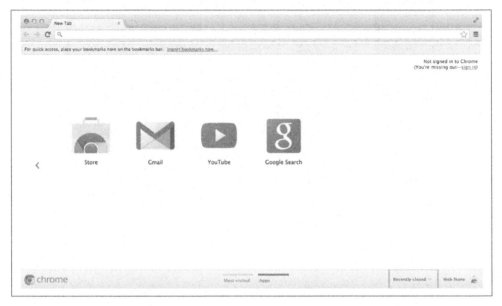

Figure 1-14. Default Chrome window

Summary

One of the most important aspects of web application development is getting used to an efficient and effective workflow. A modern workflow involves three important tools: a text editor, a version control system, and a web browser. Sublime Text is a popular, cross-platform text editor that is useful for editing source code. Git is a commonly used version control system that has a command-line interface. Chrome is an excellent web browser for web development.

Before moving on, you should have all of the previously described tools installed on your computer. You should also memorize the commands in Table 1-1 and Table 1-2, which allow you to navigate your filesystem and interact with Git from the command line.

Table 1-1. Unix commands

Command	Description
pwd	Print your current directory
ls	List the contents of your current directory
ls -a	List including all hidden files
cd [dir]	Change to the directory called [dir]
mkdir [dir]	Create a new directory called [dir]

Table 1-2. Git commands

Command	Description
git init	Initialize your repository
git status	Display the status of your repository
git add [file(s)]	Stage [files] for the next commit
git commit -m [msg]	Commit your staged files with message [msg]
git log	Show the commit history

More Practice and Further Reading

Memorization

In teaching and learning, *memorization* often has a negative connotation. In my mind, this view is mostly misguided, particularly when it relates to computer programming. If you follow the mindset that "well, I can just look that up when I need it," you'll spend more time looking up basic stuff than focusing on the more challenging things that arise. Imagine, for instance, how much more difficult long division would be if you didn't have your multiplication tables memorized!

With that in mind, I'm going to include a "Memorization" section at the end of the first few chapters that will cover the basic things that you should memorize before moving on to the next chapter. For this chapter, those things are all related to Git and the Unix command line. You should repeatedly do the following things until you can do them without looking at any documentation:

1. Create a new folder using the command line.
2. Enter that folder on the command line.
3. Create a text file in your text editor and save it as *index.html* in the new directory.
4. Initialize a Git repository from the command line.
5. Add and commit that file to the repository from the command line.

What's the best way to memorize this sequence of tasks? Simple: do it over and over again. I'll pile more onto this task throughout the next few chapters, so it's important to master these steps now.

Sublime Text

As I mentioned before, you'll be spending a lot of time in your text editor, so it's probably a good idea to move a little beyond the basics. The Sublime website has a great support page (*http://sublimetext.com/support*) that has links to documentation and videos that demonstrate advanced features of the editor. I suggest that you explore the page and see if you can level up your Sublime skills.

Emacs and Vim

Nearly every web developer will eventually have to edit a file on a remote server. This means that you won't be able to use a text editor that requires a GUI. Emacs and Vim are incredibly powerful editors that make doing so a breeze, but the learning curve on both is relatively steep. If you can find the time, it is really worthwhile to learn the basics of both editors, but it seems to me that Vim has become more common among web developers in recent years (full disclosure: I'm an Emacs user).

The GNU home page has an excellent overview of Emacs, including a tutorial for beginners (*http://www.gnu.org/software/emacs/tour*). O'Reilly also has several books on Emacs and Vim including *Learning the vi and Vim Editors* by Arnold Robbins, Elbert Hannah, and Linda Lamb and *Learning GNU Emacs* by Debra Cameron, James Elliott, Marc Loy, Eric S. Raymond, and Bill Rosenblatt.

It would be to your benefit to learn how to do the following things in both editors:

1. Open and exit the editor.
2. Open, edit, and save an existing file.
3. Open multiple files simultaneously.
4. Create a new file from within the editor and save it.
5. Search a file for a given word or phrase.
6. Cut and paste portions of text between two files.

If you take the time to do that, you'll get a pretty good sense of which editor you would prefer to spend more time with.

Unix Command Line

The Unix command line takes ages to master, but you've learned enough to get started. In my experience, it's far better to learn things in the context of solving specific problems, but there are a few other basic commands that I use regularly. Using a Google search, learn about some of these common commands: cp, mv, rm, rmdir, cat, and less. These will all come in handy at various times.

More About Git

Git is an extraordinarily powerful tool—we've only barely scratched the surface of its capabilities. Fortunately, Scott Chacon has written *Pro Git* (*http://git-scm.com/book*) (Apress, 2009), a great book that covers many aspects of Git in a lot of detail. The first two chapters cover several features that will help you move through this book more efficiently, including reverting to previously committed versions of your repository.

The third chapter of Chacon's book covers the concept of branching in detail. Branching is a bit beyond the scope of this book, but I hinted at it earlier. I encourage you to explore this topic because the ability to easily and quickly branch your repository is really one of the best features of Git.

GitHub

GitHub is an online service that will host your Git repositories. If you keep your code open source, it's free. If you want to create private Git repositories, GitHub's cheapest plan is about $7 per month. I encourage you to sign up for the free plan and explore storing Git repositories on GitHub.

GitHub's help page (*http://help.github.com*) walks you through setting up a GitHub account and connecting it to your Git repository. It also has a ton of useful information on both Git and GitHub in general. Use it to get started.

## CHAPTER 2

The Structure

Over the course of the next two chapters, we're going to get an overview of two relatively important client-side topics: HTML and CSS. Because there's no way that we can cover both of these in detail, these two chapters will be written primarily as a series of hands-on tutorials that will help you learn enough HTML and CSS to support the code examples in the remainder of the book. "More Practice and Further Reading" on page 49 will encourage you to explore other resources.

If you're already familiar with HTML and CSS, it's likely that you can comfortably move on to Chapter 4, which starts with client-side JavaScript. You may want to scan the chapters and read the summary at the end before doing so.

Hello, HTML!

HTML, which stands for HyperText Markup Language, is a technology that allows us to specify the structure of the visual elements (sometimes referred to as the *user interface*) of a web application. What do I mean when I say structure? Let's take a look at a simple example.

To get started, we'll use the command line to create a directory called *Chapter2* in our *Projects* directory. Recall that we'll use the `mkdir` command for that. Next, let's open that directory in Sublime Text using either the File menu or the shortcut keys. Create a new file called *hello.html* inside that directory. Type in the contents exactly as you see here:

```
<!doctype html>
<html>
  <head>
    <title>My First Web App</title>
  </head>

  <body>
    <h1>Hello, World!</h1>
```

```
    </body>
  </html>
```

Tags Versus Content

As you're typing, one of the things you may notice is that the document consists of two types of content. One type of content is normal text content like "My First Web App" and "Hello, World!" The other type of content, like <html> and <head>, is surrounded by angle brackets, and we refer to these elements as *tags*. Tags are a form of *metadata*, and this metadata is used to apply structure to the content of the page.

Fire up Chrome and open the file in your web browser using the Open File option in the File menu. You'll see something that looks similar to Figure 2-1.

 It's a good idea to get the hang of keyboard shortcuts because it will make your workflow more efficient. The keyboard shortcut for opening a file in Chrome is Command-O if you're in Mac OS. In Linux or Windows, it's Ctrl-O.

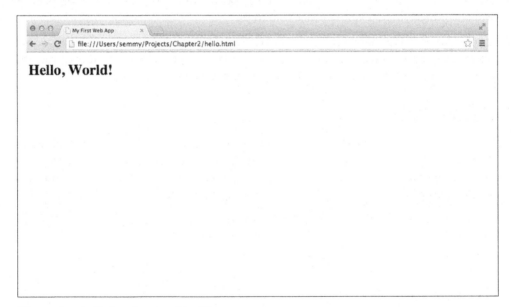

Figure 2-1. hello.html opened in Chrome

Notice that the tags don't appear, but the other content does. The "My First Web App" content appears as the title of the tab, while the "Hello, World" content appears in the body of the window.

`<p>` Is for Paragraph

Now, we'll make a minor modification by adding a paragraph with some *lorem ipsum* text, which is simply filler text that we can replace with actual copy later. You can cut and paste the text from the Wikipedia page for lorem ipsum (*http://en.wikipedia.org/ wiki/Lorem_ipsum*):

```
<!doctype html>
<html>
  <head>
    <title>My First Web App</title>
  </head>

  <body>
    <h1>Hello, World!</h1>

    <p>Lorem ipsum dolor sit amet, consectetur adipisicing elit, sed do eiusmod
       tempor incididunt ut labore et dolore magna aliqua. Ut enim ad minim
       veniam, quis nostrud exercitation ullamco laboris nisi ut aliquip ex ea
       commodo consequat. Duis aute irure dolor in reprehenderit in voluptate
       velit esse cillum dolore eu fugiat nulla pariatur. Excepteur sint
       occaecat cupidatat non proident, sunt in culpa qui officia deserunt
       mollit anim id est laborum.</p>

  </body>
</html>
```

Once we make the changes, we can save the changes to the document. Now we can go back to our browser and reload the page by clicking the circular arrow next to the address bar in Chrome. You should see the body of the browser update with the content, as illustrated in Figure 2-2.

 You can refresh this page with Ctrl-R in Windows and Command-R in Mac OS.

This will be our typical workflow when editing web pages. We'll open the file in our text editor, make some minor changes, and reload the web browser to see the changes.

Figure 2-2. Modified example1.html opened in Chrome

Comments

Comments are a convenient way to annotate our HTML. We start an HTML comment with <!-- and end a comment with -->. Here's a simple example that's built on the one in the previous section:

```
<!doctype html>
<html>
  <head>
    <title>Comment Example</title>
  </head>

  <body>
    <!-- This is the main heading -->
    <h1>Hello World!</h1>

    <!-- This is the main paragraph -->
    <p>I'm a main paragraph, most likely associated with the h1 tag since
       I'm so close to it!</p>
  </body>
</html>
```

Because computer programs are written for humans to read, it's always a good idea to annotate some of the more complicated code. You'll see examples of HTML comments peppered throughout the book and you'll likely run into commented HTML on the Web.

Headings and Anchors and Lists, Oh My!

Now that we've seen some examples of basic tags and comments, what other kinds of tags can we include in our markup?

First, we can generalize the <h1> tag by creating <h2>, <h3>, <h4>, <h5>, and <h6> tags. They represent different heading levels, and are usually reserved for important content on the page. The *most* important heading content should be contained in an <h1> tag, whereas heading content of lesser importance should appear in the others:

```
<!doctype html>
<html>
  <head>
    <title>Heading Tag Examples</title>
  </head>

  <body>
    <!-- This is the main header -->
    <h1>This is very important!</h1>

    <!--
     This is some content that might be associated with the
     important stuff
    -->
    <p>Important paragraph</p>

    <h2>This is a less important header</h2>
    <p>And here is some less important content</p>

  </body>
</html>
```

Another important tag in an HTML document is the <a> tag, which stands for *anchor* and is used to create links. The anchor tags are a unique characteristic of *hypertext* because they can link to other information, either on the current page or another web page altogether. To use anchor tags, we have to also include an HTML href *attribute*, which tells the browser where to go when a link is clicked. The href attribute goes inside the opening tag:

```
<!doctype html>
<html>
  <head>
    <title>Link Examples</title>
  </head>

  <body>
    <!--
     the href attribute tells us where to go when the anchor element
     is clicked
    -->
    <p>Here is a <a href="http://www.google.com">link</a> to Google!</p>
```

```
    <p>
      <a href="http://www.example.com">
        And this is a link that is a little longer
      </a>
    </p>
    <p>
      And here is a link to
      <a href="http://www.facebook.com">www.facebook.com</a>
    </p>
  </body>
</html>
```

When we open this page in the web browser, we'll get something that looks like Figure 2-3.

Figure 2-3. A page with links using anchor tags

All of the blue underlined text on the page is clickable, and when clicked it will take you to the page specified in the `href` attribute.

One problem with this example is that it's using paragraph elements to list content. Wouldn't it be better if we had a specific tag that represented a list? It turns out that we have two of them! The `<ol>` tag and the `<ul>` tag represent *ordered lists* and *unordered lists*, respectively. Inside these lists, we have `<li>` tags that represent *list items*. In the previous example, it doesn't look like the order of the links matters much, so perhaps an unordered list would be best:

```
<!doctype html>
<html>
  <head>
    <title>List Examples</title>
  </head>

  <body>
    <h1>List Examples!</h1>

    <!-- We'll wrap the links in an ul tag -->
    <ul>
      <li>
        Here is a <a href="http://www.google.com">link</a> to Google!
      </li>
      <li>
        <a href="http://www.example.com">
          And this is a link that is a little longer
        </a>
      </li>
      <li>
        And here is a link to
        <a href="http://www.facebook.com">
          www.facebook.com
        </a>
      </li>
    </ul>

    <!-- We can also create an ordered list tag -->

    <h3>How to make an ordered list</h3>
    <ol>
      <li>Start by opening your ol tag</li>
      <li>Then add several list items in li tags</li>
      <li>Close your ol tag</li>
    </ol>
  </body>
</html>
```

When we refresh our browser, it should look similar to Figure 2-4.

Figure 2-4. A page with an unordered and ordered list

Notice how both lists have bullets at the front of each list item, but the bullets for the ordered list are numeric.

Generalizations

We can generalize a few things from the first few examples that we've seen. The first is that all normal text content is wrapped in HTML tags.

Second, you'll probably notice that we've indented HTML tags that are contained in other HTML tags. The reason is that HTML is a hierarchical method of structuring documents. We use indentation as a visual cue to remind us where we are in the hierarchy. That's why the <head> tag and the <body> tag are indented within the <html> tag, and the <h1> tag and the <p> tags are also indented relative to the <body> tag. We've occasionally kept the links on the same line as the content, while other times we've broken the line. In HTML, white space doesn't matter in most cases.

Last, but not least, you'll see that as we are building an HTML document, we will add or modify a small amount of content, save our progress, then switch to the browser window and reload the page. Because you'll be doing this so often, it's a good idea to practice it a few times. To get started, add another few paragraphs of lorem ipsum text to the body of the document, and switch to the browser to reload the page.

Because you do it so often, it's helpful to learn the keyboard short-cuts to reload the page and switch between active windows in your environment. In Windows and most Linux environments, you can use Ctrl-Tab to switch between active windows and Ctrl-R to reload the page. In Mac OS, you use Command-Tab and Command-R.

The Document Object Model and Trees

HTML tags define a hierarchical structure called the *Document Object Model*, or DOM for short. The DOM is a way of representing objects that can be defined via HTML and then later interacted with via a scripting language like JavaScript. HTML tags define DOM *elements*, which are entities that live in the DOM.

We've already been writing our HTML in a way that helps us visualize the DOM. That's why we've been indenting our tags that are contained in other tags, because it gives us a sense of the hierarchy. Although that's helpful for our code, it doesn't always work as clearly as we might hope. For instance, consider the following HTML:

```
<!doctype html>
<html>
  <head>
    <title>Hello World!</title>
  </head>
  <body>
    <h1>Hello World!</h1>

    <div>
      <ol>
        <li>List Item</li>
        <li>List Item</li>
        <li>List Item</li>
      </ol>

      <p>This is a paragraph.</p>

      <p>This is a <span>second</span> paragraph.</p>

    </div>

    <ul>
      <li>List Item <span>1</span></li>
      <li>List Item <span>2</span></li>
      <li>List Item <span>3</span></li>
    </ul>
  </body>
</html>
```

This code includes several tags that we haven't seen, but it's not essential that you un-derstand their function yet. What is important is that you notice that even though this code is clearly indented, there are a few tags that are still not separated out on a different line. For example, the span elements are contained on the same line as the li elements. This is actually fine because the <span> tag contains a single character, but it doesn't illustrate the relationship as clearly as the indented structure does. So we need another way to think about this example.

In the previous chapter, we discussed using tree diagrams to create mental models of our computer's filesystem. It turns out that we can also use tree diagrams to create mental models of the DOM. This mental model will come in handy later when we're interacting with the DOM via JavaScript. As an example, we can use a tree diagram to represent the preceding code, as shown in Figure 2-5.

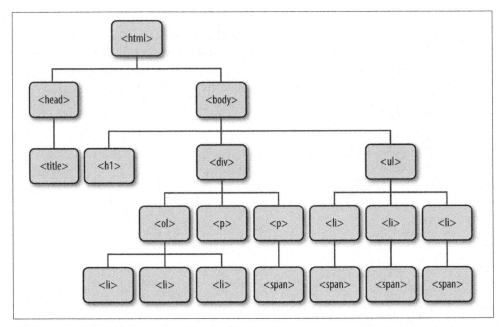

Figure 2-5. A tree representation of the preceding DOM

Note that this diagram creates a clear representation of the contents of the DOM. It also clarifies some of the relationships: we refer to DOM elements that are lower in the tree as *descendants* of DOM elements that are higher in the tree if there is a path that connects them. Immediate descendants are called *child elements*, and the element above a child element is referred to as its *parent element*.

In this example, all elements are descendants of the html element and the ul element is a descendant of the body element. The ul element is not a descendant of the the head element because there is no path starting at the head element and ending at the ul element without moving up in the hierarchy. The ul element has three children (each of the li elements) and each li element has a span element as a child.

We'll learn more about these relationships as we move forward, but for now it's good to get some practice thinking about the DOM in this way.

Using HTML Validation to Identify Problems

Like I said in the previous section, text content in our HTML document is typically enclosed by a pair of tags. An opening tag looks like <html> and a closing tag looks like </html>. The actual name of the tag is what specifies the type of the DOM element that it represents.

This can cause problems once our document gets very long. For instance, consider the following HTML document, which is a slight generalization of our previous example with some new tags:

```html
<!doctype html>
<html>
  <head>
    <title>My First Web App</title>
  </head>

  <body>
    <h1>Hello, World!</h1>

    <nav>
      <div>Login</div>
      <div>FAQ</div>
      <div>About Us</div>
    </nav>

    <p>Lorem ipsum dolor sit amet, consectetur adipisicing elit, sed do eiusmod
      tempor incididunt ut labore et dolore magna aliqua. Ut enim ad minim
      veniam, <span>quis nostrud exercitation</span> ullamco laboris nisi ut
      aliquip ex ea commodo consequat.</p>

    <p>Lorem ipsum dolor sit amet, consectetur adipisicing elit, sed do eiusmod
      tempor incididunt ut labore et dolore magna aliqua. Ut enim <span>ad
      minim veniam, quis nostrud exercitation ullamco laboris nisi ut aliquip
      ex ea commodo consequat. Duis aute irure dolor in reprehenderit in
      voluptate <span>velit esse cillum dolore eu fugiat</span> nulla
      pariatur.</p>

    <p>Lorem ipsum dolor sit amet, consectetur adipisicing elit, sed do eiusmod
      tempor incididunt ut labore et dolore magna aliqua.</p>

  </body>
</html>
```

This HTML document has an error, but if you open it in your browser you won't notice it. Spend a few moments looking and see if you can find it.

If you found it, congratulations—you have a great eye! If you didn't find it, don't feel bad. It's in the second paragraph. There's an opening <span> tag inside the second sentence, but it's never closed. Most people have a hard time finding such errors when they are first starting out. Fortunately, it turns out that there's a very nice automated way to find errors in HTML documents.

A *validation* program is a program that automatically checks to see if your code conforms to certain basic standards. If you've used a programming language like Java or C++ in the past, you may have worked with a compiler. If your code has an error, the compiler will tell you about it when you run your code through it. Languages like HTML are a bit looser in the sense that a browser will let you get away with a small number of errors. A validation program will catch these errors even when a browser won't.

But if the browser displays the page in exactly the same way with or without a closing <span> tag, why do we care? It turns out that the only way we can guarantee that it will *always* look the same in every browser is if our HTML is correct. That's why an HTML validator is a very handy tool.

We don't have to install any software to use an HTML validator. For now, we'll get started by visiting the W3C's Markup Validation Service home page (*http://validator.w3.org/*). At the time of this writing it looks something like Figure 2-6.

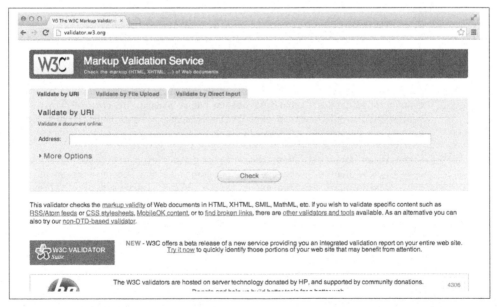

Figure 2-6. The W3C's Markup Validation Service home page

Notice that there's a tab that says "Validate by Direct Input." When we click it, we can cut and paste some of our HTML code into the text field that appears. Once we have some code pasted, we click the big Check button. We'll start by running our lorem ipsum example from earlier. If our HTML doesn't have any errors, we'll see something similar to Figure 2-7.

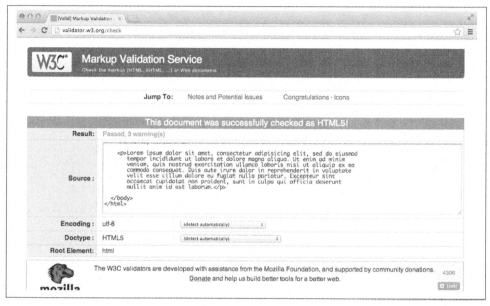

Figure 2-7. The W3C's HTML validator after being run on our lorem ipsum example

When validating your HTML, you'll most likely get three warnings even when you have no errors. The first of those warnings tells you that the validator is using the HTML5 conformance checker. Even though the HTML5 standard is relatively stable, there could be changes and this warning is just letting you know that.

The other two relate to character encoding, and can be ignored for now. If you're interested, one of the warnings links to a brief tutorial on character encoding that will show you how to specify a character encoding in your HTML document.

If the code does not pass validation, we'll see specific errors listed. For example, if we run the code that is missing a closing tag for the span element in the second paragraph, we'll see something similar to Figure 2-8.

Figure 2-8. The W3C's HTML validator after being run on our example with a mistake

If we scroll down a bit we can see the errors specifically listed. The validator isn't smart enough to tell us exactly where the problem is, but if we understand our code enough we should be able to find it. Figure 2-9 shows the validator's description of our errors.

It's always a good idea to periodically run our HTML code through the validator program to see if it is correct. Throughout the rest of this chapter, I'll periodically tell you to double-check your HTML with the validator, and you should probably do so.

Amazeriffic

For the rest of this section, we'll build an HTML splash page for a fake web app. We have a few goals in doing this. First, we'll practice the workflow that we learned in the previous chapter on an actual project. Second, we'll learn a few more important HTML tags and what they represent.

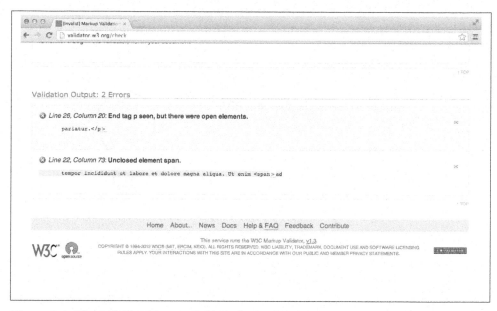

Figure 2-9. The W3C's HTML validator showing our errors

Identifying Structure

Our fake web app is called Amazeriffic, which is a portmanteau of the words *amazing* and *terrific*, and despite its silliness, it's no less ridiculous than many of the company names coming out of Silicon Valley these days. As a product, Amazerrific tracks and categorizes a set of tasks (you can think of it as a to-do list organizer). Later in the book, we'll actually work on implementing a project like this, but for now we're going to focus on the front page of the product until we get the hang of HTML. The page that we'll build looks something like Figure 2-10.

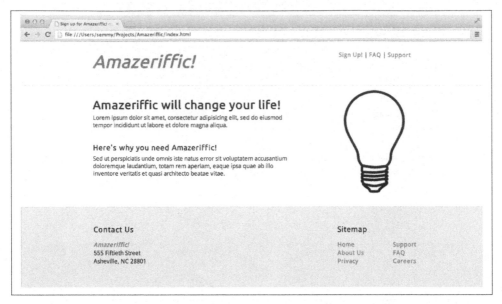

Figure 2-10. The Amazeriffic splash page that we'll build in this chapter and the next

Remember that HTML is all about the *structure* of a document. This means that even though we see numerous *stylistic* elements here (like the various fonts, the colors, and even the layout), it's best to ignore them for now because, for the most part, it should have no bearing on the HTML. For now we'll focus exclusively on the structure of the document.

Before we even sit down to code, it's helpful to see if we can identify the various parts of the structure. Using a pencil and some scratch paper, sketch this layout and label the structural elements as best as you can. If you have no idea what I'm talking about, then draw light boxes around bigger and smaller elements of the page and give them a descriptive name that describes their role in the document.

In Figure 2-11, we see an annotated version of the previous mockup with dashed lines drawn around the elements. We can easily see that some elements are contained inside other elements. This creates a relationship that specifies which elements will be descendants of other elements in the DOM, and this helps us roughly see what the HTML should look like.

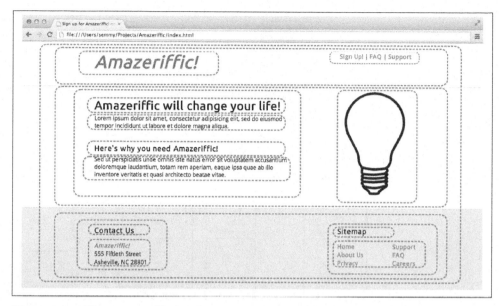

Figure 2-11. The Amazeriffic mockup, annotated to illustrate structure

Notice that I could go even further and label the circled parts. For example, it's relatively obvious where the header, the logo, the navigation links, the footer, the contact information, the sitemap, the main content, the subcontent, and the image are located. These all represent some structural element of the page.

Visualizing Structure with a Tree

Once we have identified all the structural elements, we'll need to examine how they fit together. To do this, we can create a tree diagram for the structure that will specify the contents of all the various elements. Figure 2-12 shows what a tree representation of this structure might look like.

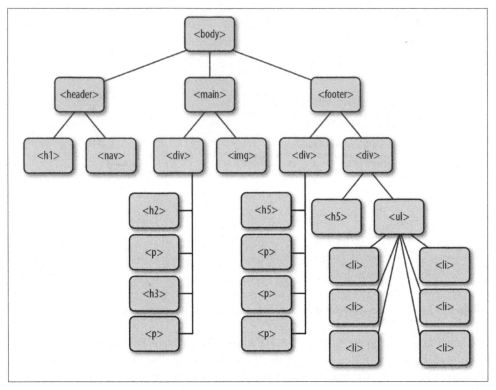

Figure 2-12. The Amazeriffic structure in the form of a tree diagram

Implementing the Structure with Our Workflow

Once we have a tree representation (either on paper or in our head), it's pretty easy to code up the HTML if we know the tags that represent these structural content elements. Because we haven't seen all the tags we'll need, I'll introduce them as we go along.

First, before we do anything, we're going to create a directory to store our project. If you followed the instructions in the first chapter, you already have a *Projects* directory in your home directory (if you're in Mac OS or Linux) or your *Documents* folder (if you're in Windows). We'll want to start by navigating to that directory from the Terminal application in Mac OS or from Git Bash in Windows. We'll use the cd command:

```
hostname $ cd Projects
```

Once we're in that directory, we'll create a directory for our Amazeriffic project. Which command do we use for that? You're right! We use the mkdir command:

```
hostname $ pwd
/Users/semmy/Projects
hostname $ mkdir Amazeriffic
```

Then we can get some visual feedback that the directory has actually been made by using the `ls` command, and finally, navigate to that directory with the `cd` command:

```
hostname $ ls
Amazeriffic
hostname $ cd Amazeriffic
```

At this point, we should be in our new project directory (we can confirm that by using the `pwd` command). The next major thing that we want to do is to put this directory under version control. We use `git init` to create a Git project:

```
hostname $ git init
Initialized empty Git repository in /Users/semmy/Projects/Amazeriffic/.git/
```

Now that we've created a directory and put it under version control, we're ready to start coding! Open up Sublime, and then open the Amazeriffic directory using the keyboard shortcuts described in the previous chapter.

Next, we can create a new HTML document by right-clicking the directory in the navigation pane and selecting New File. This will create an unnamed file that we can rename by simply typing *index.html*. After it is created and given a name, we can open the file by double-clicking it. Let's add "Hello World" to the document in order to get some content in it that we can view in the browser.

After having a basic document set up, we can fire up Chrome and open the page. If all goes well, we should see "Hello World" in the browser.

Next, we'll build a skeleton HTML document to get started. Replace the "Hello World" in your *index.html* file with the following:

```
<!doctype html>
<html>
  <head>
    <title>Amazeriffic</title>
  </head>

  <body>
    <h1>Amazeriffic</h1>
  </body>
</html>
```

Save the file and reload the browser. Once we do that, we should see something that looks similar to Figure 2-13.

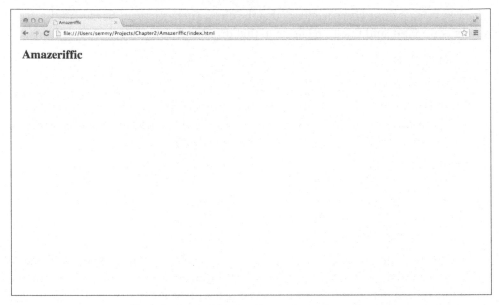

Figure 2-13. Amazeriffic, after we add a few basic elements to the page

Once that's done, we'll make our first commit. First, we'll check the status of our working directory. That's a good habit to get into, because visual feedback is always helpful. Among other things, this will tell us if we have inadvertently changed a file that we didn't intend to change. For now, though, we see that the only file that has changed is *index.html*.

```
hostname $ git status
# On branch master
#
# Initial commit
#
# Untracked files:
#   (use "git add <file>..." to include in what will be committed)
#
#   index.html
```

After that, we'll add and commit the *index.html* file.

```
hostname $ git add index.html
hostname $ git status
# On branch master
#
# Initial commit
#
# Changes to be committed:
#   (use "git rm --cached <file>..." to unstage)
#
#   new file:   index.html
```

```
hostname $ git commit -m "Add default index.html to repository."
[master (root-commit) fd60796] Add default index.html to the repository.
 1 file changed, 10 insertions(+)
 create mode 100644 index.html
```

Now we're ready to actually build the structure for the page. If we take a look at the tree, we'll see that we have a header, a main content section, and a footer. Each of these are children of the body element. It turns out that HTML has a tag representing all three of these sections of a document. The <header> and <footer> tags represent elements that appear at the top and the bottom of a document, and the <main> tag represents the main content area of a document:

```
<!doctype html>
<html>
  <head>
    <title>Amazeriffic</title>
  </head>

  <body>
    <header>
      <h1>Amazeriffic</h1>
    </header>

    <main>
    </main>


    <footer>
    </footer>
  </body>
</html>
```

Note that we've also moved the <h1> tag containing the Amazeriffic logo inside the header tag. That's because the logo is a child of the header in our tree diagram.

Next, we'll see that the upper-right corner of the page has a small navigation section with links to a Sign Up page, a FAQ page, and a Support page. Sure enough, HTML has a tag that supports a navigation element, and it's called nav. So we'll add that section to our <header> tag:

```
<header>
  <h1>Amazeriffic</h1>
  <nav>
    <a href="#">Sign Up!</a> |
    <a href="#">FAQ</a> |
    <a href="#">Support</a>
  </nav>
</header>
```

Note that the nav element contains several links that are separated by the | symbol. That symbol is right above the Enter key on your keyboard, co-located with the backslash. You'll have to press Shift to print the | symbol.

The links in the nav element are contained in <a> tags. As mentioned previously, <a> tags contain *href* attributes, which usually contain a link to the page we should be directed to when we click. Because we're not actually linking anywhere in this example, we've used the # symbol as a temporary placeholder for the link.

Because we've completed the <header> section, it's probably a good idea to commit to our Git repository. It might be helpful to do a git status first to see the changed files in our repository. Then we'll do a git add and a git commit with a meaningful commit message.

Structuring the Main Content

Now that we've completed the <header> section, we can move on to the <main> section. We'll see that, like the header, there are two main parts to the structure of the main section. There's the content on the left side, and then there's the image that is on the right side. The content on the left side is divided up into two separate sections, so we'll need to make sure to account for that.

To build out the structure of the content on the left side, we'll use four new tags. We'll use two heading tags (<h2> and <h3>), which represent heading text that is less important than an <h1> tag. We'll also use the <p> tag, which represents paragraph content. In addition, we'll use the <ul> tag, which represents an unordered list, along with its related <li> tags, which are list items.

And last but not least, we'll use the <img> tag to include the lightbulb image in our layout. Notice that the <img> tag doesn't have a closing tag associated with it. That's because HTML5 includes a set of elements referred to as *void* elements. Void elements typically do not have content and do not require a closing tag.

We'll also see that the <img> tag has a required attribute called the *alt* attribute. This attribute contains a textual description of the image. This is important to make our page accessible by the visually impaired, who often use screen readers when browsing the Internet.

You can download the lightbulb image from *http://www.learningwe bappdev.com/lightbulb.png*. To get it to appear on your page, you'll need to save it in the same directory as your *index.html* file.

Once we add the structured content to the `<main>` tag, it will look something like this:

```
<h2>Amazeriffic will change your life!</h2>
<p>Lorem ipsum dolor sit amet, consectetur adipisicing elit, sed do
   eiusmod tempor incididunt ut labore et dolore magna aliqua.</p>

<h3>Here's why you need Amazeriffic</h3>
<ul>
  <li>It fits your lifestyle</li>
  <li>It's awesome</li>
  <li>It rocks your world</li>
</ul>

<img src="lightbulb.png" alt="an image of a lightbulb">
```

When we reload the page in our browser, it should look similar to Figure 2-14.

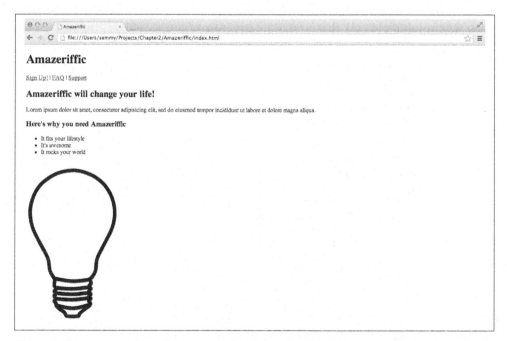

Figure 2-14. Amazeriffic, after structuring the main element

At this point, it would be a good idea to run your code through the validator and make sure you haven't inadvertently omitted anything. Once you're happy with it, make another commit to the Git repository, and we'll move on to the footer.

Structuring the Footer

The footer contains two main sections just like the other sections. One of the sections includes contact information for the company, and the other section is a set of links that we'll refer to as a *sitemap*. Furthermore, the sitemap itself is divided up into two columns.

First of all, there's no HTML element that represents contact information. That's okay, because HTML gives us two generic tags called <div> and <span> that allow us to create elements that represent some structure that we define ourselves. We'll learn the difference between the div and span elements in the next chapter.

In this case, we have two separate structures in the footer: the "Contact" information and the "Sitemap." Therefore, we'll create two <div> elements, each of which has a *class* attribute that specifies the type of the element. At this point, you can think of a class attribute as an attribute that you use to add meaning to the generic <div> and <span> tags.

In addition, we'll use another <ul> tag to create an unordered list element for the sitemap. The resulting HTML that creates the structure of our footer is as follows:

```
<footer>
  <div class="contact">
    <h5>Contact Us</h5>
    <p>Amazeriffic!</p>
    <p>555 Fiftieth Street</p>
    <p>Asheville, NC 28801</p>
  </div>

  <div class="sitemap">
    <h5>Sitemap</h5>
    <ul>
      <li><a href="#">Home</a></li>
      <li><a href="#">About Us</a></li>
      <li><a href="#">Privacy</a></li>
      <li><a href="#">Support</a></li>
      <li><a href="#">FAQ</a></li>
      <li><a href="#">Careers</a></li>
    </ul>
  </div>
</footer>
```

Add the footer content to your HTML document, run it through the HTML validator to make sure you haven't made any mistakes, and commit it to your Git repository.

We'll revisit this example in Chapter 3, where we'll style it.

Summary

In this chapter, we've learned to structure the user interface of our application using HTML. HTML is a markup language that lets us use tags to define a structure referred to as the DOM. The browser uses the DOM to create a visual rendering of the page.

The DOM is a hierarchical structure and can be easily represented using a tree diagram. It's sometimes helpful to think about the DOM in the form of a tree because it more clearly represents the descendant, child, and parent relationships between elements.

Validation is a useful tool that helps us avoid simple errors and HTML-related pitfalls.

We learned about several tags in this chapter, which are listed in Table 2-1. They all represent specific structural elements with the exception of the <div> tag. We typically attach a class attribute to a <div> tag to give it some kind of semantic meaning.

Table 2-1. HTML tags

Tag	Description
<html>	The main container for an HTML document
<head>	Contains meta-information about the document
<body>	Contains the content that will be rendered in the browser
<header>	The header of the page
<h1>	Most important heading (only one per document)
<h2>	Second most important heading
<h3>	Third most important heading
<main>	The main content area of your document
<footer>	The footer content of your document
<a>	Anchor, a link to another document or a clickable element
<ul>	A list of things where order doesn't matter
<ol>	A list of things where order matters
<li>	An element of a list
<div>	A container for a substructure

More Practice and Further Reading

Remember, if you're having trouble completing the examples in this chapter, you can see the finished HTML on our GitHub page (*http://www.github.com/semmypurewal/LearningWebAppDev*).

Memorization

Now that we've learned the basics of HTML, we can add a few more steps to our memorization goal. In addition to the five steps mentioned in the previous chapter, you should add the following to your practice:

1. Open the file in Chrome using keyboard shortcuts.

2. Modify *index.html* to include `<!doctype>`, `<html>`, `<head>`, and `<body>` tags.

3. Add a `<p>` tag that simply contains the words "Hello World."

4. Reload the file in Chrome and make sure it renders correctly (if it doesn't, fix it).

5. Commit the changes to your Git repository from the command line.

6. Add `<header>`, `<main>`, and `<footer>` tags to your `<body>` tag.

7. Confirm that it renders correctly in Chrome.

8. Validate it with the HTML validator.

9. Commit the *index.html* changes to your Git repository.

Tree Diagrams

Draw a tree diagram for the following HTML document. We'll also use this HTML document for practice problems at the end of Chapter 3 and Chapter 4:

```
<!doctype html>
<html>
  <head>
  </head>

  <body>
    <h1>Hi</h1>
    <h2 class="important">Hi again</h2>
    <p class="a">Random unattached paragraph</p>


    <div class="relevant">
      <p class="a">first</p>
      <p class="a">second</p>
      <p>third</p>
      <p>fourth</p>
      <p class="a">fifth</p>
      <p class="a">sixth</p>
      <p>seventh</p>
    </div>
  </body>
</html>
```

Build the FAQ Page for Amazeriffic

In Amazeriffic's navigation bar, there is a dead link for a *Frequently Asked Questions* page. Create a page that follows exactly the same style for the header and footer, but has a list of questions and answers as its main content. Use lorem ipsum text as a placeholder (unless you actually want to come up with questions and answers).

Save the file as *faq.html*. You can link to the page by filling out the `href` attribute in its associated `<a>` tag—set it to *faq.html*. If you include the two pages in the same directory, you should be able to click from the main splash page to get to the FAQ page. Similarly, you can link back to *index.html* from *faq.html*.

In Chapter 3 we'll style this page.

More About HTML

Throughout this book, I'll point you to the Mozilla Developer Network documentation (*https://developer.mozilla.org/en-US/docs/Web/HTML*) for more information on certain topics. Its site includes a wonderful overview of HTML. I encourage you to take a look for more in-depth documentation and advanced features.

The Style

In the previous chapter, we learned to structure the content of an HTML document and some related mental models. But the pages we created left a lot to be desired in terms of design and style.

In this chapter, we'll attempt to alleviate some of these issues and learn to change the way an HTML document is displayed using *Cascading Style Sheets* (CSS). As mentioned in the previous chapter, this will give you enough information to get started with CSS, and "More Practice and Further Reading" on page 93 will encourage you to explore other resources.

Hello, CSS!

To get our feet wet, we'll start with a very simple HTML example, similar to the ones from the beginning of the previous chapter. Open up a terminal window and create a directory called *Chapter3* in our *Projects* directory.

Now open up Sublime Text, and open the *Chapter3* directory in the same way that we did in the previous chapter. Create the following HTML file and save it in the directory as *index.html*:

```
<!doctype html>
<html>
  <head>
    <title>My First Web App</title>
    <link href="style.css" rel="stylesheet" type="text/css">
  </head>

  <body>
    <h1>Hello, World!</h1>

    <p>This is a paragraph.</p>
```

```
    </body>
</html>
```

This file defines a very simple HTML page with an h1 element and a p element contained in the body element. You'll immediately notice that the example also includes a new tag contained inside the <head> tag. The <link> tag links to an external stylesheet file that describes how the document should be displayed.

You can create the missing *style.css* file using Sublime from the file navigation window in the editor. Fill *style.css* with the following content:

```
body {
    background: lightcyan;
    width: 800px;
    margin: auto;
}

h1 {
    color: maroon;
    text-align: center;
}

p {
    color: gray;
    border: 1px solid gray;
    padding: 10px;
}
```

This is a simple example of a CSS file. This particular CSS file sets the background of the body element to a light bluish color (lightcyan) and tells the browser that the text contained in the h1 element should be rendered in a maroon color. Additionally, we give the body a width of 800 pixels and set the margin to auto so that the body is centered on the page. Last, but not least, we give the text contained in the p element a gray color and create a thin border around it.

Essentially, a CSS file describes how specific elements of the HTML should be displayed by the browser. For example, Figure 3-1 illustrates the preceding HTML file rendered with the CSS file.

Figure 3-1. index.html opened in Chrome with the added stylesheet

If we don't include the CSS file, the page would look like Figure 3-2.

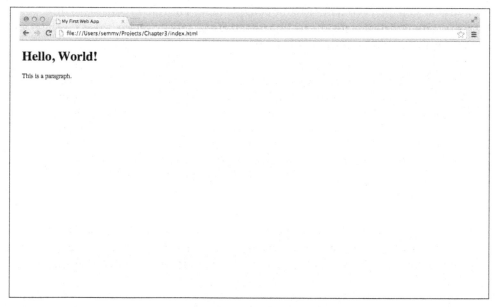

Figure 3-2. index.html opened in Chrome without the added stylesheet

If you have your *index.html* file and your *style.css* file in the same directory, you should be able to open the former in your browser and see that it looks the same as the first image. In fact, if you create a second HTML page that has different content and link the same CSS file, it will display both pages as specified by the CSS. That's one of the nice things about CSS—it allows the style for multiple pages to be defined in the same place!

Rulesets

A CSS file is a collection of *rulesets* and a ruleset is simply a collection of style rules that are applied to some subset of elements in the DOM (which you will recall is the hierarchical object defined by the HTML document). A ruleset consists of a *selector* (which we can think of as a tag name for now), an opening curly brace, a list of rules, and a final closing curly brace. Each rule consists of a specific *property*, followed by a colon, followed by a value (or a list of values separated by spaces), followed by a semicolon:

```
body {
    width: 800px;
    background: lightcyan;
    color: #ff0000;
}
```

This is an example of a ruleset that gets applied to the body element in the DOM. In this case, the selector is "body," which is just the name of the HTML element to which we want to apply the style. These rules will apply to all of the content of the body element, as well as any elements contained in the body element. The ruleset consists of three rules, one specifying the value for the width property, one specifying the value for the background property, and one specifying a value for the color property.

 In CSS, there are two ways to specify colors. The first is with CSS color names for commonly used colors (*http://www.crockford.com/wrrrld/color.html*). The second way to specify CSS colors is with a hexadecimal color code. A hex color code consists of six hexadecimal digits (0–9 or A–F). The first pair represents the amount of red in the color, the second represents the amount of green, and the third represents the amount of blue. These three colors are the primaries in the RGB color model.

An experienced CSS developer has a solid knowledge of the types of properties that can be set for a particular element, and the types of values that each property accepts. Several properties, like background and color, can be used to style most HTML elements.

Comments

Our CSS code can also include comments. Like HTML comments, CSS comments are code annotations that are completely ignored by the browser. For example, we can insert comments in the previous CSS ruleset:

```
/* Here we are styling the body */
body {
    width: 800px;           /* Set the body width to 800 pixels */
    background: lightcyan;  /* Set the background to a light bluish color */
    color: #ff0000;         /* Set the foreground color to red */
}
```

Some people will suggest that you be very liberal with your comments in all programs. I tend to think that you should let your code speak for itself as much as possible, and minimize places where comments are necessary. In fact, experienced CSS developers would find the preceding comments to be superfluous, because once you know a little these types of comments become redundant. On the other hand, there are times when it won't be obvious what your code is supposed to be doing, and in those cases it's a good idea to annotate it.

If you're just starting out with CSS, I always recommend erring on the side of more comments. I'll use comments liberally for most of the remainder of this chapter to make things easier to understand.

Padding, Border, and Margin

For the most part, HTML elements are displayed in one of two ways. The first way is *inline*, which applies to elements that have the type a or span, for example. This means (among other things) that the content will appear on the same line as the surrounding content:

```
<div>
  This is a paragraph and this <span>word</span> appears inline. This
  <a href="http://www.example.com">link</a> will also appear inline.
</div>
```

If we add this code to the <body> tag of the *index.html* file, the page will render similar to the image in Figure 3-3.

It's actually more common for elements to be *block* elements instead of inline elements. This means that the content contained inside the element will appear on a new line outside of the normal flow of text. Block elements that we've seen include the p, nav, main, and div elements:

```
<div>
  This is a paragraph and this <div>word</div> appears inline. This
  <a href="http://www.example.com">link</a> will also appear inline.
</div>
```

This code will look different, as illustrated in Figure 3-4.

Figure 3-3. An example of inline elements within a block element

Figure 3-4. An example of block elements within a block element

Both block style elements and inline elements have background and color properties. But block style elements have three other properties that come in very handy when styling the page with custom layouts. They are padding, border, and margin.

The padding property represents the spacing between the content of the element and the border, and the margin is the spacing between the element and its surrounding element. The border property represents the space between the padding and the margin. This is illustrated in Figure 3-5.

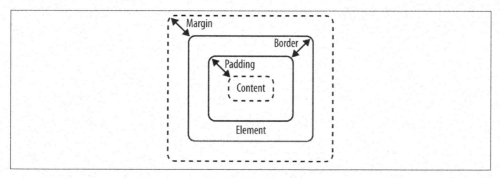

Figure 3-5. The margin, border, and padding of a block DOM element

Here's a simple example that you can use to manipulate the padding, border, and margin of a few different elements. The first file is *margin_border_padding.html*:

```
<!doctype html>
<html>
  <head>
    <title>Chapter 3 -- Margin, Border, and Padding Example</title>
    <link href="margin_border_padding.css" rel="stylesheet" type="text/css">
  </head>

  <body>
    <div>
      <p>THIS IS A PARAGRAPH CONTAINED INSIDE A DIV</p>
    </div>
  </body>
</html>
```

And here is *margin_border_padding.css*, which is referenced in the preceding HTML file. You can create these files in the same directory in Sublime, and then open the *margin_border_padding.html* file in Chrome:

```
body {
    background: linen;
    width: 500px;
    margin: 200px auto;
}
```

```
div {
  border: 5px solid maroon;
  text-align: center;
  padding: 5px;
}

p {
  border: 2px dashed blue;
}
```

If you typed everything in correctly, the page should look similar to Figure 3-6.

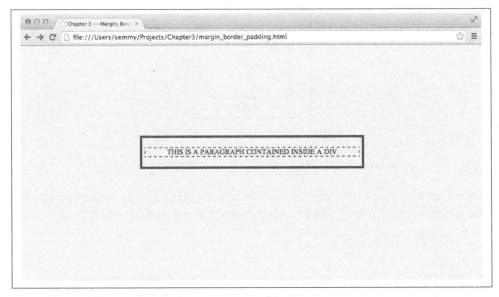

Figure 3-6. A margin/padding/border example to explore

You can see that both elements (the div and the p) are block elements so they each have their own border, margin, and padding properties. If you haven't already done it, take this opportunity to create the HTML and CSS just shown. Then spend some time changing the padding, border, and margin properties of each element to see how they affect the way the page is displayed.

Selectors

The most important aspect of CSS comes from the effective use of selectors. We've seen a basic *type* selector that uses a tag name to select all elements that have that name. For example, consider the following HTML:

```
<body>
  <h1>Hello World!</h1>
```

```
    <p>This is a paragraph.</p>

    <p>This is a second paragraph.</p>
</body>
```

And let's suppose that it's styled with the following CSS:

```
h1 {
    background: black;
    color: white;
}

p {
    color: red;
    margin: 10px;
    padding: 20px;
}
```

The first ruleset styles the h1 element, and the second ruleset styles *both* p elements. In many cases, this is exactly the behavior that we would want. In other cases, however, we may want to style the first and second paragraph tags independently.

Classes

In Chapter 2, we saw that we can add a class attribute to <div> tags to differentiate between them. It turns out that we can add a class to *any* DOM element. For example, we can rewrite the previous HTML to look as follows:

```
<body>
    <h1>Hello World!</h1>

    <p class="first">This is a paragraph.</p>

    <p class="second">This is a second paragraph.</p>
</body>
```

Now we can select the specific paragraph tag by its class name:

```
h1 {
    background: black;
    color: white;
}

p.first {
    color: red;
    margin: 10px;
    padding: 20px;
}
```

In this example, the `p.first` ruleset will only be applied to the first paragraph element. If the class only appears on a certain type of element (which is usually the case), we can omit the tag name and simply use the class:

```
.first {
    color: red;
    margin: 10px;
    padding: 20px;
}
```

Pseudoclasses

In the previous chapter, we saw that we could create clickable DOM elements with the `<a>` tag:

```
<body>
  <a href="http://www.example.com">Click Me!</a>
</body>
```

The a element can be styled just like any other DOM element via CSS. For example, we can create a CSS file that changes the color of all links:

```
a {
    color: cornflowerblue;
}
```

It's often useful, however, to have links with a different color depending on whether or not the user has already clicked them. CSS allows us to change the color of visited links by adding another ruleset:

```
a {
    color: cornflowerblue;
}

a:visited {
    color: tomato;
}
```

In this example, `visited` is an example of a CSS *pseudoclass* on the a element. It almost behaves just like a normal class in that we can style elements that have the class in the same way as a normal class. The main difference is that the browser actually implicitly adds the class for us.

One common use case for CSS pseudoclasses is changing the way a link is displayed when a user hovers over it. This can be achieved by using the `hover` pseudoclass on an a element. In the following example, we modify the previous example so that the link is underlined only when the user is hovering over it:

```
a {
    color: cornflowerblue;
    text-decoration: none; /* remove the default underline */
```

```
  }

a:visited {
    color: tomato;
}

a:hover {
    text-decoration: underline;
}
```

More Complex Selectors

As our tree diagram for the DOM gets more complicated, it becomes necessary to create more complicated selectors. For example, consider this HTML:

```
<body>
  <h1>Hello World!</h1>

  <div class="content">
    <ol>
      <li>List Item <span class="number">first</span></li>
      <li>List Item <span class="number">second</span></li>
      <li>List Item <span class="number">third</span></li>
    </ol>

    <p>This is the <span>first</span> paragraph.</p>

    <p>This is the <span>second</span> paragraph.</p>
  </div>

  <ul>
    <li>List Item <span class="number">1</span></li>
    <li>List Item <span class="number">2</span></li>
    <li>List Item <span class="number">3</span></li>
  </ul>
</body>
```

This HTML has two lists, several paragraphs, and several list items. We can easily select and style general elements as we've discussed previously. For example, if we want to create a rounded border around the ordered list (ol) element, we can apply the following ruleset:

```
ol {
    border: 5px solid darksalmon;
    border-radius: 10px;
}
```

Now suppose we wanted to make it so the list items in the ordered list are brown. To do that, our immediate intuition might be to do the following:

```
li {
    color: brown;
}
```

But this will change the li elements in both the unordered list and the ordered list. We can get more specific with our selector by *only* selecting the li elements in the ordered list:

```
ol li {
    color: brown;
}
```

If there are several ordered lists on the page, we may want to get even more specific and select only the li elements that are descendants of the content div element:

```
.content li {
    color: brown;
}
```

Now suppose we want to set the background of the first li elements in both lists to yellow. It turns out that there's a pseudoclass representing elements that are a *first-child* of their parents:

```
li:first-child {
    background: yellow;
}
```

Likewise, we can select the elements that are second, third, fourth, etc., children by using the nth-child pseudoclass:

```
li:nth-child(2) {
    background: orange;
}
```

Cascading Rules

What happens when two different rulesets use selectors that target the same element in CSS? For example, consider a p element with class greeting:

```
<p class="greeting">Hello, Cascading Rules!</p>
```

Now suppose that we have two rules that select that element and apply different styles:

```
p {
    color: yellow;
}

p.selected {
    color: green;
}
```

Which rule gets applied to the class above? It turns out that there are a set of *cascading rules* that browsers apply when conflicts arise. In this case, the more specific rule (the class) takes precedence. But what happens if we do something like the following?

```
p {
    color: yellow;
}

p {
    color: green;
}
```

In this case, the cascading rules specify that the ruleset that appears later in the CSS list will be applied. So in this case, the paragraph(s) will be green. If we swapped the rules, the paragraph(s) would be yellow.

Inheritance

If you haven't noticed by now, descendants inherit properties of their ancestors. What this means is that if we create a style on an element, all descendants of that element in the DOM will also have that style unless it is overridden by another ruleset that targets that element. So, for example, if we select the body and change the color property, all elements that are descendants of the body (which means all elements appearing on the page) will inherit that color. This is an essential part of CSS and this is why it's helpful to maintain a visualization of the DOM hierarchy in your head while styling elements:

```
body {
    background: yellow;
}

/**
 * Since h1 is a descendant of the body tag
 * it will have a yellow background.
 */
h1 {
    color: red;
}

/**
 * h2 is also a descendant of body, but
 * we'll override the background so it's
 * not yellow
 */
h2 {
    background: green;
}
```

Though most CSS properties work this way, it's worth noting that not all properties are inherited by default. The most notable noninherited properties are related to block-style elements (the margin, padding, and border rules aren't inherited from ancestors):

```
body {
    margin: 0;
    padding: 0;
}

/**
 * h1 will not inherit the margin and padding of the body,
 * even if we don't specify an alternative
 */
h1 {

}
```

Layouts with Floats

We've seen properties that affect the basic style of DOM elements. But there are other more general properties that affect the overall layout of the page relative to a single element. These properties give a developer more control over where objects appear. One of the more commonly used properties of this nature is the float property. This flexible property can allow us to create layouts that are more complicated than the stacked layout that HTML builds automatically.

The float property of a DOM element can be set to left or right. This takes the element out of the normal flow (which typically stacks block elements on top of one another) and pushes it as far to the left or right in the containing element, assuming there's enough room to do so. For example, consider the following HTML snippet:

```
<body>
  <main>
    <nav>
      <p><a href="link1">link1</a></p>
      <p><a href="link2">link2</a></p>
      <p><a href="link3">link3</a></p>
      <p><a href="link4">link4</a></p>
    </nav>

    <p class="content">Lorem ipsum dolor sit amet, consectetur adipisicing elit,
      sed do eiusmod tempor incididunt ut labore et dolore magna aliqua. Ut
      enim ad minim veniam, quis nostrud exercitation ullamco laboris nisi ut
      aliquip ex ea commodo consequat. Duis aute irure dolor in reprehenderit
      in voluptate velit esse cillum dolore eu fugiat nulla pariatur.
    </p>
  </main>
</body>
```

In this example, a nav element and a p element are contained in a main element. We also create a separate p element for each link because we want the elements to appear as block elements (one on each line). Without any styling, the elements are stacked on top of each other vertically. It looks like Figure 3-7.

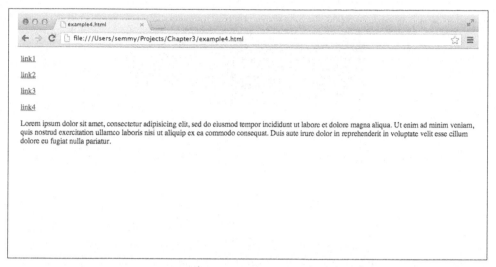

link1

link2

link3

link4

Lorem ipsum dolor sit amet, consectetur adipisicing elit, sed do eiusmod tempor incididunt ut labore et dolore magna aliqua. Ut enim ad minim veniam, quis nostrud exercitation ullamco laboris nisi ut aliquip ex ea commodo consequat. Duis aute irure dolor in reprehenderit in voluptate velit esse cillum dolore eu fugiat nulla pariatur.

Figure 3-7. The rendered page before CSS is applied

 It's definitely better to use a `ul` element along with several `li` elements for the list of links in this example, but that introduces a few subtle issues associated with list items that are unrelated to the topic at hand.

Now, suppose we applied the following CSS to this HTML:

```
main {
    width: 500px;
    margin: auto;
    background: gray;
}

nav {
    /* uncomment the next line to get a border around the nav */
    /* border: 3px solid black; */
    width: 200px;
    float: right;
}

p.content {
  margin: 0; /* zero out the default margin */
}
```

The result should look similar to Figure 3-8.

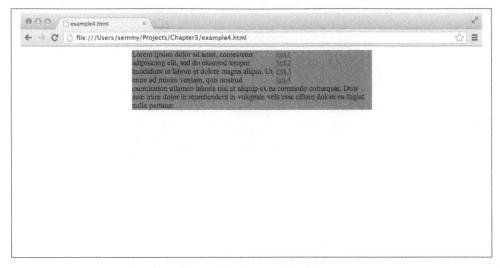

Figure 3-8. An example of an element floating to the right

Note that we've made the nav element 200 pixels wide and floated it to the right to create a sidebar layout. Notice how it removes the nav element from the standard stacked layout and moves it to the right. The content of the p element then flows around the nav div. I've also included a line that you can uncomment to add a visual border around the floated element. Give that a try!

Though simply floating an element to the right generally works well for images or other inline elements that need to have text flowing around them, we'll often want to create a two-column grid-type layout. That presents us with a slightly more interesting challenge. In this case, we'll want to float the p element to the left and make sure that the combined size of the two elements won't overtake the size of the container. Here is some CSS that will achieve this:

```
main {
    width: 500px;
    margin: auto;
    background: gray;
}

nav {
    width: 100px;
    float: right;
}

/* remove defaults on the p elements inside the nav */
nav p {
    margin: 0;
    padding: 0;
}
```

```
p.content {
    margin: 0;       /* remove the default margin on p */
    float: left;
    width: 400px;
}
```

Now if we look at this in the browser, we'll see that the two columns correctly line up, but our gray background is gone. This is because when all elements contained in an element are floated, the height of the containing element becomes 0. There's a simple fix for that—we can set the overflow property of the containing div to auto:

```
main {
    width: 500px;
    margin: auto;
    background: gray;
    overflow: auto;
}
```

This gives us a layout similar to the one illustrated in Figure 3-9.

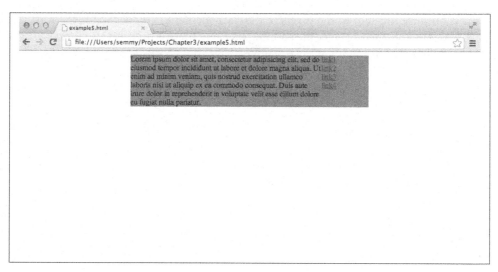

Figure 3-9. A simple two-column layout using floats

Note that we've set the sum of the widths of the left and right elements in this example to 500 pixels, which is exactly the width of the containing div. This can cause problems if we add any padding, margin, or border to either element. For example, we may want to push the text of the p element away from the edges of the element. This will require us to add padding. But if we add 20 pixels of padding to the element, we'll get something that looks like Figure 3-10.

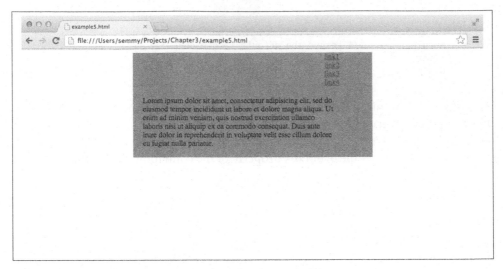

Figure 3-10. Adding padding breaks our layout

This is because the sum of the pixels in the main element is bigger than its width. We can fix this by subtracting twice the padding (because there is both left and right padding of 10 pixels) off of the width of the p element. The final CSS might look something like this:

```
main {
    width: 500px;
    margin: auto;
    background: gray;
    overflow: auto;
}

nav {
    width: 100px;
    float: right;
}

p.content {
    margin: 0; /* remove the default margin on p */
    padding: 10px;
    float: left;
    width: 380px; /* 400 - 2*10 = 380 */
}
```

This same trick must be applied whenever we add a nonzero border or margin to elements as well.

The clear Property

One interesting issue can arise when building layouts using floating elements. Here is a slightly different HTML document. This time, our goal is to set up the navigation on the left side with a footer underneath both columns:

```
<body>
  <nav>
    <p><a href="link1">link1</a></p>
    <p><a href="link2">link2</a></p>
    <p><a href="link3">link3</a></p>
    <p><a href="link4">link4</a></p>
  </nav>

  <main>
    <p>Lorem ipsum dolor sit amet, consectetur adipisicing elit, sed do
       eiusmod tempor incididunt ut labore et dolore magna aliqua. Ut enim
       ad minim veniam, quis nostrud exercitation ullamco laboris nisi ut
       aliquip ex ea commodo consequat. Duis aute irure dolor in reprehenderit
       in voluptate velit esse cillum dolore eu fugiat nulla pariatur.
    </p>
  </main>

  <footer>
    <p>This is the footer</p>
  </footer>
</body>
```

The following CSS floats the `nav` element to the left and clears out the default margins and paddings using the *universal* selector, which selects all elements in the DOM. It also sets the background of the elements to various distinguishable shades of gray:

```
* {
    margin: 0;
    padding: 0;
}

nav {
    float: left;
    background:darkgray;
}

main {
    background:lightgray;
}

footer {
    background:gray;
}
```

When we render this document using this stylesheet, we'll see something similar to Figure 3-11.

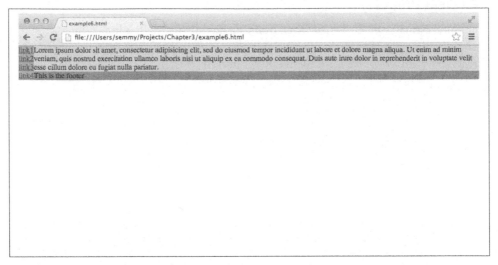

Figure 3-11. Notice that the footer is below the main section, instead of below everything

Note that the footer is actually on the right of the layout, underneath the main section. We'd like the footer to be underneath both elements. This is what the clear property does for us. We can force the footer element to be underneath a floating element on the right, the left, or under both the right and left floating elements by specifying the clear property. So we can change the footer CSS as follows:

```
footer {
    background:gray;
    clear: both;        /* or we can just use 'clear: left' in this case */
}
```

And this will render as shown in Figure 3-12.

Now the footer is underneath the floating element, as desired.

Floats tend to be one of the more confusing aspects of CSS for beginners, so I encourage you to spend some time experimenting and building layouts.

Working with Fonts

In the past, working with custom fonts on websites was problematic, because you were limited to the fonts that the viewer of your site had installed on their computer. Web fonts have made that much easier, because you can deliver the fonts over the Internet when they are needed. Google now hosts a number of custom fonts and has made using them a breeze.

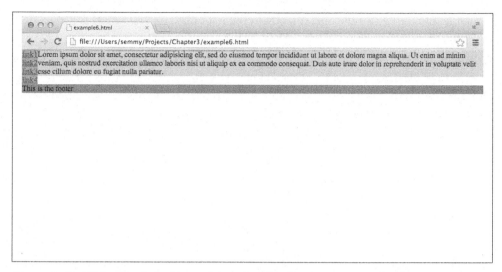

Figure 3-12. We've fixed the layout by setting the clear property in the footer

We can start by going to the Google Fonts home page (*http://www.google.com/fonts*), as shown in Figure 3-13. There we'll see a list of fonts that we can scroll through.

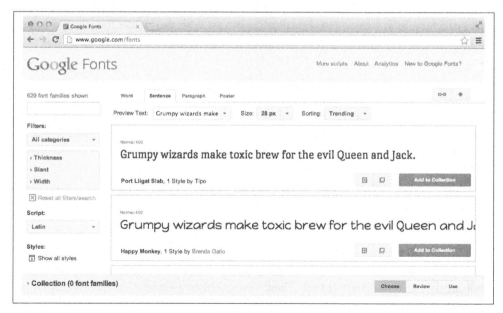

Figure 3-13. The Google Fonts home page

In this example, we'll use a font called *Denk One*, which was the first font in the list when I visited the Google Fonts home page. To use this font, we'll click the Quick-use button, which is one of the two buttons directly to the left of the big blue "Add to Collection" button.

This will bring up instructions on how to use it on our page. We'll need to add two things: first, we'll need to add a `<link>` tag to the head of our HTML. So if we're using the same example from earlier, we can cut and paste the `<link>` tag specified on the quick use page, or just add a line similar to the following:

```
<head>
  <title>Amazeriffic</title>
  <!-- There's a line break below to make things more readable -->
  <link href="http://fonts.googleapis.com/css?family=Denk+One"
        rel="stylesheet" type="text/css">
  <link href="style.css" rel="stylesheet" type="text/css">
</head>
```

 HTML allows either single quotes (') or double quotes (") to delimit strings. I've tried to consistently use double quotes throughout this book, but the cut-and-paste code from Google uses single quotes. Because they are interchangable, it doesn't matter whether you leave them as they are or change them to double quotes.

This will make the web font available on our page. Next, we can use it in our *style.css* file. For example, if we want to style our h1 element with the Denk One font, we would add a `font-family` property to our ruleset:

```
h1 {
    font-family: 'Denk One', sans-serif;
}
```

The first part of the property specifies the font (which should be loaded via the `<link>` tag) and the second one specifies the font to use if the first one is not available. So, for example, this line says "use the Denk One font if it's available, and if it's not available, use the default sans serif font installed on the user's system."

Now that we are able to easily display fonts and change their color (via the `color` property on the associated element), how do we actually change their size? In the past there were multiple ways to do it, but there's one way that is typically considered best practice.

First, we should consider that the user may change their default text size for the browser, and our pages should respect that. Therefore, in the body ruleset for the document we should set a base font size and then scale all other fonts relative to that one. Fortunately, CSS makes that pretty easy by using *em* units to specify the length:

```
body {
    font-size: 100%;      /* this sets the base font size for everything */
}
```

```
h1 {
    font-size: xx-large; /* sets it relative to the base font size */
}

h2 {
    font-size: x-large;
}

.important {
    font-size: larger;    /* makes it a little larger than the parent */
}

.onePointTwo {
    font-size: 1.2em;     /* sets it to 1.2 times the base size */
}
```

In this example, we set the base font size to 100% of the user's font size for their browser, and then scale all font sizes relative to it. We can use the CSS absolute size values xx-large and x-large (or, similarly, x-small or xx-small), which will scale the size accordingly. Likewise, we can use relative sizes like larger or smaller to make the font size relative to the current context.

If we need more fine-grained control over font sizes, we use *ems*, which are meta-units that represent a multiplier on the current font size. For example, if we set our base font size in the body to a specific size like, say, 12pt, then setting another element's font size to 1.5em will make its actual size 18pt. This is useful because the font sizes will scale according to the base font size, which means to make the text bigger or smaller on the page we simply have to change the base size. This also comes in handy for visually impaired users: they will often set a larger base font size for the browser, so using ems instead of explicit values will make the page scale appropriately.

In the preceding example, we set the paragraph font size to 1.2 times the base size. Figure 3-14 illustrates how the preceding rulesets style a document.

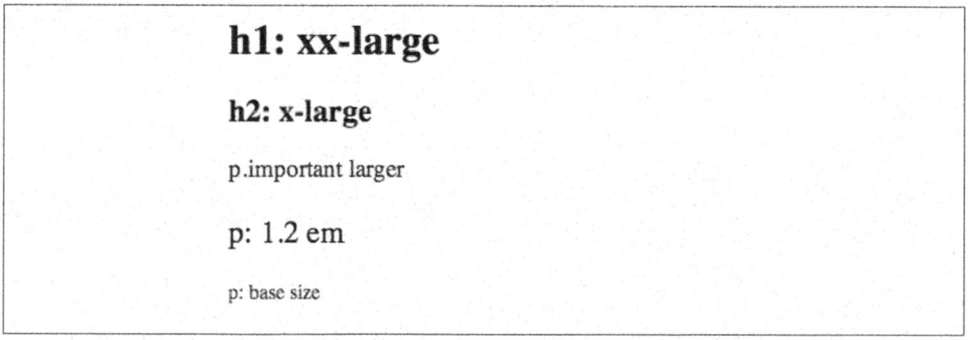

h1: xx-large

h2: x-large

p.important larger

p: 1.2 em

p: base size

Figure 3-14. Some example fonts based on the previous stylesheet

Resetting Browser Inconsistencies

One controversial tool that you will often see used is a CSS reset.

Remember our float example where we removed the default margin and padding on the paragraph tags? It turns out that various browsers implement their base CSS settings slightly differently, which can lead to your CSS rendering slightly differently in different browsers. A *CSS reset* is designed to remove all browser defaults. The best known reset is Eric Meyer's (*http://meyerweb.com/eric/tools/css/reset*).

Why are CSS resets controversial? There are several reasons, but they can be categorized into three main points. One is accessibility—for example, they can cause problems for people who are navigating via a keyboard. Another criticism is performance. Because they often use the universal selector (*), they can be relatively inefficient. And lastly, they create an awful lot of redundancy because browser defaults are often exactly what you want.

On the other hand, I think resets are excellent from a pedagogical standpoint, and that's why I'm including them here. They force beginners to explicitly state the way they want certain aspects of the page to appear instead of relying on browser defaults. Since, presumably, you're reading this because you're just starting out with CSS, I recommend that you use one.

To make things explicit, I include my reset as a separate stylesheet altogether and add an additional `link` element to my HTML. We can copy Eric Meyer's reset into another CSS file called *reset.css* and link it from the HTML:

```
<head>
  <title>Amazeriffic</title>
  <link rel="stylesheet" type="text/css" href="reset.css">
  <link rel="stylesheet" type="text/css" href="style.css">
</head>
```

It's pretty easy to see the dramatic effect that a reset can have on a page. Consider the following HTML:

```
<body>
  <h1>This is a header</h1>
  <h3>This is a slightly less important header</h3>

  <p>Lorem ipsum dolor sit amet, consectetur adipisicing elit, sed do eiusmod
      tempor incididunt ut labore et dolore magna aliqua. Ut enim ad minim
      veniam, quis nostrud exercitation ullamco laboris nisi ut aliquip ex ea
      commodo consequat.</p>

  <p>Lorem ipsum dolor sit amet, consectetur adipisicing elit, sed do eiusmod
      tempor incididunt ut labore et dolore magna aliqua. Ut enim ad minim
      veniam, quis nostrud exercitation ullamco laboris nisi ut aliquip ex ea
      commodo consequat.</p>
</body>
```

Figure 3-15 shows the page rendered in Chrome with only the default browser styling applied.

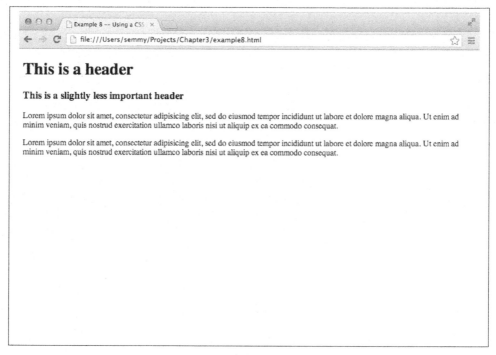

Figure 3-15. A simple page with some default styling

Notice how the h1 elements and the h3 elements already have styled fonts and margins. Likewise, the p elements have margins.

Now we'll add the reset. I copied the reset file from Eric Meyer's page and saved it as *reset.css* in the same directory as my HTML. I modified the <head> tag in my HTML to look like this:

```
<head>
  <title>Example 8 -- Using a CSS Reset</title>
  <link href="reset.css" rel="stylesheet" type="text/css">
</head>
```

Now when I reload the page, it looks like Figure 3-16.

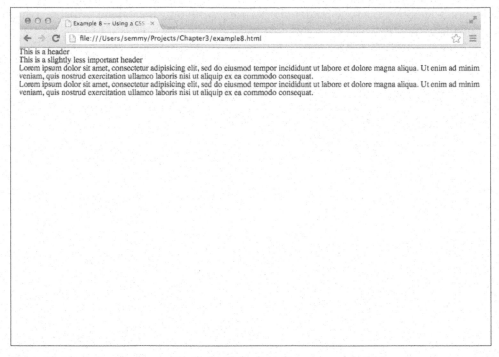

Figure 3-16. A simple page with all the default styling removed via a reset

The margins, padding, and default font sizes have been completely removed from the page. Clearly we don't want our site to look like this, but the point is that including a CSS reset file that removes the browser's default styling allows the rules that we supply in our own CSS file to always have the same end effect, regardless of the browser (and its corresponding choice of default rules) the user happens to be using.

Using CSS Lint to Identify Potential Problems

Just like with HTML, it's sometimes helpful to have a tool that helps us find potential problems with our CSS. For example, can you spot the error in this example CSS?

```
body {
    background: lightblue;
    width: 855px;
    margin: auto;


h1 {
    background: black;
    color: white;
}
```

```
p {
    color: red;
    margin: 10px
    padding: 20px;
}
```

If you found it, then you're wrong! You should have found two of them! I think that the most glaring error is that the body ruleset is missing a closing curly brace at the bottom, prior to the start of the h1 ruleset. But there's one other one.

You probably noticed the second one after a second look. But if you didn't, it's in the ruleset for the p element. There's a missing semicolon after the margin property.

Like an HTML validator, CSS Lint is a tool that will help us identify potential problems with our code. And like the W3C's online HTML validator, we don't have to install any software to use it; we simply visit *http://csslint.net* (as shown in Figure 3-17) and we cut and paste our CSS.

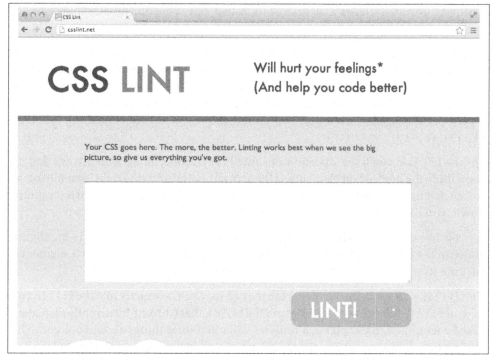

Figure 3-17. The CSS Lint home page

CSS Lint gives a lot more warnings than the HTML validation tool we studied in Chapter 2, but there are options that allow you to customize the warning level. You can see those options by clicking the down arrow right next to the Lint! button on the main page. The options are categorized by the reasons for the warnings. For example, "Disallow universal selector" is under the Performance category. That means that it might make your page render more slowly if you use this particular CSS feature, so CSS Lint warns you about it.

I typically leave all of the options checked in CSS Lint, but you may want it to be a little more flexible. I recommend leaving them all on, and as you're getting warnings, take the time to do some Google searching to find out why CSS Lint is warning you. It's almost like having a CSS expert sitting right next to you!

Interacting and Troubleshooting with the Chrome Developer Tools

As is the case with any kind of software development, things will sometimes not work the way that you intend it to. With CSS, that often means your page looks different in the browser than you expect and it's not clear why that is the case. Fortunately, the Chrome browser includes a nice set of tools that can help you troubleshoot your CSS and your HTML.

Let's start by opening up *margin_border_padding.html* in the Chrome browser. Next, go to the View menu in Chrome, select the Developer submenu, and click the Developer Tools option. This should open up the Chrome Developer Tools at the bottom of your browser window. If it's not already selected, click the Elements tab at the top of the Developer Tools subwindow and you should be presented with something that looks like Figure 3-18.

On the left side you'll see a portion of some HTML code, along with arrows that can show/hide the descendant elements. If the arrow is pointing to the right, that means you can click it to show the HTML that is contained in that element. Likewise, if it is pointing down, you can click it to hide the contained HTML.

As you hover over HTML elements, you should see the actual elements highlighted above in the display portion of the window. You can select a specific HTML element by clicking its opening tag and its associated line will then appear in blue.

The HTML you see in the Elements tab may or may not be exactly like the HTML code in your HTML file, but even if it's not, it's the HTML that Chrome is currently displaying. Like I mentioned in Chapter 2, a browser will often infer things about your code (like closing tags, for instance) and the HTML presented in the Elements tab includes all the assumptions that Chrome is making. For example, if you create an HTML document that only contains a <p> tag (and not an <html>, <header>, or <body> tag), Chrome will insert those tags for you and you will see them in the Elements tab, as shown in Figure 3-19. This can be a helpful way of bridging the sometimes confusing gap between what you actually intended and what Chrome thinks you intended.

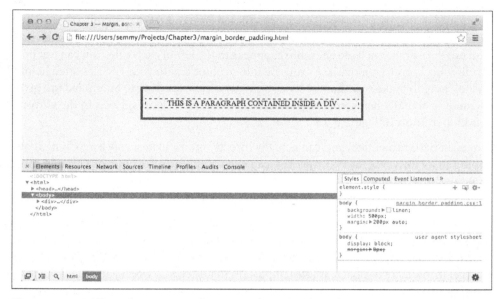

Figure 3-18. The Chrome Developer Tools opened with the margin_border_pad-ding.html example

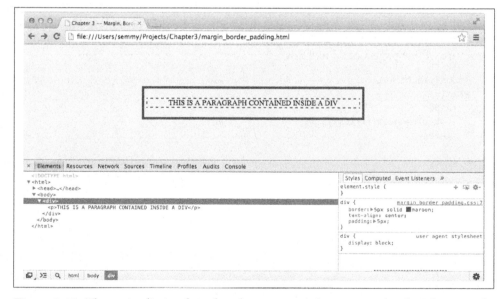

Figure 3-19. The main div is selected and you can see the associated style ruleset on the right

On the right side of the window, you can see the CSS associated with the selected HTML element. Go ahead and select the div element that contains the paragraph. On the right, you'll see the ruleset associated with it in the Matched CSS Rules subwindow, and when you hover over it, you'll see checkboxes appear to the left of each rule. You can uncheck a rule's checkbox to remove it. As you run into problems with your CSS, it's often helpful to look here to make sure that the style rule that you're expecting to be applied to a given element is actually being applied. You can see the style rules displayed in the Chrome Developer Tools in Figure 3-19.

But even better than that, you can actually directly manipulate a rule by clicking it and typing in a new value for that rule. You can even add new rules here, but keep in mind that this doesn't get reflected in your CSS file. So if you find a solution to a styling problem in this window, you'll have to go back to Sublime to include the style in your CSS file.

You should have already played around with setting the padding, border, and margin by modifying your code. Try similar manipulations, but this time in the Elements tab of the Chrome Developer Tools window. You'll see that it's much easier to try out things and get immediate feedback. It's also important to notice that when you reload the page, all of your changes will be lost and Chrome will return to the page that is defined in your HTML and CSS files.

Styling Amazeriffic

Now let's put it all together in an example. In the previous chapter, we built the structure for the home page of an app called Amazeriffic. The resulting HTML that defined the structure of our page looked like this:

```
<!doctype html>
<html>
  <head>
    <title>Amazeriffic</title>
  </head>

  <body>
    <header>
      <h1>Amazeriffic</h1>
      <nav>
        <a href="#">Sign Up!</a> |
        <a href="#">FAQ</a> |
        <a href="#">Support</a>
      </nav>
    </header>

    <main>
      <h2>Amazeriffic will change your life!</h2>
      <p>Lorem ipsum dolor sit amet, consectetur adipisicing elit, sed do
          eiusmod tempor incididunt ut labore et dolore magna aliqua.</p>
```

```
    <h3>Here's why you need Amazeriffic</h3>
    <ul>
      <li>It fits your lifestyle</li>
      <li>It's awesome</li>
      <li>It rocks your world</li>
    </ul>

    <img src="lightbulb.png">
    </main>

    <footer>
      <div class="contact">
        <h5>Contact Us</h5>
        <p>Amazeriffic!</p>
        <p>555 Fiftieth Street</p>
        <p>Asheville, NC 28801</p>
      </div>

      <div class="sitemap">
        <h5>Sitemap</h5>
        <ul>
          <li><a href="#">Home</a></li>
          <li><a href="#">About Us</a></li>
          <li><a href="#">Privacy</a></li>
          <li><a href="#">Support</a></li>
          <li><a href="#">FAQ</a></li>
          <li><a href="#">Careers</a></li>
        </ul>
      </div>
    </footer>
  </body>
</html>
```

First, we'll enter the directory that contains our Git project for Amazeriffic. If we're in our home directory, we can go directly into the *Amazeriffic* directory by using cd and giving the full path as an argument:

```
hostname $ cd Projects/Amazeriffic
```

We can use the ls command to see the contents of the directory and then follow up with git log to see our commit history from the previous chapter. Mine looks something like this:

```
hostname $ ls
index.html

hostname $ git log
commit efeb5a9a5f80d861119f5761df789f6bde0cda4f
Author: Semmy Purewal <semmy@semmy.me>
Date:   Thu May 23 1:41:52 2013 -0400

    Add content and structure to footer
```

```
commit 09a6ea9730521ed1effd135a243723a2745d3dc5
Author: Semmy Purewal <semmy@semmy.me>
Date:    Thu May 23 12:32:17 2013 -0400

    Add content to main section

commit f90c9a6bd896d1a303f6c3647a7475d6de9c4f9e
Author: Semmy Purewal <semmy@semmy.me>
Date:    Thu May 23 11:45:21 2013 -0400

    Add content to header section

commit 1c808e2752d824d815929cb7c170a04267416c04
Author: Semmy Purewal <semmy@semmy.me>
Date:    Thu May 23 10:36:47 2013 -0400

    Add skeleton of structure to Amazeriffic

commit 147deb5dbb3c935525f351a1154b35cb5b2af824
Author: Semmy Purewal <semmy@semmy.me>
Date:    Thu May 23 10:35:43 2013 -0400

    Initial commit
```

Next, we can open up the directory in Sublime, and create two new CSS files. First, we'll build a *reset.css* file based on Eric Meyer's reset. You can type in the code (as described previously) or cut and paste the code from his website (*http://meyerweb.com/eric/tools/css/reset*). We'll also create a *style.css* file that will include our custom CSS.

Before we commit, let's go ahead and link our CSS files from our HTML file by adding two link tags to the head:

```
<head>
  <title>Amazeriffic</title>
  <link rel="stylesheet" type="text/css" href="reset.css">
  <link rel="stylesheet" type="text/css" href="style.css">
</head>
```

Now we can open the file in Chrome. It should look completely unstyled due to the reset file. Mine looks something like Figure 3-20.

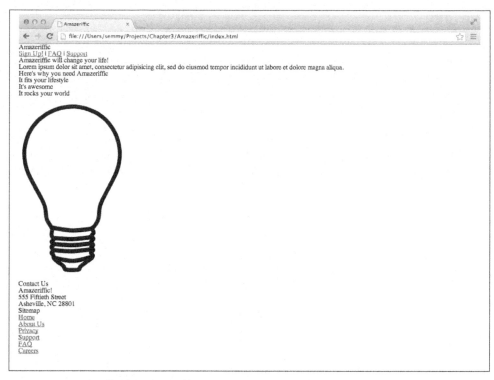

Figure 3-20. The final Amazeriffic HTML, with an included reset

Now we'll commit the changes to our Git repository:

```
hostname $ git add reset.css
hostname $ git add style.css
hostname $ git add index.html
hostname $ git status
# On branch master
# Changes to be committed:
#   (use "git reset HEAD <file>..." to unstage)
#
#       modified:   index.html
#       new file:   reset.css
#       new file:   style.css
#
hostname $ git commit -m "Add reset.css and style.css, link in index.html"
[master b9d4bc9] Add reset.cssand style.css, link in index.html
 3 files changed, 142 insertions(+), 2 deletions(-)
 create mode 100644 reset.css
 create mode 100644 style.css
```

The Grid

Now let's examine the style for Amazeriffic. Notice that the content is horizontally aligned in two columns. The first column takes up about two-thirds of the content area, while the second column takes up about one-third of the content area. Next, notice that the content is vertically aligned in about three rows. This defines a styling grid over the content, which is one basic approach to design layouts.

Another aspect of the design that's hard to get across in a book is that it's a fixed width design. This means that as we resize our browser window, the content of the page remains centered at the same width regardless. Figure 3-21 and Figure 3-22 show Amazeriffic in two browser windows of different sizes.

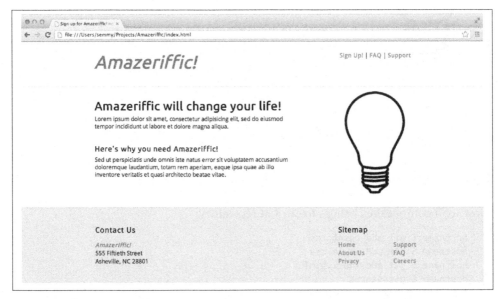

Figure 3-21. Amazeriffic in a 1,250 × 650 browser window

This means the design is not *responsive*, which is a modern approach to CSS layout that allows the layout to rearrange itself depending on the width of the browser. This is important when designing for the Web, because many people will view the design on a mobile phone or tablet. We're not going to spend much time on responsive design here, but you'll have the opportunity to try a few tools that simplify the responsive design process in the exercises at the end of this chapter.

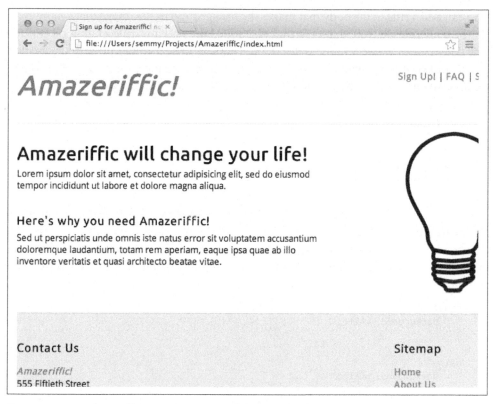

Figure 3-22. Amazeriffic in an 800 × 575 browser window

Our goal is to build this two-column, fixed width design using CSS. To start with, we'll need to make it so that the rows (which in this case are our `header`, `main`, and `footer` elements) have the fixed width property. The first thing that we can do to assist us in this is to create a ruleset for all of these elements. In our *style.css* file, we'll add a ruleset that looks as follows:

```
header, main, footer {
    min-width: 855px;
}
```

The `min-width` property makes it so that if the browser is resized to a viewport smaller than 855 px, the remaining part of the page will be hidden from view. Try it out.

Next, notice that the footer has a yellowish color that should fill the bottom of the page as the browser window is expanded vertically. This means that the yellow color will have to be the background color of the entire page, and we'll need to change the color of the `header` and the `main` elements to white later.

We can add a rule to the body that makes the background of the image that yellow color in the body ruleset. Note that even though I added the previous ruleset first, I'll still add the body ruleset above it in the *style.css* file. That's because it comes prior to the `header`, `main`, and `footer` elements in the HTML file. Keeping the locations (relatively) consistent between these two files makes it easier to find issues and make changes:

```
body {
    background: #f9e933;
}

header, main, footer {
    min-width: 855px;
}
```

Now we'll see that the entire page is the off-yellow color, so we'll change the backgrounds of the `header` and `main` elements to be white. To do this, we'll add two new rulesets for the `header` and `main` elements in addition to the one that contains the `min-width` rule. We'll separate them because we'll want to add different styling rules to each as we move forward:

```
header {
    background: white;
}

main {
    background: white;
}
```

So now we've got things looking similar to Figure 3-23.

 As of this writing, the `<main>` tag is not rendering correctly in the Safari browser. If you're using that browser and having problems, try adding a ruleset for `main` that includes the `display: block;` rule.

Now that we have some basic styling set up, it's probably a good idea to commit the changes to your Git repository. Start by checking the status. The only file that should have changed is *style.css*. Stage that file (with the `add` command) and then commit the change with a meaningful commit message.

Figure 3-23. Amazeriffic after some (very) basic styling

Next, we'd like the following things to happen. We'd like to have the content centered and fixed at 855 px wide. We're choosing 855 px because we'd like to have the number of pixels divisible by 3 (because the columns are about two-thirds and one-third wide). Because 855/3 is 285, this gives us the ability to work with whole numbers.

Here's a potential approach to solving this problem. We could add a `max-width` rule to the ruleset styling the `header`, `main`, and `footer`, set the `width` of the body to `855px`, and then set the `margin` on the `body` to `auto`. Before moving on, try that and see what happens.

If you actually did it, you probably realized that the header and main content areas are now not stretching to fit the full size of the page and so the background color is filling the spaces to the left and right. This is not what we want.

How do we fix this? This is a case where we'll want to add a `div` element to the DOM so we can style the elements independently. We want the `header` and `main` elements to span the entire width of the page, but the content contained inside to be 855 px. So we'll create a container class inside those two elements to hold the content. Go ahead and modify the HTML so that the `header`, `main`, and `footer` elements contain a class called `container`, which contains the content elements. For example, here's what we would do with the `header` div:

```
<header>
  <div class="container">
    <h1>Amazeriffic</h1>
    <nav>
```

```
            <a href="#">Sign Up!</a> |
            <a href="#">FAQ</a> |
            <a href="#">Support</a>
        </nav>
      </div>
    </header>
```

Now we can make the container content have a max width of 855 px and an automatic margin. When we're finished, our rulesets should look something like this:

```
body {
    background: #f9e933;
}

header, main, footer {
    min-width: 855px;
}

header .container, main .container, footer .container {
    max-width: 855px;
    margin: auto;
}

header {
    background: white;
}

main {
    background: white;
}
```

Now as we resize our browser, our content will remain at a fixed width! This is a good point to drop to the terminal window and commit your changes to your Git repository. This time you have modified two files, so you'll need to add both to your Git repository before committing.

Creating the Columns

The next thing that we want to do is to create the columns in the content elements. To do this, we'll float the content that is in the right column to the right, and specify the widths for the right column to be 285 px and the width of the left column to be 570 px. We'll also set the `overflow` property to `auto` so that the element won't shrink to zero when we float both children elements.

When we finish the header rulesets, they will look something like this:

```
header {
    background: white;
    overflow: auto;
}
```

```
header h1 {
    float: left;
    width: 570px;
}

header nav {
    float: right;
    width: 285px;
}
```

The header is a little unique because it only contains two child elements—the h1 element and the nav element. This is not true of the main and footer elements. If you're thinking about this correctly, you'll most likely need to add additional div elements to both of them in order to package the floating left and right content into a single element. And on the right side of the footer, you'll need to create a left-right layout within the footer layout to style the sitemap. This is by design—you should be able to do this with the skills you have learned in this chapter.

I would work on one section at a time: get the header looking correct, then get the main content area looking correct, and then get the footer looking correct. You should make intermediate commits to your Git repository. I would also periodically run your code through CSS Lint (and the HTML validator, if you're modifying the HTML) to make sure you don't have any potential problems.

When we finish with this section, we'll have something that looks like Figure 3-24 (with the exception of the sitemap, which is still unstyled in this image).

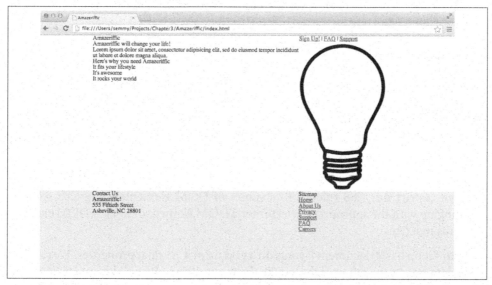

Figure 3-24. Amazeriffic after a little more styling

Once your page looks like this and you've identified any potential problems by running your CSS through CSS Lint, it is a good time to make another commit to your Git repository.

Adding and Manipulating Fonts

Next, we'll add two Google Fonts. For this example, I've used the *Ubuntu* and the *Droid Sans* fonts. The header tags (<h1>, <h2>, <h3>, and <h4>) are all styled with the Ubuntu font, and the rest of the page content is styled with Droid Sans. This will require us to add two link tags to our HTML file and then rules in the CSS.

After you have the fonts set correctly, commit the changed files to your Git repository. Once you do that, set up a base font size of 100% and modify the font sizes of the elements in an attempt to get them looking as close as possible to the original mock-up image.

After getting the font sizes looking correct, validate your HTML and run your CSS through Lint to try to identify problems. Once you do that, commit the changes to your Git repository.

A Few More Modifications

Finally, you'll need to add padding and margins to get everything lined up and spaced correctly. This will require experimenting with the margins and padding on various elements. I encourage you to do that in the Chrome Developer Tools. You'll also need to style the links on the page. All of the links are red and not underlined unless the cursor is hovering over them. That will require you to manipulate the hover pseudoclass of the a elements.

Summary

In this chapter, we used CSS to add style to the structure of our user interface and content. The basic idea behind CSS is that we attach stylistic *rulesets* to elements in the DOM. Most of these rulesets are *inherited*, meaning that when we apply them to a certain element in the DOM, they also apply to all descendant DOM elements unless overridden in a ruleset specific to that element. In cases where there's ambiguity, *cascade* rules are applied.

We can restrict our CSS rulesets to a subset of DOM elements using CSS *selectors*. Coming up with the appropriate selector for a DOM element or a set of DOM elements requires practice.

We can set up basic document layouts on a grid using CSS float properties. We can float CSS elements to the left or right to take them out of the normal document flow. If an element has two child elements, and we float one child element to the left and one to the right, they will appear side-by-side, assuming they don't overlap. We can ensure that they don't overlap by specifying their width.

CSS Lint is a tool that helps us to avoid common CSS pitfalls and errors, while Chrome has a rich set of interactive CSS tools built in.

More Practice and Further Reading

There are still a couple of issues to fix with Amazeriffic. I encourage you to fix those issues and get it looking as similar to the mock-up as possible.

Memorization

We'll start by adding a few more steps to our practice. Remember, your goal is to *memorize* how to do this along with the previous steps listed in the previous chapters:

1. Create a simple *style.css* file that uses the universal selector to zero out the margin and padding on all elements and change the background of the page to a slightly off-white color.

2. Link the *style.css* file to your HTML document in the <head> tag, and reload the page to confirm that it's working correctly.

3. Commit *style.css* and your *index.html* changes to your Git repository.

4. Add some basic styling to the header, main, and footer elements.

5. Commit the changes to your repository.

CSS Selectors Practice

Type up the following HTML document and save it in a file called *selectorpractice.html*:

```
<!doctype html>
<html>
  <head>
  </head>

  <body>
    <h1>Hi</h1>
    <h2 class="important">Hi again</h2>
    <p class="a">Random unattached paragraph</p>


    <div class="relevant">
      <p class="a">first</p>
      <p class="a">second</p>
      <p>third</p>
      <p>fourth</p>
```

```
      <p class="a">fifth</p>
      <p class="a">sixth</p>
      <p>seventh</p>
    </div>
  </body>
</html>
```

Next, attach a CSS file via a link. In the CSS, add a single selector:

```
* {
  color: red;
}
```

This changes the text color of every element to red. We'll use this file to practice our CSS selectors. Replace the * with a selector that selects the following element(s) and confirm that only the selected elements change to red:

1. Select the <h1> element.

2. Select the <h2> element by its class.

3. Select all of the relevant paragraphs.

4. Select the first paragraph of the relevant paragraphs.

5. Select the third paragraph of the relevant paragraphs.

6. Select the seventh relevant paragraph.

7. Select all of the paragraphs on the page.

8. Select only the random, unattached paragraph.

9. Select all of the paragraphs with the a class.

10. Select only the relevant paragraphs with the a class.

11. Select the second and fourth paragraphs (HINT: use a comma).

The Mozilla developer documentation has a great tutorial on selectors (*https://develop er.mozilla.org/en-US/docs/Web/Guide/CSS/Getting_started/Selectors*). Their tutorial covers much more than we've seen here. Once you're comfortable with the selectors I've introduced, I encourage you to read it.

Style the FAQ Page for Amazeriffic

If you completed the questions at the end of Chapter 2, you built a FAQ page for Amazeriffic. Link the *style.css* file to *faq.html* and add additional style rules to style the content portion of the page. If the structure of the header and footer is the same, you shouldn't have to modify those rules. You'll simply add additional rules for the main section to style the FAQ page.

Cascading Rules

In this chapter, I covered CSS's cascading rules at a very high level. I think that they are pretty intuitive for the most part. On the other hand, knowing the rules in detail is often helpful when troubleshooting CSS issues. The W3C has the rules clearly specified (*http://www.w3.org/TR/CSS2/cascade.html#cascade*). I encourage you to read them and commit them to memory, particularly if you find yourself doing a lot of work with CSS.

Responsiveness and Responsive Libraries

One major topic relating to CSS that we haven't learned is *responsive design*. A design is said to be *responsive* if it changes its layout based on the height and width of the browser in which it is displayed. This is important in this day and age because of the number of people who view web applications and web pages on mobile phones and tablets.

It's possible to build responsiveness into your CSS using *media queries*. But this goes a little beyond the scope of this book. You can read about them on Mozilla's developer website (*https://developer.mozilla.org/en-US/docs/Web/Guide/CSS/Media_queries*). I encourage you to do so.

In addition, several CSS frameworks are available that allow you to build responsive designs with minimal work. I've used both Twitter Bootstrap (*http://getboot strap.com*) and Zurb's Foundation (*http://foundation.zurb.com*). If you've enjoyed working with layouts and CSS in this chapter, you may want to read the documentation for both of these frameworks and try to rebuild the Amazeriffic layout as a responsive design using one of them. These two frameworks are also great to keep in mind as starting points for future projects.

## CHAPTER 4

The Interactivity

So far, we've studied three very important aspects of web application development. Sadly, however, we haven't built an application that actually *does* anything. We've just been able to structure content and then style it so it looks interesting.

In this chapter, we're going to start exploring interactivity. This will allow us to go beyond building web pages that don't change. Instead, we'll begin building dynamic applications that respond to user input.

To this end, we'll learn a little bit about JavaScript, the scripting language that runs inside every web browser, and jQuery, a JavaScript library that's useful for manipulating the DOM (among other things). In addition, we'll spend some time learning the basics of JavaScript as a language, with an emphasis on using and manipulating arrays.

Hello, JavaScript!

Let's start with an example. As before, we'll create a directory in *Projects* called *Chapter4*. In this directory, we'll start by creating a subdirectory called *Example1* and open that directory in Sublime. Next, we'll create three files: *index.html*, *style.css*, and *app.js*. We'll start with *index.html*:

```
<!doctype html>
<html>
  <head>
    <title>App Name</title>
    <link href="style.css" rel="stylesheet" type="text/css">
  </head>

  <body>
    <h1>App Name</h1>
    <p>App Description</p>

    <script src="http://code.jquery.com/jquery-2.0.3.min.js"></script>
```

```
            <script src="app.js"></script>
          </body>
        </html>
```

Everything in *index.html* should be familiar with the exception of the `<script>` tags at the bottom of the `body` element. Like the `link` element, `script` elements allow you to associate external files with your HTML, but the `script` elements typically point to JavaScript files. Another important thing to note is that unlike the `<link>` tag, `<script>` will always require a closing tag.

We choose to place the `<script>` tags in the `body` element instead of the `head` for a technical reason: the browser displays the page in a top-down fashion, creating the DOM elements as it comes across them in the HTML document. By placing the `<script>` tags at the end, the JavaScript files will be one of the last things the page loads. Because JavaScript files are often very large and take a bit of time to load, we like to do that last so that the user will get visual feedback from the other elements as fast as possible.

The first `<script>` tag includes a commonly used client-side library called *jQuery*, which we're going to learn a lot about in the coming sections. It loads jQuery from *http://code.jquery.com*, a *content delivery network*. This means we're not keeping a copy of jQuery on our local machine. Instead, we tell the browser to download it from an external site similar to the way we handled Google Fonts in the previous chapter. So our computer will need to be connected to the Internet for this example to work properly.

The second `script` element includes the *app.js* script that contains the JavaScript code that we write. We'll create that file next.

We also have a linked CSS file, which we've set up to remove the default margin and the padding of all the elements on the page. Using the universal selector will cause CSS Lint to give us a warning, but we'll ignore the warning for the time being:

```
* {
    margin: 0;
    padding: 0;
}
```

Our *app.js* file is the one we are most interested in, and its content is shown in the following code. Before we discuss it, go ahead and type it in exactly as you see here, and then open up *index.html* in your web browser:

```
var main = function () {
    "use strict";

    window.alert("hello world!");
};

$(document).ready(main);
```

If you typed in everything correctly, you should see an alert dialog box that says *hello world!* when the page loads, as shown in Figure 4-1.

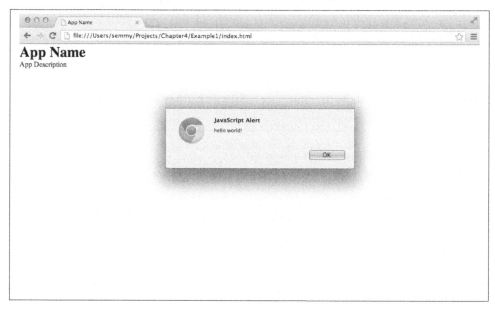

Figure 4-1. Our first (sort of) interactive app

This is a basic skeleton that we'll use in all of our JavaScript programs. It does two primary things that you can generalize to the rest of the client-side app code in this book: (1) it defines a global function called `main`, which is the entry point for the execution of our program, and (2) it uses jQuery to set up the execution of the `main` function once the HTML document is fully loaded and ready.

The code is also set up to run in *strict* mode, which disallows certain bad aspects of JavaScript that have caused problems for programmers in the past. This will always be the first line in our `main` function. The script also creates the "hello world!" dialog, but that's just for this example.

Our First Interactive App

Now we'll use jQuery to create something a little more interesting. Our goal is to create a simple app that allows the user to enter some text, which subsequently will be appended to the page in a different place. This example will demonstrate that it's very easy to make interesting things happen in a few lines of code.

Let's start by creating a new directory in our *Chapter4* directory called *Example2*. Initialize an empty Git repository and open the directory in Sublime. Re-create the three example files from the preceding section (*index.html*, *style.css*, and *app.js*). As has been discussed in previous chapters, it's a good idea to memorize this basic skeleton structure so that you can create it from scratch without having to copy any code.

Once you have the skeleton project set up, go ahead and make your initial commit to your Git repository.

The Structure

Let's take a quick look at the user interface before we get started. It is shown in Figure 4-2.

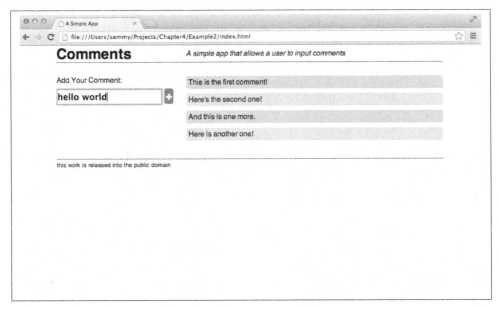

Figure 4-2. The user interface for our first interactive app

You'll see that the structure consists of three primary elements: the `header`, the `footer`, and `main`. With this in mind, we can modify our HTML to outline our user interface:

```
<!doctype html>
<html>
  <head>
    <title>A Simple App</title>

    <link href="style.css" rel="stylesheet" type="text/css">
  </head>

  <body>
    <header>
    </header>
```

```
<main>
  <!-- note that we use a dash here for our CSS class name
       that contains multiple words, that's a CSS convention -->
  <section class="comment-input">
  </section>

  <section class="comments">
  </section>
</main>

<footer>
</footer>

<script src="http://code.jquery.com/jquery-2.0.3.min.js"></script>
<script src="app.js"></script>
</body>
</html>
```

Once you modify your HTML to look similar to the preceding code, commit it to your Git repository. Next, fill in the header and footer elements, along with the primary part of the main content on the left side, to correspond with the design in Figure 4-2. Hopefully you can see that some of the sections will have an `<h1>`, `<h2>`, or `<h3>` tag along with some content. Add those now.

For the comment-input section, we'll use a new HTML tag: `<input>`. The input element represents an input text box, and doesn't require a closing tag. Add an empty `<input>` tag to the comment-input section. You can also add the paragraph with our "Add Your Comment:" prompt:

```
<section class="comment-input">
  <p>Add Your Comment:</p>
  <input type="text">
</section>
```

In the .comments section, add a few example comments that will simply be paragraph tags. This will help us with the styling. So, for example, we may modify our comments section to look something like this:

```
<section class="comments">
  <p>This is the first comment!</p>
  <p>Here's the second one!</p>
  <p>And this is one more.</p>
  <p>Here is another one</p>
</section>
```

Finally, we'll add a button element labeled with a + character. Although we haven't seen the button element yet, there's nothing particularly special about it until we attach a JavaScript behavior to it. To add a button, we'll add the `<button>` tag immediately following the `<input>` tag. The code contained in my `comment-input` section looks something like this:

```
<section class="comment-input">
  <p>Add Your Comment:</p>
  <input type="text"><button>+</button>
</section>
```

Once we have the structure defined, let's commit it to our Git repository and move on to styling the page.

The Style

The style consists of a few simple things. First, it might be helpful to use a reset, but don't feel obligated to do so for this example. At minimum you'll want to keep the simple CSS starting point where we've zeroed out the default margin and padding.

The width of the body is 855 pixels in this example, with the left column taking up a third of that. The other two-thirds of the body consists of the comments.

One interesting aspect of the comments section is that we've alternated colors for comments. In other words, the even-numbered comments are one color, and the odd-numbered comments are another. We can achieve this effect using pure CSS—we'll simply use the `nth-child` pseudoclass along with the even or odd value. For example, if we want to alternate the colors `lavender` and `gainsboro`, we can create CSS rulesets that look like this:

```
.comments p:nth-child(even) {
    background: lavender;
}

.comments p:nth-child(odd) {
    background: gainsboro;
}
```

If you've added some example comments, you should see the background colors alternate once you add this ruleset to the CSS. Notice that we've also given our comments a slight `border-radius` to make them have rounded edges.

Other than that, the rest of this layout should follow previous examples pretty closely. Finish styling the interface as best as you can and commit your code to the Git repository so we can move on to making it interactive. If you have trouble, you can see it in our GitHub repository (*http://bit.ly/1fY92Fe*).

The Interactivity

Now we're ready to work on the interactivity. We'll build this example step by step, making Git commits along the way.

Handling click events

Let's start by doing the following: when the user clicks the + button, we'll insert a new comment into the comments section. To do this, we'll begin by modifying our *app.js* code to look like this:

```
var main = function () {
    "use strict";

    $(".comment-input button").on("click", function (event) {
        console.log("Hello World!");
    });
};


$(document).ready(main);
```

Open up your page in your browser and open the Chrome Developer Tools as described in the previous chapter. Once there, click the Console tab in the top bar of the Developer Tools. Now, when you click the + button on the page, you should see "Hello World!" appear in the console! If everything is set up and working correctly, it's a good time to commit your progress to your Git repository.

What's happening here? This code is attaching an *event listener* to the DOM element referenced in the call to the $ function. Notice that the contents of the $ look a lot like a CSS selector—and that's no coincidence! That's exactly what it is! jQuery allows you to easily target elements in the DOM using CSS selectors, and then manipulate them using JavaScript.

The event for which we're listening on the `button` element is the "click" event. The listener itself is a function that simply prints "Hello World!" to the console. So we can translate the code into English as follows: *when the user clicks the +, print "Hello World!" to the console.*

Of course, we don't actually want to print "Hello World!" to the console—we want to add a comment to the comments section. To move toward making that happen, we'll modify our code slightly, replacing the `console.log` with another line of jQuery that appends a DOM element to the comments section:

```
var main = function () {
    "use strict";

    $(".comment-input button").on("click", function (event) {
        $(".comments").append("<p>this is a new comment</p>");
    });
};


$(document).ready(main);
```

Reload your browser window, and if all goes well you should be able to click + and see "this is a new comment" added to the comments section. You'll notice that the jQuery code (which starts with the $) selects the comments section in the same way that we select it in our CSS file, and then appends some HTML code to it. If everything is working, commit your code with a meaningful commit message. If it's not working, go back and make sure you've typed it in correctly.

Dynamically manipulating the DOM

We've made some progress toward our goal, but every time we click the button it adds the exact same content. We want to change the text in the paragraph based on the content contained in the input box. We'll start by creating a variable to hold the DOM element that we're going to append:

```
var main = function () {
    "use strict";

    $(".comment-input button").on("click", function (event) {
        var $new_comment = $("<p>");

        $new_comment.text("this is a new comment");
        $(".comments").append($new_comment);
    });
};

$(document).ready(main);
```

This modification hasn't actually changed anything that our code is doing: it simply *refactored* it so that we can more easily customize the text content of the paragraph tag. Specifically, we've added a *variable* declaration and assignment. The variable name $new_comment can be anything that we want, but if the variable will hold a jQuery object, it's sometimes helpful to distinguish it by using the $ as the first character.

The first line of the new code creates a new paragraph element as a jQuery object, and the second line changes the text content of the new paragraph element to "this is a new comment." Because jQuery allows for *chaining* function calls, we can actually do both lines in a single line if we'd prefer:

```
var $new_comment = $("<p>").text("this is a new comment");
```

Even if we do use the chaining feature in jQuery, it's important to remember that two things are happening here—a new paragraph element is being created, and then the text content of the paragraph element is being changed to "this is a new comment."

Next, we'd like to get the content of the input box to store it in the variable that we've created. Before moving on, however, take a moment and try to figure out how to target the input element that is contained in the .comment-input section with jQuery.

Hopefully you gave it a try using CSS selectors! The answer is the following:

```
$(".comment-input input");
```

Just like in CSS, this line targets the elements with the `.comment-input` class, and then drills down to target the `input` elements that are descendants of the `.comment-input` sections. Because only one element meets this criteria, it is the only element that will be selected.

Now that we know that, we can get the content out. It turns out that jQuery has a function that returns the content of an input box, and that function is called `val`, which is just shorthand for value. We can access the content of the input box by using the following code:

```
$(".comment-input input").val();
```

Now we just need to do something with it! In this case, we're going to make the content of the input box the text value of our new paragraph element. So we can refactor our code to look like this:

```
var main = function () {
    "use strict";

    $(".comment-input button").on("click", function (event) {
        var $new_comment = $("<p>"),
            comment_text = $(".comment-input input").val();

        $new_comment.text(comment_text);

        $(".comments").append($new_comment);
    });
};

$(document).ready(main);
```

And if we'd like, we can do much of this in a single line without using an intermediate variable to store the result of the call to the `val` function:

```
var $new_comment = $("<p>").text($(".comment-input input").val());
```

Now open the app in your browser. If everything is working correctly you should be able to type content into the text box, and then click the button and see the content added to the comment section. If something isn't working, you can double-check to make sure you have all your semicolons and parentheses in the correct place, and then open up the Chrome Developer Tools to check to see if there are any errors in the console. The error might give you clues to what you've typed incorrectly.

Once you get everything working to your satisfaction, commit the changes to your Git repository with a meaningful commit message.

At this point everything should be roughly working. For our users, however, the experience leaves a lot to be desired and we can make a few minor changes that would substantially improve it.

Squashing a bug

You probably didn't realize that there's a bug in our code yet, but it turns out that there is! It's probably useful to take a moment to think about the expected behavior of the application and see if you can find it.

If you still haven't found it, here it is: when we click the add button and there is no content in our input box, our jQuery program adds an empty p element to the DOM. How does this bug present itself? It actually appears as a problem with the even/odd coloring scheme that we applied in our CSS.

To see this bug rear its ugly head, start by reloading the page. Next, type in one comment using the input box, clear out the box, click the add button, and then add another comment. If you followed those directions, you'll see that the two comments that show up are the same color! That's because the empty comment is taking the odd color and it doesn't show up.

We can also verify the bug is caused by the empty p element by using the Elements tab in the Chrome Developer Tools window. Start by opening the Chrome Developer Tools and clicking the Elements tab. Next, drill down into the main element and then into the comments section. After you have that section open, click the button with no content in the input box. You'll see the empty p elements added.

How can we fix this? Basically, we'll insert a check to see if the content of the input box is empty before we do anything with it. We can do this using an if statement:

```
$(".comment-input button").on("click", function (event) {
    var $new_comment;

    if ($(".comment-input input").val() !== "") {
        $new_comment = $("<p>").text($(".comment-input input").val());
        $(".comments").append($new_comment);
    }
});
```

The !== confirms that the content of the input box does *not* equal the empty string, which is basically equivalent to checking to see if the input box is empty. So the if statement only executes the code if the input box is not empty. This simple change should fix the bug, and once we do that, it's a good idea to go ahead and make a commit to your Git repository.

 Notice that we moved the variable declaration above the if statement. It's always a good idea to keep your variables declared at the top of your function definitions.

Clearing out the input box

The next major user experience problem is that the input box is not clearing out when users click the button. If they want to enter a second comment, they have to manually delete the content that was there previously. It's actually pretty easy to clear it out: if we call the `val` method of the jQuery object with an explicit value, it will fill the box with that value. In other words, we can clear out the current content by sending the empty string to the `val` method:

```
$(".comment-input input").val("");
```

So one more line of code will add this feature:

```
$(".comment-input button").on("click", function (event) {
    var $new_comment;

    if ($(".comment-input input").val() !== "") {
        $new_comment = $("<p>").text($(".comment-input input").val());
        $(".comments").append($new_comment);
        $(".comment-input input").val("");
    }
});
```

Making the Enter key work as expected

Another thing that users will expect is that the Enter key on the keyboard should submit the comment. This is often true when we're interacting with a chat program, for example.

How can we make that happen? We can add an additional event handler that listens for the keypress event on the `input` element itself. We can add this directly after our click event handler:

```
$(".comment-input input").on("keypress", function (event) {
    console.log("hello world!");
});
```

Note that two main differences exist between this listener and our previous listener. The first is that this listener is set up to listen for the keypress event instead of the click event. The second is that we're listening for an event on a different element: in this case we're listening on the input box, whereas in the previous example we were listening on the button element.

If you try out this code, you'll see that "Hello World!" gets logged to the Chrome developer console every time we type a key. We want to ignore most key presses in the input box and only react when the user presses the Enter key. To do this we can use the event local variable that we ignored in the previous handler—that holds the value of the key pressed. How can we see that value? Let's modify our code slightly:

```
$(".comment-input input").on("keypress", function (event) {
    console.log("this is the keyCode " + event.keyCode);
});
```

Note that the C in `keyCode` is capitalized. This is an example of *camelCase*: when we have a variable name that has multiple words in it, we capitalize each word after the first.

In the output, we're using + to concatenate the value of the `keyCode` to the string that starts "this is the keyCode." When your code is running, you'll see the actual value of the `keyCode` in the output.

Now when we reload the browser and start typing into the input box, we'll see the keyCodes scroll up the screen. We can use this to figure out the keyCode for the Enter key. Once we do that, we can wrap our code in an `if` statement to only respond to the Enter key:

```
$(".comment-input input").on("keypress", function (event) {
    if (event.keyCode === 13) {
        console.log("this is the keyCode " + event.keyCode);
    }
});
```

This code only prints out the `keyCode` when the Enter key is pressed. Finally, we can copy the code from our other event listener that adds a new comment:

```
$(".comment-input input").on("keypress", function (event) {
    var $new_comment;

    if (event.keyCode === 13) {
        if ($(".comment-input input").val() !== "") {
            var $new_comment = $("<p>").text($(".comment-input input").val());
            $(".comments").append($new_comment);
            $(".comment-input input").val("");
        }
    }
});
```

Fading in our new comment

Now all of our important features should be working. But let's add one more aspect to the experience: instead of the new comment just appearing immediately, let's have it fade in. Fortunately, jQuery makes this very easy because every jQuery element has a `fadeIn` method built in. But in order to have the element fade in, we'll need to ensure that it's hidden first. To do that, we'll call the `hide` method on the element before appending it to the DOM. The following code does exactly that:

```
$(".comment-input button").on("click", function (event) {
    var $new_comment;

    if ($(".comment-input input").val() !== "") {
        $new_comment = $("<p>").text($(".comment-input input").val());
        $new_comment.hide();
        $(".comments").append($new_comment);
```

```
        $new_comment.fadeIn();
        $(".comment-input input").val("");
    }
});
```

Now, when we add a comment with the button, we'll see it fade in slowly instead of appearing. We should also modify our keypress event to do the same thing. Once you get that working, go ahead and commit your code.

Refactoring for simplicity

At this point, my *app.js* file looks like this, and yours should look similar:

```
var main = function () {
    "use strict";

    $(".comment-input button").on("click", function (event) {
        var $new_comment;

        if ($(".comment-input input").val() !== "") {
            $new_comment = $("<p>").text($(".comment-input input").val());
            $new_comment.hide();
            $(".comments").append($new_comment);
            $new_comment.fadeIn();
            $(".comment-input input").val("");
        }
    });

    $(".comment-input input").on("keypress", function (event) {
        var $new_comment;

        if (event.keyCode === 13) {
            if ($(".comment-input input").val() !== "") {
                $new_comment = $("<p>").text($(".comment-input input").val());
                $new_comment.hide();
                $(".comments").append($new_comment);
                $new_comment.fadeIn();
                $(".comment-input input").val("");
            }
        }
    });
};

$(document).ready(main);
```

One thing you'll immediately notice is that we have duplicated code. In particular, our code that adds a comment is duplicated in both event handlers, and when we changed one of them to fade in the text, we had to change the other as well. This violates a principle of software development known as the *DRY* (Don't Repeat Yourself) principle. Whenever we are cutting and pasting code, a little red light should go off in our mind to warn us that there's probably a better way to do what we're trying to do. In this case, we can rearrange our code to look like this:

```
var main = function () {
    "use strict";

    var addCommentFromInputBox = function () {
        var $new_comment;

        if ($(".comment-input input").val() !== "") {
            $new_comment = $("<p>").text($(".comment-input input").val());
            $new_comment.hide();
            $(".comments").append($new_comment);
            $new_comment.fadeIn();
            $(".comment-input input").val("");
        }
    };

    $(".comment-input button").on("click", function (event) {
        addCommentFromInputBox();
    });

    $(".comment-input input").on("keypress", function (event) {
        if (event.keyCode === 13) {
            addCommentFromInputBox();
        }
    });
};

$(document).ready(main);
```

In this example, we abstract the duplicated code as a reusable function and then call the function in each of the event listeners. We do this by declaring a variable to store the function and then defining the function. This leads to code that is much more maintainable: now when we have to make a change to the comment-adding behavior, we only have to do it in one place!

jQuery Generalizations

Wow—that example was pretty intense, but hopefully you made it through in one piece! On the bright side, we got to see a lot of the types of things that jQuery can do. Now let's take a step back and examine some of the things that we can generalize from that example. Essentially, jQuery offers us three things:

- A streamlined, expressive approach to DOM manipulation
- A consistent approach to DOM event handling
- A simplified approach to AJAX

We'll study the first two in this chapter, and the third in the next. It's also worth mentioning that jQuery also has a tremendous number of third-party plug-ins that can quickly and easily enhance websites.

Setting Up a Project

Before we begin, let's start by discussing a little more about our workflow. Generally, the client-side portion of our application can span multiple HTML, CSS, and JavaScript files. Therefore, it's often helpful to keep those things organized in a meaningful way.

From here on out, we'll keep all of our HTML files in the root of our project directory, and then we'll have three subdirectories called *stylesheets*, *images*, and *javascripts*. We'll make sure that their content appropriately reflects their names.

This changes things slightly when we're linking stylesheets or importing scripts. Here's an example of how this change affects our HTML:

```
<!doctype html>
<html>
  <head>
    <link href="stylesheets/reset.css" rel="stylesheet">
    <link href="stylesheets/style.css" rel="stylesheet">
  </head>

  <body>
    <script src="http://code.jquery.com/jquery-2.0.3.min.js"></script>
    <script src="javascripts/app.js"></script>
  </body>
</html>
```

Note that we've had to explictly qualify the location of our script and CSS files by prepending them with a forward slash and the directory name.

Comments

Before we start typing in real code, it's probably good to start with a discussion of JavaScript comments. Just like in HTML and CSS, we can put comments in our JavaScript to annotate our code for human readers. There are two types of comments: a single-line comment and a multiline comment. Single-line comments are created by using two forward slashes next to each other, and multiline comments look just like CSS comments:

```
// this is a single-line comment, which runs to the end of the line

var a = 5; // this is a single-line comment following some actual code

/* This is a multiline comment that will run until
   we close it. It looks like a CSS comment */
```

Selectors

As we've seen in the previous example, jQuery selectors are very similar to CSS selectors. In fact, we can use any CSS selector as a jQuery selector. So, for example, the following jQuery selectors select exactly what we'd expect:

```
$("*");              // selects all elements in the document
$("h1");             // selects all of the h1 elements
$("p");              // selects all of the p elements
$("p .first");       // selects all paragraph elements with the class 'first'
$(".first");         // selects all elements with the class 'first'
$("p:nth-child(3)"); // selects all paragraph elements that are the third child
```

It turns out that jQuery selectors aren't identical to CSS selectors in all cases. In fact, jQuery adds a rich set of pseudoclasses and pseudoelements that are not currently available in CSS. Additionally, certain valid CSS identifiers have to be represented differently when used in jQuery (special characters such as . must be escaped by two backslashes). But for our purposes, we are going to think of jQuery selectors as CSS selectors that return DOM elements that we can manipulate in our JavaScript. If you're interested in learning more, you can check out the jQuery selector documentation (*http://api.jquery.com/category/selectors/*).

DOM Manipulation

Once we've successfully used selectors to add elements to the DOM, it's likely that we're going to want to manipulate them in some way. jQuery makes that pretty easy.

Adding elements to the DOM

To get started, it's helpful to remember our tree mental model for the DOM. For instance, consider this HTML snippet:

```
<body>
  <h1>This is an example!</h1>
  <main>
  </main>

  <footer>
  </footer>
</body>
```

Note that our main and footer elements are empty. We can draw a tree diagram as shown in Figure 4-3.

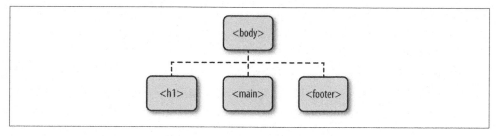

Figure 4-3. A tree diagram of the DOM before any manipulation is done with jQuery

To create an element, we use the same $ operator that we use to select an element. Instead of sending in a selector, however, we send in the tag representing the element we'd like to create:

```
// By convention, I start jQuery object variables with a $
var $newUL = $("<ul>"); //create a new ul element
var $newParagraphElement = $("<p>"); // create a new p element
```

Once we've created an element, we can add things to it, including other HTML elements. For example, we can add text to our p element like this:

```
$newParagraphElement.text("this is a paragraph");
```

After we execute that code, our paragraph DOM element will be equivalent to the following HTML:

```
<p>this is a paragraph</p>
```

The ul and the p elements that we've created are not part of the DOM that appears on the page yet, so our tree diagram would have those new elements floating off in space, but referenced by their associated jQuery variables. This is illustrated in Figure 4-4.

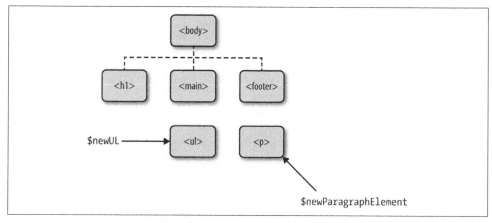

Figure 4-4. After the ul and p elements are created, but not yet attached to the DOM

We can add it to the page by selecting the element to which we want to append it, and then calling the append function on the jQuery object. For example, if we want to add this element as a child of the `footer` element, we can do the following:

```
$("footer").append($newParagraphElement);
```

Now our content should appear in the footer because the element is connected to the tree diagram! It looks something like Figure 4-5.

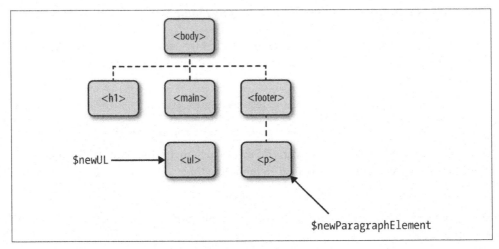

Figure 4-5. The DOM, after the p element is added to the footer

We can actually build far more complicated DOM structures before we make them appear on the page. For example, we can add `li` elements to the `ul` element we created previously:

```
// we can chain our creation and call to add the text
var $listItemOne = $("<li>").text("this is the first list item");
var $listItemTwo = $("<li>").text("second list item");
var $listItemThree = $("<li>").text("OMG third list item");

// now we'll append these elements to the ul element we created earlier
$newUL.append($listItemOne);
$newUL.append($listItemTwo);
$newUL.append($listItemThree);
```

At this point, we have a new *subtree* disconnected from the rest of the tree. It looks something like Figure 4-6.

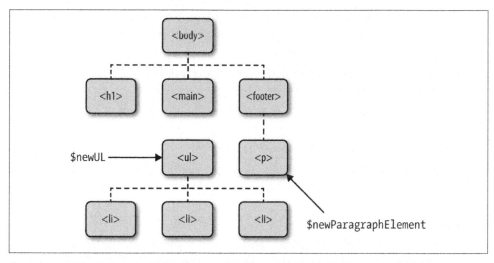

Figure 4-6. The DOM, with an unconnected subtree that represents a ul element

Now suppose we want to attach this subtree to the body as part of the main element. We follow the same pattern as before, but we only have to attach the *root* of our subtree!

```
$("main").append($newUL);
```

Now our DOM tree looks like Figure 4-7.

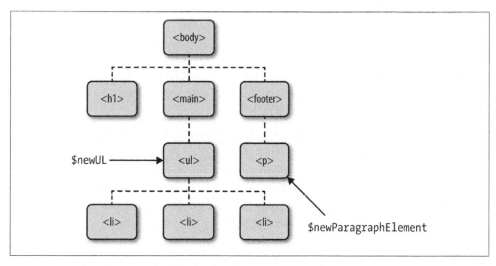

Figure 4-7. The DOM, with the ul subtree now connected

jQuery provides some flexibility in adding things once we have a DOM element select-ed. For instance, we can prepend elements instead of appending them, which makes them the first child of the parent node:

```
var $footerFirstChild = $("<p>").text("I'm the first child of the footer!");
$("footer").prepend($footerFirstChild);
```

In addition, we can use `appendTo` or `prependTo` to change the way our code reads:

```
// this is equivalent to the previous line
$footerFirstChild.appendTo($("footer"));
```

Don't forget that we can also use the Elements tab in the Chrome Developer Tools to confirm that our DOM is updated as described in the previous section.

Removing elements from the DOM

Removing elements is almost as easy, and jQuery provides a couple ways of doing this. One thing we can do is just use the `remove` function on a selector, which will remove the selected element(s) from the DOM:

```
// remove the first list item from
// the list we created previously
$("ul li:first-child").remove();
```

We can also delete all children of an element by using the `empty` function on a jQuery object. So, for instance, to clear the list items that we created in the previous example we could do the following:

```
// remove all children from the
// list we created previously
$newUL.empty();
```

In the first example, we learned that we could use `fadeIn` to have an invisible element fade in. In addition to that, we can make elements disappear using `fadeOut` or `slideUp` before removing them from the DOM!

```
// this will remove the footer paragraph from the DOM.
$("footer p").fadeOut();
```

It turns out that `fadeOut` doesn't actually remove the element from the DOM—it just hides it. To remove it, we have to call `remove` on the element, but we have to do it *after* it is finished fading out. This means we have to schedule it to happen asynchronously, which we'll learn how to do in the next section.

Events and Asynchronicity

In the first example of this chapter, we saw how to process both the *click* event and the *keypress* event. In general, we can process any event using the on pattern. For example, we can respond to the `dblclick` event, which is triggered when a user double-clicks:

```
$(".button").on("dblclick", function () {
    alert("Hey! You double-clicked!");
});
```

In general, this style of programming is called *event-driven* or *asynchronous* programming. How is that different from traditional programming? We're likely used to our code executing like this:

```
console.log("this will print first");
console.log("this will print second");
console.log("this will print third");
```

With asynchronous programming, certain event-related functions take *callbacks*, or functions that are to be executed later, as arguments. This makes it so the execution order is not always so clear:

```
console.log("this will print first");

$("button").on("click", function () {
    console.log("this will only print when someone clicks");
});

console.log("this will print second");
```

Here is another example that doesn't rely on user input for callbacks to be executed. We've already seen the `ready` function, which waits until the DOM is ready to execute the callback. The `setTimeout` function behaves similarly, but it executes the callback after the specified number of milliseconds have passed:

```
// This is a jQuery event that executes the callback
// when the DOM is ready. In this example, we're using
// an anonymous function instead of sending the main
// function as an argument
$(document).ready(function () {
    console.log("this will print when the document is ready");
});

// This is a built-in JavaScript function that executes
// after the specified number of milliseconds
setTimeout(function () {
    console.log("this will print after 3 seconds");
}, 3000);

// this will print before anything else, even though
// it appears last
console.log("this will print first");
```

Right now, event-driven programming based on user interaction probably makes sense, and the examples involving `setTimeout` and the `ready` function should be relatively easy to understand. The problems start to arise when we want to sequence events. For example, consider a situation where we are using jQuery's `slideDown` function to animate some text sliding down:

```
var main = function () {
    "use strict";

    // create and hide our content as a div
    var $content = $("<div>Hello World!</div>").hide();

    // append the content to the body element
    $("body").append($content);

    // slide the content down for 2 seconds
    $content.slideDown(2000);
};

$(document).ready(main);
```

Now suppose we'd like to fade in a second message *after* the content slides down. We might immediately try to do something like this:

```
var main = function () {
    "use strict";

    // create and hide our content as a div
    var $content = $("<div>Hello World!</div>").hide();
    var $moreContent = $("<div>Goodbye World!</div>").hide();

    // append the content to the body element
    $("body").append($content);

    // slide the content down for 2 seconds
    $content.slideDown(2000);

    // append the second content to the body
    $("body").append($moreContent);

    // fade in the second content
    $moreContent.fadeIn();
}

$(document).ready(main);
```

Type in this code and run it. You'll see that the "Goodbye World!" div fades in *while* the "Hello World!" div is sliding down. This is not what we wanted. Take a moment and think about why that is happening.

You've probably figured out that the `slideDown` function is happening asynchronously. This means that the code that follows is being executed *while* the slide down is occurring! Fortunately, jQuery offers us a workaround—most asynchronous functions accept an optional callback parameter as its last argument, which allows us to sequence asynchronous events. So we can achieve the effect we're shooting for by modifying our code as follows:

```javascript
var main = function () {
    "use strict";

    // create and hide our content as a div
    var $content = $("<div>Hello World!</div>").hide();
    var $moreContent = $("<div>Goodbye World!</div>").hide();

    // append the content to the body element
    $("body").append($content);

    // slide the content down for 2 seconds
    // and then execute the callback which
    // contains the second content
    $content.slideDown(2000, function () {
        // append the second content to the body
        $("body").append($moreContent);

        // fade in the second content
        $moreContent.fadeIn();
    });
};

$(document).ready(main);
```

We would use the same approach to finish off our example from the previous section. To remove the p element from the footer when it is finished fading out, we would do something like this:

```javascript
$("footer p").fadeOut(1000, function () {
    // this will happen when the p element
    // is finished fading out
    $("footer p").remove();
});
```

Later on in the book, we'll see other examples of asynchronous programming with Node.js, but for now it's good to get the hang of these functions and understand the patterns.

JavaScript Generalizations

A number of frontend developers know a lot about HTML and CSS, and then enough jQuery to get plug-ins working and do some basic DOM manipulation. A knowledge of those three things can get you pretty far in frontend web development. On the other hand, it's a good idea to learn as much about JavaScript as possible in order to be a highly effective frontend engineer and to build more complex web applications.

In this section, we'll review some of the basics of JavaScript. My plan is to keep it short and to focus on the most important aspects of the language. We'll see an example that ties all of these ideas together at the end of the chapter.

Interacting with JavaScript in the Chrome JavaScript Console

It turns out that we don't have to create an entire project to start playing around with JavaScript. Chrome has a pretty nice interactive JavaScript interpreter built into its Developer Tools!

Let's start by opening a new window or tab in our browser and open the Chrome Developer Tools as described in the previous chapter (go to View → Developer and click Developer Tools). Next, click the Console tab at the top. You should be greeted with a prompt that looks similar to Figure 4-8.

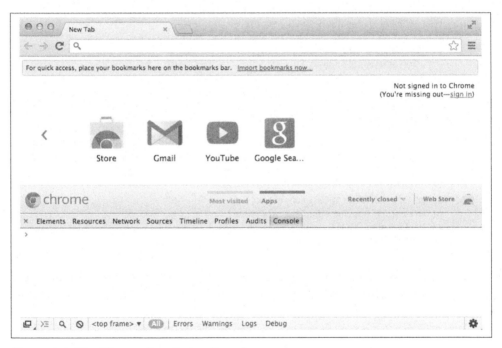

Figure 4-8. The Chrome JavaScript Console

We can now interact with the JavaScript Console. For example, type in the following code, pressing Enter after each line:

```
5+2;
//=> 7

Math.random();
//=> 0.3896130360662937
```

```
console.log("hello world!");
//=> hello world!
```

The first line should print out 7, because the numerical expression evaluates to 7. The second line should print out a random decimal number between 0 and 1.

The last line should print out "hello world!" followed by a line that says "undefined." That's okay—Chrome always prints out the result of evaluating the last line. The console.log statement does something, but it doesn't actually *evaluate* to anything, which is why Chrome prints out undefined.

For the rest of this section, you can type the examples directly into the JavaScript Console with one minor caveat. If you need to type in something that appears on multiple lines (like an if statement or a for loop), you'll need to press Shift-Enter instead of just Enter at the end of the line. Give it a try by typing in the following code:

```
var number = 5;

if (number >= 3) {
    console.log("The number is bigger than or equal to 3!");
}
//=> The number is bigger than or equal to 3!
```

Also note that you can press the up and down arrows on your keyboard to navigate through your previously typed code snippets (just like you can navigate your command history in your terminal window).

Variables and Types

JavaScript is not a strongly typed language. This means that variables can hold any data of any type (like integers, strings, and numbers with decimals). This is different from languages like Java or C++, where variables have to be declared to hold specific types:

```
// This holds a string
var message = "hello world!";

// These hold numbers
var count = 1;
var pi = 3.1415;

// This holds a boolean
var isFun = true;

console.log(message);
//=> hello world!

console.log(pi);
//=> 3.1415
```

```
    console.log(isFun);
    //=> true
```

Variable declarations/definitions can be defined as a single statement separated by commas. As I mentioned before, it's a good idea to put them at the top of your function definition. This convention creates consistency that adds to the readability of your code:

```
var main = function () {
    "use strict";

    var message = "hello world!",
        count = 1,
        pi = 3.1415,
        isFun = true;

    console.log(message);
};
```

Functions

We've seen a lot of examples of functions so far. Unlike C++ and Java, functions are *first-class* citizens. That means we can assign functions to variables, send in functions as parameters to other functions, and define *anonymous* functions (which are simply functions without names):

```
// define a function and store it
// in a variable called sayHello
var sayHello = function () {
    console.log("hello world!");
}

// execute the function in the sayHello variable
sayHello();
//=> "hello world!"
```

Similar to other languages, JavaScript functions can have *inputs* and an *output*. The inputs are often referred to as *arguments* or *parameters* and they are specified inside the parentheses of the function definition. The output is often referred to as the *return value* and is always preceded by the keyword return:

```
// define a function called add which
// accepts two inputs: num1 and num2
// and has one output: the sum of the
// two numbers
var add = function (num1, num2) {
    // add the inputs, and store the result in sum
    var sum = num1 + num2;

    // return the sum
    return sum;
}
```

```
// execute the add function with 5 and 2 as inputs
add(5,2);
//=> 7
```

One interesting consequence of the fact that functions are first-class objects in JavaScript is that we can use other functions as inputs to functions. We've utilized this pattern by sending in anonymous functions as callbacks, but we've also used named functions. For example, we sent in a function called `main` to the `ready` function in jQuery:

```
// the main entry point of our program
var main = function () {
    "use strict";
    console.log("hello world!");
};

// set up main to run once the DOM is ready
$(document).ready(main);
```

Although C++ has function pointers, it doesn't easily admit anonymous functions so code patterns like those that we've seen aren't often used. Likewise, at least at the time of this writing, Java has no easy mechanism for creating functions that accept other functions as parameters.

In the next chapters, we'll have the opportunity to write functions that take other functions as parameters. This becomes helpful when we're doing more complex asynchronous programming.

Selection

One of the first control structures we learn in any language is the `if` statement. This lets us tell the interpreter that a block of code should only be executed if some condition is true:

```
var count = 101;

if (count > 100) {
    console.log("the count is bigger than 100");
}
//=> the count is bigger than 100

count = 99;

if (count > 100) {
    console.log("the count is bigger than 100");
}
//=> prints nothing
```

An `else` statement allows us to do something different if the condition is false:

```
var count = 99;

if (count > 100) {
    console.log("the count is bigger than 100");
} else {
    console.log("the count is less than 100");
}
//=> the count is less than 100
```

Sometimes we'll find that we want to do multiple mutually exclusive things depending on different conditions. When that's necessary, the if-else-if pattern often comes in handy:

```
var count = 150;

if (count < 100) {
    console.log("the count is less than 100");
} else if (count <= 200) {
    console.log("the count is between 100 and 200 inclusive");
} else {
    console.log("the count is bigger than 200");
}
//=> the count is between 100 and 200 inclusive
```

Best of all, conditions don't have to be simple. We can use the && (and), || (or), and ! (not) operators to build more complex conditions. As mentioned in Chapter 2, the | key is found right above the Enter key on your keyboard—you'll have to hold down Shift to get it instead of the backslash:

```
// check to see if *any* of the conditions are true
if (cardRank === "king" || cardRank === "queen" || cardRank === "jack") {
    console.log("that's a high ranking card!");
} else {
    console.log("not quite royalty!");
}

// check if the card is the ace of spades
if (cardRank === "ace" && cardSuit === "spades") {
    console.log("THAT'S THE ACE OF SPADES!");
} else {
    console.log("Sadly, that's not the ace of spades");
}

// check if the card is *not* the ace of spades
// by flipping the output using the ! operator
if (!(cardRank === "ace" && cardSuit === "spades")) {
    console.log("That card is not the ace of spades!");
}
```

In JavaScript, a single equals sign represents an assignment statement, and a triple equals sign represents a comparison that returns true or false if the left and right sides of the expression are equivalent. We'll talk more about that later.

Iteration

Often, we'll have to do things multiple times. For example, suppose we want to print out the first 100 numbers. Obviously we can do this in a pretty naive way:

```
console.log(0);
console.log(1);
console.log(2);
// ... ugh
console.log(99);
console.log(100);
```

That's a lot of code! It's much easier to use a looping structure to print out all 100 numbers:

```
var num; // this will be the number that we print out

// print 101 numbers starting with 0
for (num = 0; num <= 100; num = num + 1) {
    console.log(num);
}
```

This achieves the same thing as the preceding code, but in a much more concise way. This is an example of a for loop.

A for loop consists of four (pun intended) things. Three of them are in the parentheses that follow the word for and I refer to those as the *initialization statement*, the *continuation condition*, and the *update statement*. The fourth is the *loop body*, which is the code that is in between the curly braces. The initialization statement occurs just before the loop body runs for the first time. The update statement runs each time the loop body completes. And the continuation condition is checked right before the loop body is run (even the first time).

Here are two annotated for loops that achieve the same result—printing out the even numbers less than 100:

```
var i;

// initialization: i gets set to 0
// continuation: keep going as long as i is smaller than 100
// update: add 2 to i
// body: print out i
// in other words, print out only the even numbers starting with 0 and ending
// with 98
```

```
for (i = 0; i < 100; i = i + 2) {
    console.log(i);
}

// initialization: i gets set to 0
// continuation: keep going as long as i is smaller than 100
// update: add 1 to i
// body: print out i only if the remainder when dividing i by 2 is 0
// print out only the even numbers starting with 0 and ending with 98
for (i = 0; i < 100; i = i + 1) {
    if (i%2 === 0) {
        console.log(i);
    }
}
```

In the second example, we use the remainder operator (%), which yields the remainder from integer division. In other words, 5%2 evaluates to 1 because 5/2 is 2 with a remainder of 1. In the example, we're using this operator to check for divisibility by 2 (which tells us the number is even). Even though this operator may *seem* esoteric, it's actually extremely useful. In fact, it's so useful for experienced programmers that questions involving it are often asked at job interviews for programming positions (see the FizzBuzz practice problem at the end of this chapter).

If you're familiar with while and do...while loops from Java or C++, you'll be pleased to know that JavaScript supports these as well. I like keeping it simple, so I'll only use for loops (and forEach loops on arrays) for the remainder of this book.

Arrays

Loops are interesting in general, but extraordinarily useful in the context of *arrays*. Arrays are simply indexed collections of JavaScript entities. One way of thinking of arrays is as a single variable that can hold multiple values. Here's a simple example that creates an array:

```
var greetings = ["hello", "namaste", "hola", "salut", "aloha"];
```

We can generalize this example pretty easily: we create an array literal by using the square brackets and then listing out the elements separated by commas. This array has five elements in it, each of which is a string. Here's an example with an array of integers:

```
var primes = [2, 3, 5, 7, 11, 13, 17, 19, 23, 29];
```

We can index into the arrays to get certain elements by using the variable name followed by square brackets. The indexing for arrays always starts at 0 and ends at one less than the length of the array:

```
console.log(greetings[1]);
//=> 'namaste'

console.log(greetings[0]);
```

```
//=> 'hello'

console.log(primes[4]);
//=> 11

console.log(greetings[4]);
//=> 'aloha'
```

Likewise, we can set individual elements of the array by using the same indexing trick:

```
greetings[3] = "bonjour"; // changes 'salut' to 'bonjour'
```

What if we want to print all the elements of the array? One approach is to use the length property of the array to build a continuation condition for a for loop:

```
var index;

for (index = 0; index < greetings.length; index = index + 1) {
    console.log(greetings[index]);
}
```

This is a perfectly valid approach, and one that is often used in JavaScript along with other languages like Java. But JavaScript has a slightly nicer *JavaScripty* way of achieving the same thing. Every array has a forEach loop attached to it, which takes in a function that operates on each element:

```
// the forEach loop takes a function as an argument
// and calls it for each element of the array
greetings.forEach(function (element) {
    console.log(element);
});
```

This is nicer because it removes the need to maintain an extra variable such as index in the previous example. It's often the case that removing a variable declaration will make our code less error prone.

In addition to including the forEach function, JavaScript arrays have some other advantages over raw arrays in C++ or Java. First, they can grow and shrink dynamically. Second, they have several functions built in that let us do some common operations. For example, we'll commonly want to add elements to the end of our array. We can use the push function to do that:

```
// create an empty array
var cardSuits = [];

cardSuits.push("clubs");
console.log(cardSuits);
//=> ["clubs"]

cardSuits.push("diamonds");
console.log(cardSuits);
//=> ["clubs", "diamonds"]
```

```
cardSuits.push("hearts");
console.log(cardSuits);
//=> ["clubs", "diamonds", "hearts"]

cardSuits.push("spades");
console.log(cardSuits);
//=> ["clubs", "diamonds", "hearts", "spades"]
```

There are many other built-in functions on JavaScript arrays, but we'll leave it with push for now. We'll learn a few others as we move forward.

Arrays and loops are pretty essential tools no matter what programming language you're working in. The only way to master them is to practice creating them and using them. Several practice problems at the end of this chapter will get you creating and manipulating arrays using loops.

Using JSLint to Identify Potential Problems

Like HTML and CSS, it's pretty easy to write JavaScript code that *works* but doesn't conform to best practices. In fact, this is really easy to do when you're first starting out with the language. For example, consider the following code:

```
cardRank = "king";

if (cardRank = "king") {
    console.log("the card is a king!");
} else {
    console.log("the card is not a king!");
}
//=> the card is a king!
```

At first glance, this code looks just fine, and it *seems* to work! Type it into the Chrome JavaScript Console and you'll see the output that you would expect! But let's change the code slightly—let's set cardRank to "queen":

```
cardRank = "queen";

if (cardRank = "king") {
    console.log("the card is a king!");
} else {
    console.log("the card is not a king!");
}
//=> the card is a king!
```

Now the error is probably a little more clear. The problem is that our if statement contains an assignment statement instead of a comparison, and the assignment statement is evaluating to a *truthy* value. It's not essential that we understand what a *truthy* value is at this point, or why it causes the if statement to execute its code block, but we do have to understand that the error comes from the fact that we've accidentally used = (assignment) instead of === (comparison).

We can fix this by changing the assignment to a comparison:

```
if (cardRank === "king") {
    console.log("the card is a king!");
} else {
    console.log("the card is not a king!");
}
```

There's actually another subtle problem with this code. Fortunately, there's a JavaScript analog to CSS Lint called (not surprisingly) JSLint. The JSLint home page is shown in Figure 4-9.

Let's cut and paste our original code into JSLint (*http://www.jslint.org*) and see what it tells us. It should respond as shown in Figure 4-10.

Figure 4-9. The home page for JSLint

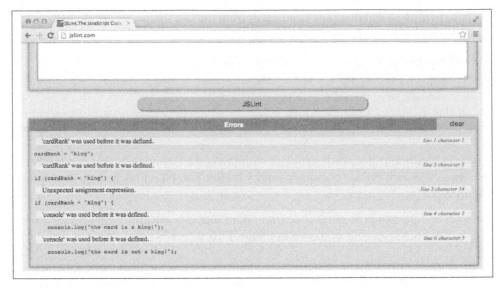

Figure 4-10. Our first errors in JSLint!

The first errors that we see are related to the subtle error that I mentioned earlier. Java-Script does not absolutely require that we declare variables before we use them, but this can often lead to unintended consequences. It's better to make sure we declare all variables with the var keyword. So let's modify our code so that it declares the variable in addition to defining it:

```
var cardRank = "king";
```

Once we do that and re-Lint our code, we'll see the first two errors go away. The next one is the assignment problem that I mentioned before. Once we fix that one we're left with the last two.

The last two errors are about the global variable console being used before it is defined. We can't simply add the word var in front of that variable because we didn't create it. Instead, we can go down to the JSLint options and turn on the console, alert, ... globals option and those errors will go away.

Like CSS Lint, JSLint is about as close as you can get to having a professional JavaScript programmer looking over your shoulder while you code. Lots of times, its warnings will be strange and you'll have to do some work to figure out how to fix them (Google is a great starting point for this), but it's well worth it and you'll learn how to write better JavaScript code much more efficiently.

Adding Interactivity to Amazeriffic

Let's put some of these ideas together in an example. We'll flesh out our idea for Amazeriffic as an app that keeps track of a to-do list. To achieve this, we'll build a tabbed interface with three tabs—the first tab will display our to-do list with the newest items first, as shown in Figure 4-11.

The second tab will display the same list, but have the list appear with the oldest items first, as shown in Figure 4-12.

And the last tab will have an input box where we can add new to-do items, as shown in Figure 4-13.

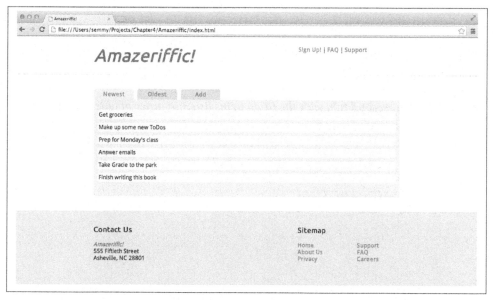

Figure 4-11. Our first tab, with the to-do items listed in order of newest to oldest

Figure 4-12. Our second tab, with the to-do items listed in order of oldest to newest

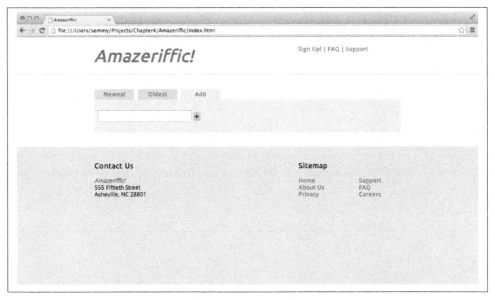

Figure 4-13. The tab that lets us add another to-do item

Getting Started

Because we've seen several examples with Git up to this point, I'll let you decide the appropriate times and places to update your repository in this example. Just make sure that you actually create a Git repository and update it regularly as we work our way through the example.

You'll also see that I've reused much of the design from the last example in the previous chapter. Therefore, you should be able to copy your work (namely, the HTML and the CSS) from the previous chapter. In this case, though, we'll want to create our *javascripts* and *stylesheets* directory to keep our code organized.

The Structure and Style

We can start by modifying the `main` element to contain our UI. My HTML for the `main` element looks like this:

```
<main>
  <div class="container">
    <div class="tabs">
      <a href="#"><span class="active">Newest</span></a>
      <a href="#"><span>Oldest</span></a>
      <a href="#"><span>Add</span></a>
    </div>
    <div class="content">
      <ul>
        <li>Get Groceries</li>
        <li>Make up some new ToDos</li>
        <li>Prep for Monday's class</li>
        <li>Answer recruiter emails on LinkedIn</li>
        <li>Take Gracie to the park</li>
        <li>Finish writing book</li>
      </ul>
    </div>
  </div>
</main>
```

You can use this basic structure for the `main` element, along with your work from Chapter 3 to style the page. Here are the style rules for my tabs:

```
.tabs a span {
    display: inline-block;
    border-radius: 5px 5px 0 0;
    width: 100px;
    margin-right: 10px;
    text-align: center;
    background: #ddd;
    padding: 5px;
}
```

You'll see one new thing here: I've set the display property to inline-block. Recall that inline elements like span don't have a width property, whereas block elements do, but they appear on a new line. The inline-block setting creates a hybrid element, giving the span a width property that I set to 100px. This makes it so every tab has the same width.

Of course, I also have an extra ruleset for the active tab. This makes the active tab have the same color as the content background, which gives the interface some visual depth:

```
.tabs a span.active {
    background: #eee;
}
```

The Interactivity

Let's move on to the really interesting part: the JavaScript! Of course, at this point we should have included both jQuery and */javascripts/app.js* via a script element at the bottom of our body element in the HTML. So we can start our *app.js* with our basic skeleton program:

```
var main = function () {
    "use strict";

    console.log("hello world!");
};

$(document).ready(main);
```

Recall that if we open this in our browser window, we should see *hello world!* in the JavaScript Console if everything is set up properly. Go ahead and do that.

Creating the tab functionality

If everything is working correctly, let's get our tabs—for lack of a better word—tabbing. We'll start with some code that responds to click events for each tab:

```
var main = function () {
    "use strict";

    $(".tabs a:nth-child(1)").on("click", function () {
        // make all the tabs inactive
        $(".tabs span").removeClass("active");

        // make the first tab active
        $(".tabs a:nth-child(1) span").addClass("active");

        // empty the main content so we can recreate it
        $("main .content").empty();

        // return false so we don't follow the link
```

```
        return false;
    });

    $(".tabs a:nth-child(2)").on("click", function () {
        $(".tabs span").removeClass("active");
        $(".tabs a:nth-child(2) span").addClass("active");
        $("main .content").empty();
        return false;
    });

    $(".tabs a:nth-child(3)").on("click", function () {
        $(".tabs span").removeClass("active");
        $(".tabs a:nth-child(3) span").addClass("active");
        $("main .content").empty();
        return false;
    });
};
```

If you're paying close attention, you'll notice that we've violated the DRY principle here —there's definitely some copy-pasting going on. That should tell us that we need to abstract some part of this as a function. You should give that a try now, without looking ahead. Go on. I'll wait.

Refactoring the code using a function

I hope you at least took the time to think about it before looking at the solution! Did it occur to you to use a function that takes an argument that represented the tab number? If so, great! If not, that's okay—you'll get it eventually. It just takes practice.

It's okay if your solution looks different from mine, but the key is that you understand how my solution works:

```
var main = function () {
    "use strict";

    var makeTabActive = function (tabNumber) {
        // construct the selector from the tabNumber
        var tabSelector = ".tabs a:nth-child(" + tabNumber + ") span";
        $(".tabs span").removeClass("active");
        $(tabSelector).addClass("active");
        $("main .content").empty();
    };

    $(".tabs a:nth-child(1)").on("click", function () {
        makeTabActive(1);
        return false;
    });

    $(".tabs a:nth-child(2)").on("click", function () {
        makeTabActive(2);
        return false;
    });
```

```
    $(".tabs a:nth-child(3)").on("click", function () {
        makeTabActive(3);
        return false;
    });
};
```

You may have tried to put the `return false` inside the `makeTabActive` function, but that will cause problems. We have to leave it inside the click handler, because the listener *has* to return false or else the browser will try to follow the link.

Refactoring the code using a loop

We've cut our number of code lines down a bit and, in doing so, made it so it's less likely that we've made errors. But we can do even better. Notice how we've set up three tabs using numbers: 1, 2, 3. If we package that in a `for` loop which iterates over those numbers, we can easily remove more repeated code!

In the code below, I use the `event` object that is sent into the click handler as we did in the `keyPress` events above. I use this to get the target DOM element that is clicked, add the `active` class to that element. Note that this removes the need for the `makeTabAc` `tive` function altogether, because we're packaging the important lines of code in the loop.

```
var main = function () {
    "use strict";

    var tabNumber;

    for (tabNumber = 1; tabNumber <= 3; tabNumber++) {
        var tabSelector = ".tabs a:nth-child(" + tabNumber + ") span";
        $(tabSelector).on("click", function (event) {
            $(".tabs span").removeClass("active");
            $(event.target).addClass("active");
            return false;
        });
    }
};
```

Refactoring the code using a forEach loop

It turns out that there's even another solution! jQuery allows us to select a set of elements and then iterate over it as an array! In this simplification, we'll iterate over all of our `span` elements inside the tabs, creating a `click` handler for each:

```
var main = function () {
    "use strict";

    $(".tabs span").toArray().forEach(function (element) {
        // create a click handler for this element
```

```
$(element).on("click", function () {
    $(".tabs span").removeClass("active");
    $(element).addClass("active");
    $("main .content").empty();
    return false;
  });
});
};
```

 The array that jQuery creates is an array of DOM elements, not jQuery objects. We have to turn them into jQuery objects by wrapping them in a $() function call.

So that's three ways of making the same thing happen. There may even be other solutions, but I think these last two are pretty good—they are short, easily understandable (if you understand looping, that is) and they make it easy to add more tabs.

Manipulating content

Now we have another problem to solve. The tabs are going to fill the main .content element with different content depending on which tab is clicked. This is pretty easy if we know which child of the .tabs elements we're on. For example, if we're the first child of the .tabs element we do one thing, and if we're the second we do something different. But it turns out this is a little tricky, because inside our click handler we have access to the span element that's a child of the a element that we're interested in. A tree diagram for our situation would look something like Figure 4-14.

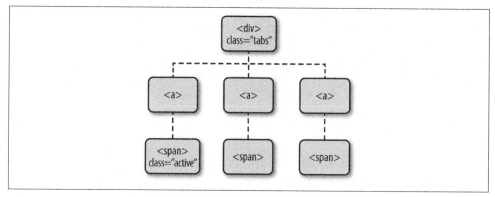

Figure 4-14. We need to know the index of the span element on which we click

It turns out that jQuery gives us a really nice way of selecting the parent of a jQuery object—it's the appropriately named parent function! But then we need to determine which child it is. It turns out that jQuery also gives us the is function, which allows us to test a selector against the current jQuery object. This is probably challenging to understand in the abstract, but it's pretty readable when you see it in action. Here's a quick example:

```
// test whether the parent of the $me jQuery object
// is the first child of its parent
if ($me.parent().is(":first-child")) {
    console.log("MY PARENT IS A FIRST CHILD!!");
} else {
    console.log("my parent is not a first child.");
}
```

We can use this pattern and the :nth-child selector to determine what we need to do in our tab example:

```
var main = function () {
    "use strict";

    $(".tabs a span").toArray().forEach(function (element) {
        // create a click handler for this element
        $(element).on("click", function () {
            // since we're using the jQuery version of element,
            // we'll go ahead and create a temporary variable
            // so we don't need to keep recreating it
            var $element = $(element);

            $(".tabs a span").removeClass("active");
            $element.addClass("active");
            $("main .content").empty();

            if ($element.parent().is(":nth-child(1)")) {
                console.log("FIRST TAB CLICKED!");
            } else if ($element.parent().is(":nth-child(2)")) {
                console.log("SECOND TAB CLICKED!");
            } else if ($element.parent().is(":nth-child(3)")) {
                console.log("THIRD TAB CLICKED!");
            }

            return false;
        });
    });
};
```

When you run this with the Chrome JavaScript Console opened, you should see the appropriate message appear when its associated tab is clicked! Easy peasy!

Setting up the tab content

Setting up the tab content requires a little bit of work. First of all, we'll start by storing the to-dos themselves as strings in an array. To make this happen, we'll add a variable in our `main` function that holds an array literal with our to-do items:

```
var main = function () {
    "use strict";

    var toDos = [
        "Finish writing this book",
        "Take Gracie to the park",
        "Answer emails",
        "Prep for Monday's class",
        "Make up some new ToDos",
        "Get Groceries"
    ];

    //... other tab-related stuff
};
```

Now when we add to-dos, all we have to do is push them onto the end of the array. That has the consequence that it keeps the oldest to-dos earlier in the array, which means the newest ones are last. Therefore, the second tab (Oldest) will list them in the order they appear in the array, while the first tab will list them backward.

To start, I'll show you how to set up the content when the second tab is clicked, and will leave construction of the content of the other tabs to you. To build the content for the first and second tab, we'll simply create a `ul` element, and then loop over the to-dos adding an `li` element for each of them. Note that for the first tab, however, we'll have to loop over the elements backward, so we'll use a traditional `for` loop in that case. For the second tab, however, we can use the preferable `forEach` loop. The code will change to look something like this:

```
$(element).on("click", function () {
    var $element = $(element),
        $content;

    $(".tabs a span").removeClass("active");
    $element.addClass("active");
    $("main .content").empty();

    if ($element.parent().is(":nth-child(1)")) {
        console.log("FIRST TAB CLICKED!");
    } else if ($element.parent().is(":nth-child(2)")) {
        $content = $("<ul>");
        toDos.forEach(function (todo) {
            $content.append($("<li>").text(todo));
        });
        $("main .content").append($content);
    } else if ($element.parent().is(":nth-child(3)")) {
```

```
        console.log("THIRD TAB CLICKED!");
    }
});
```

Like I mentioned before, building the content for the first tab will be similar. Once we do that, we actually no longer need the hardcoded content in the HTML at all! We can trigger a *fake* click on the first tab by adding a single line at the end of our `main` function, right after we set up the click handlers. This will dynamically construct our content:

```
$(".tabs a:first-child span").trigger("click");
```

Once we have that set up correctly, we can remove the hardcoded to-do elements in *index.html*.

For the third tab, we'll need to do something a little different—we'll need to create an `input` element and a `button` element just as we had in the comments example at the beginning of this chapter. But for this example, we should practice building the DOM subtree using jQuery instead of incorporating it into the HTML. We'll also have to add an event listener to the button. In this case, instead of adding an element to the DOM as we did in the earlier example, we will just add it to our `toDo` array by using the `push` function.

You can see the finished example in our GitHub repository (*http://github.com/semmy purewal/LearningWebAppDev/tree/master/Chapter4/Amazeriffic*).

Summary

In this chapter, we've learned about adding interactivity to a web application by using jQuery and JavaScript. jQuery is a widely used library that abstracts some of the difficulties of manipulating the DOM and event handling (among other things). The event-driven nature of a user interface running in the browser creates the need to write *asynchronous* code. The easiest way to get started with this is by attaching *callback* functions to events.

JavaScript is the full-featured programming language supported by all web browsers. As a beginning web app developer and programmer, it's important to work toward mastering a few fundamental concepts, including variables, `if` and `if-else` statements, and various looping structures. Arrays are another essential component of all programming languages, so understanding how to create and manipulate them is also important.

JSLint is a tool that is similar to CSS Lint or the HTML validator—it keeps you from falling into common JavaScript traps. It's a good idea to run your code through it periodically.

More Practice and Further Reading

Memorization

Let's add a few steps to your memorization practice:

1. Create a directory called *javascripts* to store your *.js* files.
2. Create a simple JS program and store it in a file called *app.js*. The file should either `alert` "hello world" or print it to the console. This should happen in a `main` function, which should be called with jQuery's `document.ready` function.
3. Import your script along with jQuery into your HTML document at the bottom of the <body> tag.
4. Reload the page in Chrome to confirm that it behaves correctly.
5. Add the file and HTML changes to your Git repository.

jQuery Plug-ins

Part of the reason that jQuery is so popular is the fact that it has a huge community of web developers who create plug-ins that allow you to include incredible effects on your page. I encourage you to visit *http://plugins.jquery.com* to see the types of plug-ins that are available. I also encourage you to experiment with a few jQuery plug-ins. You'll have to read the plug-ins' documentation to see if you can make them work, but it's well worth your time.

One of my favorite plug-ins is called *colorbox*, which allows you to easily include an animated photo gallery on your page. The author has written very clear documentation for getting it to work (*http://www.jacklmoore.com/colorbox*).

jQuery Selectors

Type up the following HTML document and store it in a file called *selectorpractice.html*:

```html
<!doctype html>
<html>
  <head>
  </head>

  <body>
    <h1>Hi</h1>
    <h2 class="important">Hi again</h2>
    <p>Random unattached paragraph</p>

    <div class="relevant">
      <p class="a">first</p>
      <p class="a">second</p>
      <p>third</p>
      <p>fourth</p>
      <p class="a">fifth</p>
      <p class="a">sixth</p>
      <p>seventh</p>
    </div>
  </body>
</html>
```

Next, create a simple *app.js* file with the following content. Use two `<script>` tags to import jQuery and then this file at the bottom of the body element:

```javascript
var main = function () {
    "use strict;"

    $("*").css("color","red");
};
$(document).ready(main);
```

The `css` function allows us to change the style of the selected elements using jQuery. The default code uses the universal CSS selector to make every element in the DOM red. For the following questions we'll change the jQuery selector to make only the specified elements turn red. For example, if we want to make the `<h1>` tag red, we would use the following selector:

```javascript
$("h1").css("color","red");
```

The last few steps are much easier if you take a look at the jQuery selector documentation (*http://api.jquery.com/category/selectors/*). Along with the selectors we've seen in this chapter, you'll want to pay special attention to the `:not` and `:gt` selectors:

1. Select the h2 element by its class.
2. Select the first paragraph of the relevant paragraphs.

3. Select the third paragraph of the relevant paragraphs.

4. Select all of the paragraphs on the page.

5. Select all of the relevant paragraphs.

6. Select the second, fourth, and sixth relevant paragraphs.

7. Select the seventh relevant paragraph.

8. Select the fifth, sixth, and seventh relevant paragraphs.

9. Select the relevant paragraphs that are not of class a.

FizzBuzz

If you're thinking about applying for a job as a computer programmer, you should really understand how to solve the FizzBuzz problem. As far as I know, the FizzBuzz problem was popularized in a blog post by Jeff Atwood entitled *Why Can't Programmers...Program? (http://bit.ly/1fYbhZd)*. In this post, he laments the fact that so many people who apply for jobs as programmers can't solve a simple problem.

The problem is essentially this:

Write a program that prints the numbers from 1 to 100. But for multiples of three print "Fizz" instead of the number and for the multiples of five print "Buzz." For numbers which are multiples of both three and five print "FizzBuzz."

Based on the background and tools I introduced to you in this chapter, you should be able to solve this problem using a for loop, along with a series of if-else statements and the remainder operator.

I should add that I'm not sure this is a particularly good test of whether or not someone can program, nor am I sure that the inability to solve this problem on the spot should disqualify someone from a programming position. There are numerous reasons that a person may not be able to solve this problem that have nothing to do with their ability to write computer programs at the junior level. But it is what it is, and you'll likely be asked this question at some point. It's a good idea to memorize the solution.

Array Practice

Another common source of job interview questions are arrays. There's a good reason for this: they are definitely the most commonly used data structure in computer programs, and every programming language has them in some form. Try to answer every question in this section using the material from this chapter. I'll start with a simple one and include a few different answers:

Write a function that accepts an array of numbers as an argument and returns their sum.

The simplest solution to this question would look something like this:

```
var sum = function (nums) {
    var sumSoFar = 0,
        i;

    // loop over the array, adding the sum
    for (i = 0; i < nums.length; i++) {
        sumSoFar = sumSoFar + nums[i];
    }

    // now that we've finished traversing the array
    // the sumSoFar variable should have the sum
    // of all the numbers
    return sumSoFar;
};

sum([1,2,3,4]);
//=> 10
```

Similarly, we could use a forEach loop:

```
var sum = function (nums) {
    var sumSoFar = 0;

    // use a forEach loop
    nums.forEach(function (value) {
        sumSoFar = sumSoFar + value;
    });

    return sumSoFar;
};

sum([1,2,3,4]);
//=> 10
```

The forEach loop is preferable here, because it removes the need to maintain the i variable. In general, this is a good thing—removing a variable that regularly changes its state in our program makes our code less error prone. In fact, if we want to get rid of all of the temporary local variables, we can use an array function called reduce that wraps a lot of this up nicely:

```
var sum = function (nums) {
    return nums.reduce(function (sumSoFar, value) {
        return sumSoFar + value;
    }, 0);
};

sum([1,2,3,4]);
//=> 10
```

I'm not going to spend any more time talking about the reduce function, but if this intrigues you I encourage you to read more about it on the Web.

It's also worth noting that we're not checking the inputs to our function. For example, what happens if we try to send in something that's not an array?

```
sum(5);
//=> TypeError!

sum("hello world");
//=> TypeError!
```

There are lots of ways we can correct for this, but let's not spend a lot of time worrying about it now. If you're writing code for a job interview, however, it's always a good idea to check inputs to any function.

Here's a series of questions that will allow you to practice with arrays:

1. Write a function that accepts an array of numbers as an argument and returns their average.

2. Write a function that accepts an array of numbers as an argument and returns the largest number in the array.

3. Write a function that accepts an array of numbers and returns true if it contains at least one even number, false otherwise.

4. Write a function that accepts an array of numbers and returns true if *every* number is even, false otherwise.

5. Write a function that accepts two arguments—an array of strings and a string—and returns true if the string is contained in the array, false otherwise. For example, your function should behave as follows:

```
arrayContains(["hello", "world"], "hello");
//=> true

arrayContains(["hello", "world"], "goodbye");
//=> false

arrayContains(["hello", "world", "goodbye"], "goodbye");
//=> true
```

6. Write a function that is similar to the previous one, but returns true only if the array contains the given string at least twice:

```
arrayContainsTwo(["a","b","a","c"], "a");
//=> true

arrayContainsTwo(["a","b","a","c"], "b");
//=> false
```

```
arrayContainsTwo(["a","b","a","c","a"], "a");
//=> true
```

Once you have that working, write a function called `arrayContainsThree` that behaves similarly, but for three instead of two. Now, we'll generalize the previous
problem. Write a function that accepts three arguments and returns `true` if the
array contains the element n times, where n is the third argument:

```
arrayContainsNTimes(["a","b","a","c","a"], "a", 3);
//=> true

arrayContainsNTimes(["a","b","a","c","a"], "a", 2);
//=> true

arrayContainsNTimes(["a","b","a","c","a"], "a", 4);
//=> false

arrayContainsNTimes(["a","b","a","c","a"], "b", 2);
//=> false

arrayContainsNTimes(["a","b","a","c","a"], "b", 1);
//=> true

arrayContainsNTimes(["a","b","a","c","a"], "d", 0);
//=> true
```

Project Euler

Another great source of practice problems is Project Euler (*http://projecteuler.net*). It
has a series of programming problems that don't require advanced knowledge to solve
correctly. Most of the problems boil down to finding a single number. Once you find
that number, you type it into the website, and—if you're correct—you'll be given access
to a discussion board where other people post solutions and discuss the best way to
solve the problem.

I was once presented with a question that was taken nearly word-for-word from a Project
Euler problem when I was interviewing with a well-known software company.

Other JavaScript References

JavaScript is a popular language, and because of this there are numerous books that
cover it. Unfortunately, Doug Crockford claims that the majority of these books "are
quite awful. They contain errors, poor examples, and promote bad practices." I tend to
agree with him (although I hope he wouldn't put my book into that category!).

That being said, I haven't found a good book that covers JavaScript programming for
novice programmers, or people who know very little about programming in general.
On the other hand, there are several excellent books for intermediate to advanced

JavaScript programmers. I can highly recommend Crockford's book *JavaScript: The Good Parts* (O'Reilly, 2008) as one of the better books on the JavaScript language in general. I also think David Herman's *Effective JavaScript* (Addison-Wesley, 2012) has a lot of good practical advice for intermediate-level JavaScript programmers.

If you're looking for general practical information relating to JavaScript software development, I encourage you to take a look at Nick Zackas's *Maintainable JavaScript* (O'Reilly, 2012). And once you get the hang of object-oriented programming in JS, you may want to check out Michael Fogus's *Functional JavaScript* (O'Reilly, 2013), which offers a different, but completely engaging, perspective.

## CHAPTER 5

The Bridge

We've mostly finished our journey through the client-side portion of a web application. Although I haven't stated it explicitly, when I refer to the *client-side* portion of a web app, I'm talking about the part of the program that runs in your web browser. The other side of the story is the *server-side* part of the application, which runs and stores information outside of your web browser, usually on a remote computer.

This chapter is not about the server-side part of a web application, but it is about a collection of technologies that allow the client and server to more easily exchange information. I like to think of this set of technologies as *the bridge* between the client and the server.

Specifically, we'll study JavaScript objects, JSON (JavaScript Object Notation), and AJAX (Asynchronous JavaScript And XML—a misnomer of sorts). These topics will prepare us for Node.js, which we'll study in the next chapter.

Hello, JavaScript Objects!

Before we start talking about transferring data between computers, we need to discuss one more important JavaScript primitive: objects. You may have heard of *object-oriented programming* in the past, and if you've programmed in C++ or Java you've most likely seen the topic in detail.

Though these ideas are very important for software engineering in general, object-oriented programming in JavaScript is a different beast altogether, so it's best to forget about them when you're first learning. Instead, we're going to take a slightly naive view of objects for the time being: they are simple collections of variables relating to one particular entity. Let's start with an example.

Representing Playing Cards

In the previous chapter, we saw some examples involving playing cards. A playing card has two basic attributes: a suit (one of clubs, diamonds, hearts, or spades), and a rank (two through ten or a face card, which is one of jack, queen, king, or ace). Now suppose that we want to take this example a bit further and create a web app that plays poker. This will require us to represent a five-card hand in JavaScript.

The most basic approach using the tools that I've presented would involve keeping 10 variables, one for each card rank and one for each card suit:

```
var cardOneSuit = "hearts",
    cardOneRank = "two",
    cardTwoSuit = "spades",
    cardTwoRank = "ace",
    cardThreeSuit = "spades",
    cardThreeRank = "five",
    // ...
    cardFiveSuitRank = "seven";
```

Hopefully you realize that this is a tedious solution. And if you went through the previous chapter carefully, I hope you're thinking that an array of five elements might simplify things! But the problem is that each card has two attributes, so how can we do that with an array?

You might consider a solution that looks like this:

```
var cardHandSuits = ["hearts", "spades", "spades", "clubs", "diamonds"],
    cardHandRanks = ["two", "ace", "five", "king", "seven"];
```

This is definitely better, but it still has a major issue in common with the previous solution: there is nothing associating a single suit with a single rank in our program—we have to keep track of the connection in our head. Whenever there are entities in our program that are strongly related, but only in the programmer's mind instead of in some programmatic structure, we're adding a lot of complexity. And it turns out it's completely unnecessary if we use objects!

An *object* is simply a collection of multiple variables that are related in some way. To create one we use curly braces, and then we can access the internal variables of an object by using the dot (.) operator. Here's an example that creates a single card:

```
// create a card object with a rank of 'two'
// and a suit of 'hearts'
var cardOne = { "rank":"two", "suit":"hearts" };

// print the rank of cardOne
console.log(cardOne.rank);
//=> two

//print the suit of cardOne
```

```
console.log(cardOne.suit);
//=> hearts
```

Once we create the object, we can always change it later. For example, we can change the rank and suit of cardOne:

```
// change the card to the ace of spades
cardOne.rank = "ace";
cardOne.suit = "spades";

console.log(cardOne);
//=> Object {rank: "ace", suit: "spades"}
```

Like an array, we can create an empty object and then add attributes to it later:

```
// create an empty object
var card = {};

// set the rank to ace
card.rank = "ace";

console.log(card);
//=> Object {rank: "ace"}

// set the suit to hearts
card.suit = "hearts";

console.log(card);
//=> Object {rank: "ace", suit: "hearts"}
```

Now if we want to represent a hand of cards, we can create an array and populate it with card objects instead of keeping two separate arrays!

```
// create an empty array
var cards = [];

// push the two of hearts onto the array
cards.push( {"rank": "two", "suit":"hearts"} );
cards.push( {"rank": "ace", "suit":"spades"} );
cards.push( {"rank": "five", "suit":"spades"} );
cards.push( {"rank": "king", "suit":"clubs"} );
cards.push( {"rank": "seven", "suit":"diamonds"} );

// print the first and third card in the hand
console.log(cards[0]);
//=> Object {rank: "two", suit: "hearts"}

console.log(cards[2]);
//=> Object {rank: "five", suit: "spades"}
```

If we prefer, we can also create one long array literal to build a hand of cards:

```
// create an array of cards
// with a big array literal
```

```
var cards = [
    {"rank": "two", "suit":"hearts"},
    {"rank": "ace", "suit":"spades"},
    {"rank": "five", "suit":"spades"},
    {"rank": "king", "suit":"clubs"},
    {"rank": "seven", "suit":"diamonds"}
];
```

Generalizations

As I mentioned before, we can think of JavaScript objects as collections of variables, each of which have a name and a value. To create an empty object, we simply use the open and closing curly braces:

```
// create an empty object
var s = {};
```

And then we can add variables to the object using the dot . operator:

```
s.name = "Semmy";
```

The variables inside an object can be of any type, including strings (which we've seen in all the previous examples), arrays, or even other objects!

```
s.age = 36;   // a number

s.friends = [ "Mark", "Emily", "Bruce", "Sylvan" ];

s.dog = { "name":"Gracie", "breed":"Shepherd Mix" };

console.log(s.age);
//=> 36

console.log(s.friends[1]);
//=> "Emily"

console.log(s.dog);
//=> Object {name: "Gracie", breed: "Shepherd Mix"}

console.log(s.dog.name);
//=> "Gracie"
```

We can also create object literals, which are simply full objects defined in code!

```
var g = {
    "name": "Gordon",
    "age": 36,
    "friends": ["Sara", "Andy", "Roger", "Brandon"],
    "dog": {"name":"Pi", "breed":"Lab Mix" }
}

console.log(g.name);
//=> "Gordon"
```

```
console.log(g.friends[2]);
//=> "Roger"

console.log(g.dog.breed);
//=> "Lab Mix"
```

On occasion, we'll need to use the special null value that represents "no object":

```
var b = {
    "name": "John",
    "age" : 45,
    "friends" : [ "Sara", "Jim" ],
    "dog" : null
}
```

In this example, John does not have a dog. We may also want to use null to signify that we're finished with an object:

```
// assign currentPerson to the object g
var currentPerson = g;

// ... do some stuff with currentPerson

// set currentPerson to null
currentPerson = null;
```

We'll use a null reference as a placeholder for an object, particularly in Chapter 6 when we start talking about errors. Specifically, our callback functions will be called with null when there was no error associated with the request.

Speaking generally, objects give us a lot of flexibility in terms of storing and manipulating data. It's also worth noting that because function variables in JavaScript behave just like any other variables, we can store them in objects. For example, we've already seen how we can access functions that are attached to jQuery objects:

```
// get a dom element
var $headerTag = $("h1");

// $headerTag is an object which has a function
// attached called fadeOut
$headerTag.fadeOut();
```

Objects with functions attached are a pretty incredible tool for abstraction (which leads to the idea of object-oriented programming), but we're going to defer that discussion for the time being. Instead, in this chapter we're going to focus on using objects to exchange information with other web applications.

Communication Between Computers

It's nearly impossible to build a web application today without tapping into other previously existing applications. As an example, you may want your application to allow users to log in via their Twitter accounts. Or you may want to make your application post updates to a user's Facebook feed. This means that your application will need to have the ability to exchange information with these services. The standard format that is used on the Web today is the JSON format, and if you understand JavaScript objects, you already understand JSON!

JSON

A JSON object is nothing more than a JavaScript object literal in the form of a string (with some technical caveats—but we can ignore most of them for now). This means that when we want to send some information to another service, we simply build a JavaScript object in our code, convert it into a string, and send it! Most of the time, AJAX libraries will take care of the majority of this for us, so to a programmer it looks like the programs are simply exchanging objects!

For example, suppose I want to define a JSON object in an external file—I can simply encode it just as I would inside a JavaScript program:

```
{
  "rank":"ten",
  "suit":"hearts"
}
```

It turns out that taking a JSON string and converting it into an object that a computer program can use is very easy in most programming languages! In JavaScript, however, it's super easy, because the format itself is just a string version of an object literal. Most JavaScript environments offer a JSON object that we can interact with. For example, open up the Chrome console and type in the following:

```
// we create a JSON string with single quotes
var jsonString = '{"rank":"ten", "suit":"hearts"}'

// JSON.parse converts it into an object
var card = JSON.parse(jsonString);

console.log(card.rank);
//=> "ten"

console.log(card.suit);
//=> "hearts"
```

Note that we've created the `jsonString` string by using single quotes instead of our usual double quotes. It turns out that JavaScript doesn't care which you use, but JSON does. Because we need to create a string within a string, we use single quotes on the outside and double quotes on the inside.

We can also convert a JSON object into a string by using the `stringify` function:

```
console.log(JSON.stringify(card));
//=> {"rank":"ten","suit":"hearts"}
```

So now that we understand how to create JSON objects in external files and as strings inside our program, let's see how we exchange them between computers.

AJAX

AJAX stands for *Asynchronous JavaScript And XML* which, as I said in the introduction, is a bit of a misnomer. The common data-interchange format that preceded JSON was called *XML*, which looked much more like HTML. And although XML is still widely used in many applications, there has been a major move to JSON since AJAX was invented.

Despite the fact that it's an acronym full of technical words, it's actually not very complicated. The basic idea behind AJAX is that your application can send and receive information to other computers without reloading the web page. One of the first examples of this (and still one of the best) is Google's Gmail web app, which arrived on the scene about 10 years ago! If you've used that, you've seen how new mail just *magically* appears in your inbox—in other words, you don't have to reload the page to get new messages. That's an example of AJAX.

Accessing an External JSON File

OK, enough with the theory. Let's see an example of AJAX in action. First, let's create a skeleton application. We'll ignore CSS for the time being just to get the example up and running. Hopefully, at this point, you can create an HTML page from memory that says "Hello World!" in an `h1` element and has an empty `main` element. We'll also want to include a `script` element with a link to jQuery from a CDN (which we explained in Chapter 4) and a `<script>` tag containing a link to *app.js*, our basic JavaScript application. That file should live in a directory called *javascripts* and it will look something like this:

```
var main = function () {
    "use strict";

    console.log("Hello World!");
}
```

```
$(document).ready(main);
```

Open up your basic app in Chrome and open the JavaScript console. As always, if everything is working correctly, you should see "Hello World!" printed.

Next, we'll create a new directory inside our example directory called *cards*. Inside that directory, we'll create a file called *aceOfSpades.json*, which will look just like one of the previous JavaScript object definitions:

```
{
  "rank" : "ace",
  "suit" : "spades"
}
```

Now we want to access this file in our program via AJAX, which—for the time being—will present a bit of a problem.

Overcoming Browser Security Restrictions

When JavaScript was invented, it was designed to be run in a web browser. This meant that, due to security restrictions, it was not allowed to access the local files stored on your computer. You can imagine the types of problems that might arise if that were to be allowed—any website you visited would have full access to your computer!

Needless to say, that's a security concern that continues to this day. On the other hand, we're allowed to access certain types of files from the same server that delivered the JavaScript file. JSON files are the perfect example of this: I can do an AJAX request to a server and access any JSON files that it makes available. Sadly, we won't be running a server until the next chapter, so for the time being we're going to use a straightforward workaround using Chrome.

 It's probably not a good idea to surf the Web with these security safeguards turned off. Make sure you restart your browser normally before visiting sites other than those that you build yourself.

To start Chrome without this particular security restriction turned on, we'll start by completely shutting it down. Next, if we're in Mac OS we'll open a terminal and type the following command:

```
hostname $ open -a Google\ Chrome --args --allow-file-access-from-files
```

If we're running Windows, we can do the same thing by clicking the Start menu, typing *run* in the search bar, and then entering the following command into the run box:

```
%userprofile%\AppData\Local\Google\Chrome\Application\chrome.exe
-allow-file-access-from-files
```

This should open Chrome with the previously mentioned security restriction turned off. Like I said, we'll only use this trick for this example in this chapter—in the next chapter, we'll actually be running a real server and this won't be necessary. For the time being, however, let's verify that it's working.

The getJSON Function

If we've successfully disabled Chrome's cross-site scripting security restriction, we can easily get access to the local JSON file in our program. To do so, we'll use jQuery's getJSON function. Like many of our JavaScript examples, this jQuery request will be asynchronous so we'll have to add a callback:

```
var main = function () {
    "use strict";

    // getJSON even parses the JSON for us, so we don't need to
    // call JSON.parse
    $.getJSON("cards/aceOfSpades.json", function (card) {
        // print the card to the console
        console.log(card);
    });
};

$(document).ready(main);
```

If we've done everything correctly, when we open our page in Chrome (with the cross-site scripting restrictions turned off), we should see the card appear in the console window. Now we can use it in our program just like any other JavaScript object!

```
var main = function () {
    "use strict";

    console.log("Hello World!");

    $.getJSON("cards/aceOfSpades.json", function (card) {
        // create an element to hold the card
        var $cardParagraph = $("<p>");

        // add text to the paragraph element
        $cardParagraph.text(card.rank + " of " + card.suit);

        // append the card paragraph to main
        $("main").append($cardParagraph);
    });
}

$(document).ready(main);
```

A JSON Array

We can even have more complex JSON objects in the file. For example, it can consist of an array of objects instead of a single object. To see this in action, create the following file called *hand.json*:

```
[
    { "suit" : "spades",   "rank" : "ace" },
    { "suit" : "hearts",   "rank" : "ten" },
    { "suit" : "spades",   "rank" : "five" },
    { "suit" : "clubs",    "rank" : "three" },
    { "suit" : "diamonds", "rank" : "three" }
]
```

Now add the following `getJSON` right below your previous one:

```
var main = function () {
    "use strict";

    console.log("Hello World!");

    $.getJSON("cards/aceOfSpades.json", function (card) {
        // create an element to hold the card
        var $cardParagraph = $("<p>");

        // create the card text
        $cardParagraph.text(card.rank + " of " + card.suit);

        // append the card paragraph to main
        $("main").append($cardParagraph);
    });

    $.getJSON("cards/hand.json", function (hand) {
        var $list = $("<ul>");

        // hand is an array, so we can iterate over it
        // using a forEach loop
        hand.forEach(function (card) {
            // create a list item to hold the card
            // and append it to the list
            var $card = $("<li>");
            $card.text(card.rank + " of " + card.suit);
            $list.append($card);
        });

        // append the list to main
        $("main").append($list);
    });
};

$(document).ready(main);
```

In this example, we reuse the card variable in the forEach loop of the second call to getJSON. This is because the variable goes *out-of-scope* at the end of the first call to getJSON. We're not going to belabor JavaScript scoping rules here, but I thought it would be worthwhile to point out in case it causes confusion.

When we run our application, our page should look something like Figure 5-1.

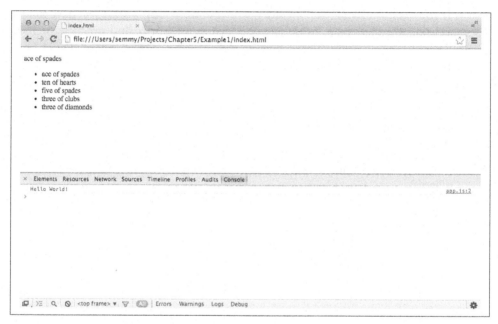

Figure 5-1. Our first AJAX application!

So What?

I realize that this example is not super exciting. In fact, you're probably thinking it would be just as easy to simply define those objects inside our code. Why bother with the separate file?

Well, imagine if the data was coming from another computer. In that case, we wouldn't be able to explicitly define it in our code. In fact, we may not even know what the object looks like in advance! For example, suppose we wanted to get the most recently posted dog pictures from Flickr.

Getting Images from Flickr

Let's create another skeleton application, this time with a CSS file. Open up Sublime and go into the *Chapter5* directory of your *Projects* directory. Create a directory called *Flickr*. Inside of that create your usual *javascripts* and *stylesheets* directories along with your *app.js* and *style.css* files. Make it so *app.js* prints out hello world to the JavaScript console. Create an *index.html* file that links all the files together to create a basic web application.

Wow! If you can do all that from memory, you've come a long way! If you have to look back occasionally, that's okay, but it's a good idea to memorize and practice the basic setup. The more basic stuff you can do from memory, the more you can let your brain focus on some of the more difficult stuff.

My HTML file looks like this:

```
<!doctype html>
<html>
  <head>
    <title>Flickr App</title>
    <link rel="stylesheet" href="stylesheets/style.css">
  </head>
  <body>
    <header>
    </header>

    <main>
     <div class="photos">
     </div>
    </main>

    <footer>
    </footer>
    <script src="http://code.jquery.com/jquery-2.0.3.min.js"></script>
    <script src="javascripts/app.js"></script>
  </body>
</html>
```

Now we're going to attempt to generalize an example that's right out of the jQuery documentation, which is available at *http://api.jquery.com*. We'll change it a little to fit our narrative better. In this example, we'll use JavaScript to pull images from Flickr, Yahoo!'s photo-sharing service. Before we do that, open your web browser and type in the following URL:

http://api.flickr.com/services/feeds/photos_public.gne?tags=dogs&format=json

The response should appear directly in your web browser as JSON. For me, the response looked something like this:

```
jsonFlickrFeed({
    "title": "Recent Uploads tagged dogs",
    "link": "http://www.flickr.com/photos/tags/dogs/",
    "description": "",
    "modified": "2013-10-06T19:42:49Z",
    "generator": "http://www.flickr.com/",
    "items": [
        {
            "title": "Huck and Moxie ride stroller",
            "link": "http://www.flickr.com/photos/animaltourism/10124023233/",
            "media": {"m":"http://bit.ly/1bVvkn2"},
            "date_taken": "2013-09-20T09:14:25-08:00",
            "description": "...description string...",
            "published": "2013-10-06T19:45:14Z",
            "author": "nobody@flickr.com (animaltourism.com)",
            "author_id": "8659451@N03",
            "tags": "park dog beagle dogs brooklyn ride stroller prospect hounds"
        },
        {
            "title": "6th Oct Susie: \"You know that thing you\'re eating?\"",
            "link": "http://www.flickr.com/photos/cardedfolderol/10123495123/",
            "media": {"m":"http://bit.ly/1bVvbQw"},
            "date_taken": "2013-10-06T14:47:59-08:00",
            "description": "...description string...",
            "published": "2013-10-06T19:14:22Z",
            "author": "nobody@flickr.com (Cardedfolderol)",
            "author_id": "79284220@N08",
            "tags": "pets dogs animal mammal canine"
        },
        {
            "title": "6th Oct Susie ready to leave",
            "link": "http://www.flickr.com/photos/cardedfolderol/10123488173/",
            "media": {"m":"http://bit.ly/1bVvpXJ"},
            "date_taken": "2013-10-06T14:49:59-08:00",
            "description": "...description string...",
            "published": "2013-10-06T19:14:23Z",
            "author": "nobody@flickr.com (Cardedfolderol)",
            "author_id": "79284220@N08",
            "tags": "pets dogs animal mammal canine"
        }
    ]
});
```

You'll see that it looks a lot more complicated than the examples we've seen so far, but the basic structure/format remains the same. It starts out with some basic information about the request, and then has a property called items, which is an array of images. Each element of the array contains another object called media, which has a property, m, that includes a link to the image. In the second chapter, we learned we could add an image to our HTML document with the <img> tag. We'll do that now.

Let's take this step by step. First, we're going to add a line to our `main` function that sets up the URL in a variable, and then we're going to call jQuery's `getJSON` function as we did before:

```
var main = function () {
    "use strict";

    // this is actually just one string,
    // but I spread it out over two lines
    // to make it more readable
    var url = "http://api.flickr.com/services/feeds/photos_public.gne?" +
              "tags=dogs&format=json&jsoncallback=?";

    $.getJSON(url, function (flickrResponse) {
        // we'll simply print the response to the console
        // for the time being
        console.log(flickrResponse);
    });
};

$(document).ready(main);
```

Now if we've set everything up correctly, when we run this, the object that Flickr responds with will be printed in the console and we can examine it by drilling down into it with the drop-down arrows. This will help us troubleshoot if we run into problems as we move forward.

Next, we're going to modify the code so that instead of printing out the entire object, we'll just print out each URL individually. In other words, we'll iterate over the `items` object using a `forEach` loop:

```
$.getJSON(url, function (flickrResponse) {
    flickrResponse.items.forEach(function (photo) {
        console.log(photo.media.m);
    });
});
```

This should print out a sequence of URLs in the console—you should even be able to click them and see the image! Next, we'll actually insert them into the DOM. To do so, we'll be using the jQuery `attr` function, which we haven't used yet. We'll use this to manually set the `src` attribute in our `<img>` tag:

```
$.getJSON(url, function (flickrResponse) {
    flickrResponse.items.forEach(function (photo) {
        // create a new jQuery element to hold the image
        var $img = $("<img>");

        // set the attribute to the url
        // contained in the response
        $img.attr("src", photo.media.m);
```

```
            // attach the img tag to the main
            // photos element
            $("main .photos").append($img);
        });
    });
```

Now when we reload the page, we'll actually see the images from Flickr! And if we change the original URL to a tag different from dog, the entire page will change! As usual, we can easily add jQuery effects to make things happen in a slightly nicer way:

```
$.getJSON(url, function (flickrResponse) {
    flickrResponse.items.forEach(function (photo) {
        // create a new jQuery element to hold the image
        // but hide it so we can fade it in
        var $img = $("<img>").hide();

        // set the attribute to the url
        // contained in the response
        $img.attr("src", photo.media.m);

        // attach the img tag to the main
        // photos element and then fade it in
        $("main .photos").append($img);
        $img.fadeIn();
    });
});
```

Now the images will fade in when the page loads. In the practice problems at the end of the chapter, we'll modify this so that the page cycles through the images, displaying one image at a time.

Adding a Tags Feature to Amazeriffic

Now that we understand how to use JavaScript objects and JSON, it might be helpful to integrate some of what we've learned into our Amazeriffic application. In this example, we'll add tags to each to-do item. We can use these tags to sort our to-do list in a different, but still meaningful, way. In addition, we can initialize our to-do list from a JSON file instead of having the array hardcoded.

To start with, we can copy our entire *Amazeriffic* directory from our *Chapter4* directory into our *Chapter5* directory. This will give us a solid starting point so we don't have to rewrite all of that code.

Next, let's add a JSON file with our to-do list. We can save this in a file called *to-dos.json* in the root directory of our project (the root directory is the one that contains the *index.html* file):

```
[
    {
        "description" : "Get groceries",
```

```
        "tags"   : [ "shopping", "chores" ]
    },
    {

        "description" : "Make up some new ToDos",
        "tags"   : [ "writing", "work" ]
    },
    {

        "description" : "Prep for Monday's class",
        "tags"   : [ "work", "teaching" ]
    },
    {

        "description" : "Answer emails",
        "tags"   : [ "work" ]
    },
    {

        "description" : "Take Gracie to the park",
        "tags"   : [ "chores", "pets" ]
    },
    {

        "description" : "Finish writing this book",
        "tags"   : [ "writing", "work" ]
    }
]
```

You'll see that this JSON file contains an array of to-do items, and that each item has an array of strings that are tags. Our goal is to have the tags work as a secondary method of organizing our to-do list.

To incorporate this new feature, we'll need to add some jQuery code that reads our JSON file. But because our main function from the previous chapter depends on the to-dos, we'll need to modify it so that it calls getJSON before it calls main. To do that, we'll add an anonymous function to our document.ready call that calls getJSON and then calls main with the result:

```
var main = function (toDoObjects) {
    "use strict";

    // now main has access to our toDo list!
};

$(document).ready(function () {
    $.getJSON("todos.json", function (toDoObjects) {
        // call main with the to-dos as an argument
        main(toDoObjects);
    });
});
```

One minor issue is that our code won't work because we've changed the structure of our to-do object. Previously, it was an array of strings that was the description of the to-do item, but now it is an array of objects. If we just want our code to work the way it did before, we can create our old array type from the new array type using the map function.

The map Function

The map function takes an array and creates a new array from it by applying a function to each element. Fire up your Chrome console and try the following:

```
// we'll create an array of numbers
var nums = [1, 2, 3, 4, 5];

// now we'll apply the map function
// which creates a new array
var squares = nums.map(function (num) {
    return num*num;
});

console.log(squares);
//=> [1, 4, 9, 16, 25]
```

In this example, the function that returns num*num is applied to each element to create the new array. This may seem like an esoteric example, but here's a more interesting one:

```
// we'll create an array of names
var names = [ "emily", "mark", "bruce", "andrea", "pablo" ];

// now we'll create a new array of names
// where the first letter is capitalized
var capitalizedNames = names.map(function (name) {
    // get the first letter
    var firstLetter = name[0];
    // return the uppercased first letter along
    // with the string starting at index 1
    return firstLetter.toUpperCase() + name.substring(1);
});

console.log(capitalizedNames);
//=> [ "Emily", "Mark", "Bruce", "Andrea", "Pablo" ]
```

So you can see that we've created an array of capitalized names without even iterating over the array ourselves!

Now that we understand how map works, it's almost trivial to create our old array from the new one:

```
var main = function (toDoObjects) {
    "use strict";

    var toDos = toDoObjects.map(function (toDo) {
        // we'll just return the description
        // of this toDoObject
        return toDo.description;
    });
```

```
    // now all of our old code should work exactly as it did!
    // ...
};

$(document).ready(function () {
    $.getJSON("todos.json", function (toDoObjects) {
        // we'll call main with toDos as an argument
        main(toDoObjects);
    });
});
```

Now that we have all of our old code working exactly as it did before, we can create a Tags tab.

Adding a Tags Tab

We'll start by adding a Tags tab to our UI. Because we've built our code to be (relatively) flexible, that's not all that difficult. We simply have to start by going into *index.html* and adding code for a tab called "Tags" between our "Oldest" and "Add" tabs:

```
<div class="tabs">
  <a href=""><span class="active">Newest</span></a>
  <a href=""><span>Oldest</span></a>
  <a href=""><span>Tags</span></a>
  <a href=""><span>Add</span></a>
</div>
```

That additional line will add a tab to our UI and (almost) everything will work exactly as we'd expect. The only problem is that we built our tabs based on their location in this list. So, when we click the Tags tab, we'll see the interface for the Add button. This is definitely not our expected behavior, but—fortunately—requires only a minor modification.

All we need to do is add an additional else-if block in the middle of our tab code and rearrange the numbers slightly. When I did that in my code, the relevant section ended up looking like this:

```
} else if ($element.parent().is(":nth-child(3)")) {
    // THIS IS THE TAGS TAB CODE
    console.log("the tags tab was clicked!");
} else if ($element.parent().is(":nth-child(4)")) {
    $input = $("<input>"),
    $button = $("<button>").text("+");

    $button.on("click", function () {
        toDos.push($input.val());
        $input.val("");
    });
    $content = $("<div>").append($input).append($button);
}
```

Building the UI

Now that we know how to set that up, let's take a quick look at our goal for this tab in Figure 5-2.

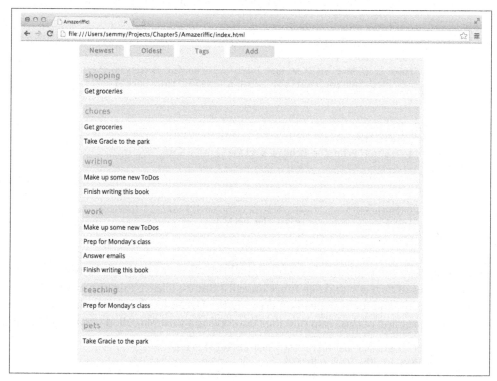

Figure 5-2. Our goal for the Tags tab

For this tab, we're planning to list out all of the tags as headers, and then add the to-do descriptions that are tagged with that category. That means our to-do descriptions can appear in multiple places.

The problem here, however, is that our JSON object isn't really stored in a way that makes this very easy. It would be easier if our toDoObjects were stored in a format organized by tags:

```
[
    {
        "name": "shopping",
        "toDos": ["Get groceries"]
    },

    {
        "name": "chores",
```

```
            "toDos": ["Get groceries", "Take Gracie to the park"]
    },

    {
        "name": "writing",
        "toDos": ["Make up some new ToDos", "Finish writing this book"]
    },

    {
        "name": "work",
        "toDos": ["Make up some new ToDos", "Prep for Monday's class",
                   "Answer emails", "Finish writing this book"]
    },

    {
        "name": "teaching",
        "toDos": ["Prep for Monday's class"]
    },

    {
        "name": "pets",
        "toDos": ["Take Gracie to the park"]
    }
]
```

Fortunately, we can easily modify our original `toDoObjects` object to be in this format using a series of `forEach` and `map` function calls! But we'll leave this transformation for the next section and focus instead on creating the UI. So let's hardcode this (or maybe a simplified version of this) into our Tags tab code as a variable called `organizedByTag`:

```
} else if ($element.parent().is(":nth-child(3)")) {
    // THIS IS THE TAGS TAB CODE
    console.log("the tags tab was clicked!");

    var organizedByTag = [
        {
            "name": "shopping",
            "toDos": ["Get groceries"]
        },

        {
            "name": "chores",
            "toDos": ["Get groceries", "Take Gracie to the park"]
        },

        /* etc */
    ];

}
```

Now our goal is to iterate over this object, adding a new section to the `.content` element of our page as we do so. To do this, we simply add an h3 element along with a ul and a list of `li` elements for each tag. The `ul` and `li` elements are built just like they were in the previous chapter, so the style should stay exactly the same. I also added styling for my h3 element to the *style.css* file to get it to look the way it does in the previous example:

```
    } else if ($element.parent().is(":nth-child(3)")) {
        // THIS IS THE TAGS TAB CODE
        console.log("the tags tab was clicked!");

        var organizedByTag = [
            /* etc */
        ]

        organizedByTag.forEach(function (tag) {
            var $tagName = $("<h3>").text(tag.name),
                $content = $("<ul>");


            tag.toDos.forEach(function (description) {
                var $li = $("<li>").text(description);
                $content.append($li);
            });

            $("main .content").append($tagName);
            $("main .content").append($content);
        });
    }
```

Now we have two things left to do. We'll need to modify the Add tab to accept a list of categories with a to-do item, and we'll need to figure out how to modify our current list of to-do objects into a list of items organized by the tag names. Let's start with the latter first, so that our app will dynamically update when we add new items.

Creating an Intermediate Tags Data Structure

When I'm confronted with a problem that seems like it's going to need to be solved in more than a few lines of code, that usually clues me in that I should abstract it as a function. In this case, we want to build a function called `organizeByTags` that takes an object stored in our program like this:

```
[
    {
        "description" : "Get groceries",
        "tags"        : [ "shopping", "chores" ]
    },
    {
        "description" : "Make up some new ToDos",
        "tags"        : [ "writing", "work" ]
    },

    /* etc */
]
```

and converts it into an object that's stored like this:

```
[
        {
            "name": "shopping",
            "toDos": ["Get groceries"]
        },

        {
            "name": "chores",
            "toDos": ["Get groceries", "Take Gracie to the park"]
        },

        /* etc */
]
```

Once we have the function, we can simply modify it and put it in the place of our hard-coded object like this:

```
} else if ($element.parent().is(":nth-child(3)")) {
    // THIS IS THE TAGS TAB CODE
    console.log("the tags tab was clicked!");

    var organizedByTag = organizeByTag(toDoObjects);
}
```

Setting up a test bed

We could try to get something like this working in the Chrome console, but that becomes a bit cumbersome when functions get long or complicated. My preferred way of setting this up is to build an external JavaScript program that contains the function and test it out by printing stuff to the console. Once I'm happy with the way it's working, I'll incorporate it into my working code.

To do this, it's sometimes nice to have a simple unused HTML file lying around in our file hierarchy. This file does nothing more than add a script file that we can use for trying things out. The HTML file doesn't even need any of our usual boilerplate content:

```
<script src="http://code.jquery.com/jquery-2.0.3.min.js"></script>
<script src="test.js"></script>
```

Now if we save that file as *index.html* and create *test.js* with the following content, we should see "organizeByTag called" on the console, along with the example object that we've set up:

```
var toDoObjects = [
    {
        "description" : "Get groceries",
        "tags"    : [ "shopping", "chores" ]
    },
    {
        "description" : "Make up some new ToDos",
```

```
            "tags"  : [ "writing", "work" ]
        },
        /* etc */
    ];


    var organizeByTags = function (toDoObjects) {
        console.log("organizeByTags called");
    };

    var main = function () {
        "use strict";

        organizeByTags(toDoObjects);
    };

    $(document).ready(main);
```

Once you have this set up, I encourage you to spend some time trying to solve this problem on your own. It's tricky, but once you see the solution I expect that you'll understand it. Trying it out yourself will help you get a good sense of how much you can do.

I'll also add that there are several ways to solve this, which is often the case when it comes to computer programming. I'm going to show you my solution, but it's often instructive to see how your solution differs from mine.

My solution

My solution is relatively easy to explain in two parts. First, I create an array that contains all the possible tags by iterating over the initial structure using a forEach loop. Once I have that, I use the map function to map the tags array to my desired object by iterating over the to-dos and finding the ones that have that tag.

Let's start with the first part. The only new thing we use here is the indexOf function that is included with all arrays. We can see how it works by interacting with the Chrome console:

```
var nums = [1, 2, 3, 4, 5];

nums.indexOf(3);
//=> 2

nums.indexOf(1);
//=> 0

nums.indexOf(10);
//=> -1
```

We can generalize this behavior: if the object is contained in the array, the function returns the index (starting with 0) of the object. If it's not in the array, the function returns –1. We can use it on strings as well:

```
var msgs = ["hello", "goodbye", "world"];

msgs.indexOf("goodbye");
//=> 1

msgs.indexOf("hello");
//=> 0

msgs.indexOf("HEY!");
//=> -1
```

We'll use this function to keep from adding duplicates to our tags array:

```
var organizeByTags = function (toDoObjects) {
    // create an empty tags array
    var tags = [];

    // iterate over all toDos
    toDoObjects.forEach(function (toDo) {

        // iterate over each tag in this toDo
        toDo.tags.forEach(function (tag) {

            // make sure the tag is not already
            // in the tag array
            if (tags.indexOf(tag) === -1) {
                tags.push(tag);
            }
        });
    });

    console.log(tags);
};
```

When we run this, it should print out the tag names without duplicates. That means we're halfway there! In the second part of the solution I use the map function:

```
var organizeByTags = function (toDoObjects) {
    /* the first part from above */

    var tagObjects = tags.map(function (tag) {
        // here we find all the to-do objects
        // that contain that tag
        var toDosWithTag = [];
        toDoObjects.forEach(function (toDo) {

            // check to make sure the result
            // of indexOf is *not* equal to -1
            if (toDo.tags.indexOf(tag) !== -1) {
```

```
                toDosWithTag.push(toDo.description);
            }
        });

        // we map each tag to an object that
        // contains the name of the tag and an array
        return { "name": tag, "toDos": toDosWithTag };
    });
    console.log(tagObjects);
};
```

Now that we have the function created and working correctly, we can incorporate it into the `main` function of our app code and it should work! Like I mentioned before, this problem admits several different solutions, so it's good to try to come up with some others!

Tags as Part of Our Input

So now we've managed to get the to-do objects organized and displayed by tags, but how can we add tags to the new elements that we input in the Add tab? That requires us modifying the code that displays the tab interface. I'd like to set it up so it looks like Figure 5-3.

Figure 5-3. Our goal for the Add tab

As you can see, it now has two input boxes. In the second one, we'll let the user input a comma-separated list of tags, which we'll incorporate into the object when we add it.

If you finished the final example in the previous chapter, you probably have code that looks something like this:

```
} else if ($element.parent().is(":nth-child(4)")) {
    var $input = $("<input>"),
        $button = $("<button>").text("+");

    $button.on("click", function () {
        toDos.push($input.val());
        $input.val("");
    });

    $content = $("<div>").append($input).append($button);
}
```

To make the UI look like it does in Figure 5-3, we need to add an additional input box and the labels. Then we need to modify the $button handler to create an array out of the tags and insert those into the objects.

One thing that we'll need to know is how to split the string object. It turns out that all strings have a built-in function called split that does just that—it splits a single string into an array of strings. And just like most of the other functions we've learned, we can see how it works inside the Chrome console:

```
var words = "hello,world,goodbye,world";

// this splits the array on a comma
var arrayOfWords = words.split(",");

console.log(arrayOfWords);
//=> ["hello","world","goodbye","world"]

arrayOfWords[1];
//=> "world"

arrayOfWords[0];
//=> "hello"
```

We'll let the user input a string of comma-separated words that are tags and then add them as an array to the object.

Last, but not least, we'll need to re-create our toDos array from the new toDoObjects array. To do this, I cut and pasted the code that we used at the top of the main function (and in doing so, violated the DRY principle—I encourage you to try to fix that). My code ended up looking like this:

```
} else if ($element.parent().is(":nth-child(4)")) {
    var $input = $("<input>").addClass("description"),
        $inputLabel = $("<p>").text("Description: "),
        $tagInput = $("<input>").addClass("tags"),
        $tagLabel = $("<p>").text("Tags: "),
```

```
    $button = $("<button>").text("+");

$button.on("click", function () {
    var description = $input.val(),
        tags = $tagInput.val().split(","); // split on the comma

    toDoObjects.push({"description":description, "tags":tags});

    // update toDos
    toDos = toDoObjects.map(function (toDo) {
        return toDo.description;
    });

    $input.val("");
    $tagInput.val("");
});

$content = $("<div>").append($inputLabel)
                     .append($input)
                     .append($tagLabel)
                     .append($tagInput)
                     .append($button);
}
```

Summary

In this chapter, we studied three major topics at a rudimentary level: JavaScript objects, JSON, and AJAX. I introduced JavaScript objects as a way to store related data as a single entity in a program. Objects are created using curly braces, and properties are added and accessed using the . (dot) operator.

You can think of JSON as simply a string representation of a JavaScript object that can be processed by any programming language. JSON is used to transfer data between computer programs—in our case between the web browser (the client) and the server. In addition, many web services (including Flickr, Twitter, and Facebook) offer *application programming interfaces* (APIs) that allow us to send and request information to and from their services using the JSON format.

Typically, when we want to send or receive information to or from a server-side program, we use a technology called AJAX. This allows us to dynamically update the information on our web page without actually reloading the page. jQuery offers several AJAX functions that we'll learn in later chapters, but we looked at the getJSON function in this chapter.

More Practice and Further Reading

Flickr Slideshow

In this problem, you'll build a simple application that allows the user to enter a search term, and then presents a series of images from Flickr that have that tag. The images should fade out and fade in sequentially.

To do this, we'll use the `setTimeout` function that was mentioned briefly in Chapter 4. This function allows us to schedule an event to happen after a specified period of time. For example, suppose we wanted to log "hello world!" after five seconds. We could do this as follows:

```
// print 'hello world' after five seconds
setTimeout(function () {
    console.log("hello world!");
}, 5000);
```

Notice that the arguments to this function are backward from what we're used to—typically the callback goes at the end. This is a quirk that we just have to remember. Also notice that the second argument represents the number of *milliseconds* that we should wait before executing the callback function.

Now suppose that we simply wanted to fade in and fade out an array of messages:

```
var messages = ["first message", "second message", "third", "fourth"];
```

We could start with a simple HTML body:

```
<body>
  <div class="message"></div>
</body>
```

Then we can set up our `main` function in *app.js* to do the following:

```
var main = function () {
    var messages = ["first message", "second message", "third", "fourth"];

    var displayMessage = function (messageIndex) {
        // create and hide the DOM element
        var $message = $("<p>").text(messages[messageIndex]).hide();

        // clear out the current content
        // it would be better to select the current
        // paragraph and fade it out.
        $(".message").empty();

        // append the message with messageIndex to the DOM
        $(".message").append($message);

        // fade in the message
        $message.fadeIn();
```

```
    setTimeout(function () {
        // In 3 seconds call displayMessage again with the next index
        messageIndex = messageIndex + 1;
        displayMessage(messageIndex);
    }, 3000);
};

displayMessage(0);
};


$(document).ready(main);
```

This will fade in the messages in order, cycling once every three seconds. There is, however, a minor problem with this—once we get to the end, we'll start seeing the word undefined appear because we've fallen off the end of the array. We can fix this by including an if statement to check if we're at the end and, if we are, setting the index back to 0.

 We probably don't want to actually add this effect to a web page. It's a modern equivalent to the maligned <blink> tag that was removed from HTML because it was super annoying.

Now we can generalize this. First, we should do an AJAX request to get the image data from Flickr, and then instead of adding a paragraph element to the DOM, we'll add an img element instead of a p element. We'll set the src attribute of the img element to the Flickr image.

Once we have that working, we'll create an interface that lets the user enter a tag to search for, and then generates the slideshow with images that include the specified tag. This is a nice exercise that should take you some time, especially if you decide to add some basic styling and really coordinate the images correctly. I encourage you to give it a try!

Object Practice

One of my favorite problems to share with beginning programmers relates to identifying poker hands. If you're not familiar with the family of card games based on poker, that's OK. They are all related to patterns that occur in hands of five playing cards. The hands are as follows:

Pair
    Two cards of the same rank

Two pair
> Two cards of the same rank, plus two cards of another rank

Three of a kind
> Three cards of the same rank

Straight
> Five ranks in order, but an ace can count as the highest or lowest rank

Flush
> Five cards of the same suit

Full house
> Two cards of the same rank, plus three cards of another rank

Four of a kind
> Four cards of the same rank

Straight flush
> Five cards of the same suit, where the ranks form a straight

Royal flush
> A straight flush, where the straight starts at a 10 and ends at an ace

We'll refer to any hand that doesn't meet one of these criteria as a *bust*. Note that the hands are not mutually exclusive—a hand that contains a *three of a kind* also contains a *pair*, and a *full house* contains *two pair*. In this set of problems, we'll write JavaScript functions that test whether an array of five cards has one of these properties.

There are many ways to solve these problems, and some are way more efficient or require much less code than others. But our goal here is to practice with objects, arrays, and conditional statements. So we'll follow an approach that allows us to build a series of helper functions that we can use to determine if a set of five cards matches a certain type of hand.

To start, let's see what a hand might look like:

```
var hand = [
    { "rank":"two", "suit":"spades" },
    { "rank":"four", "suit":"hearts" },
    { "rank":"two", "suit":"clubs" },
    { "rank":"king", "suit":"spades" },
    { "rank":"eight", "suit":"diamonds" }
];
```

In this example, our hand contains a pair of twos. It might be a good idea to construct an example for each of the other types of hands before going any further.

How do we determine if a hand meets one of the criteria? We're going to reduce it to a problem that we solved at the end of Chapter 4! If you finished those problems, you'll remember that I had you write a function called containsNTimes that accepted three arguments: an array, an item to search for, and a minimum number of times that it needed to appear. Now imagine if we sent in an array of ranks to that function:

```
// there are 2 twos
containsNTimes(["two","four","two","king","eight"], "two", 2);
//=> true
```

This tells us that the array of ranks has a pair! We can similarly use this to determine if there's a three of a kind or a four of a kind!

```
// there are not 3 twos
containsNTimes(["two","four","two","king","eight"], "two", 3);
//=> false
```

So now we've reduced the problem to turning our array of card objects into an array of ranks. It turns out that's pretty easy using the map function that we learned in this chapter:

```
// our "hand" is the hand array defined above
hand.map(function (card) {
    return card.rank;
});
//=> ["two","four","two","king","eight"]
```

So we can assign the result of the call to map as a variable, and then send that into our containsNTimes function to determine if it has a pair of twos:

```
var handRanks,
    result;

handRanks = hand.map(function (card) {
    return card.rank;
});

//result holds 'true'
result = containsNTimes(handRanks, "two", 2);
```

To finish this off, we create an array of all possible ranks, and use a forEach loop to determine if the hand contains a pair of *any* of them:

```
// this is all of our possible ranks
var ranks = ["two","three","four","five","six","seven","eight",
             "nine","ten","jack","queen","king","ace"];

var containsPair = function (hand) {
    // we'll assume that it doesn't have a pair
    // until we find evidence to the contrary
    var result = false,
        handRanks;

    // create our array of hand ranks
    handRanks = hand.map(function (card) {
        return card.rank;
```

```
    });

    // search for a pair of any rank
    ranks.forEach(function (rank) {
        if (containsNTimes(handRanks, rank, 2)) {
            // we found a pair!
            result = true;
        }
    });

    // this is set to true if we found a pair
    // it's false if we didn't
    return result;
};
```

Now that we've seen an example, try generalizing it to write a function for each of the other ranks (e.g., `containsThreeOfAKind`). For two pair and a full house, you'll need to keep track of the actual ranks of the elements you find. For the flush, you'll need to extract the suits from the array of objects instead of the ranks.

A straight is a little harder, but here's a hint: a straight does not contain a pair (which you can determine by flipping the result of the `containsPair` function using the `!` operator), and the difference between the highest card and the lowest card is 4. So it would be good to write a couple of helper functions to find the highest card rank and the lowest card rank as numbers (for instance, a jack would be 11, a queen would be 12, a king 13, and an ace would be 14). Once you have those functions, you can determine if a hand has a straight by confirming that it doesn't contain a pair and the difference between the high card and low card is 4.

You can also build up all of the rest of the functions by using existing functions. For instance, a straight flush is just a flush that also contains a straight. And a royal flush is a straight flush where the high card is an ace (or the low card is a 10).

Other APIs

Now that you've seen that you can easily pull in data from Flickr and play with the results, it's sometimes fun to pull data in from other APIs. It turns out that many APIs allow you to access data in the same way we accessed the Flickr data.

Programmable Web (*http://www.programmableweb.com*) keeps a list. For the site to work with jQuery's `getJSON` function, it needs to support a technology called *JSONP*. You can pull up a list of APIs that support JSONP (*http://www.programmableweb.com/apis/directory/1?format=JSONP*) and you can read more about JSONP on Wikipedia (*http://en.wikipedia.org/wiki/JSONP*).

You'll need to read the documentation for the specific API to determine how to format your query URL, but playing around with other APIs is a great way to practice your AJAX skills.

## CHAPTER 6

The Server

At this point, we've seen the major technologies associated with the client-side part of a web application. We've also learned a bit about how the browser communicates with a server using JSON and AJAX. Next, we're going to delve into server-side programming.

Understanding the server-side part of the application will require us to learn more about the client-server model, the HTTP protocol, and Node.js. Node.js is a relatively new (and exciting) technology that allows us to easily build event-driven servers using JavaScript.

Setting Up Your Environment

Setting up a development environment that supports building database-driven applications can be a daunting task, and describing the procedure for Windows, Mac OS, and Linux is way beyond the scope of this book. To simplify the process, I've created a set of scripts that will get you up and running relatively quickly using Vagrant and VirtualBox.

Vagrant is a tool that helps build a development environment using a virtual machine. You can think of a virtual machine as a separate computer running completely within the confines of your computer. We'll elaborate more on this in "Mental Models" on page 187. For now, just understand that we'll be using Vagrant along with VirtualBox to build a virtual server-side development environment. This environment will include the majority of the tools that we'll use throughout the rest of this book.

Obviously, part of this process is about convenience: even though installing a Node.js development environment on your local machine is pretty easy (and I will encourage you to do it in the practice problems at the end of the chapter), adding a full server-stack including MongoDB and Redis is nontrivial and takes a bit of time and patience.

Another reason we're doing this is consistency. Because I'm writing the scripts, I have a little more control over the versions of Node.js, MongoDB, and Redis that are installed. Furthermore, using Vagrant allows us to have the same development environment running whether you're using Windows, Mac OS, or Linux. This will (hopefully) minimize any issues arising due to OS differences.

I also think that running our development environment inside of VirtualBox separates out the server part of the application in a very clear way. This makes it a useful pedagogical abstraction for someone learning the basics of web application development.

Installing VirtualBox and Vagrant

First, you'll need to install the latest version of VirtualBox. At the time of this writing, the latest version is 4.2.18. You can go to *http://www.virtualbox.org* (shown in Figure 6-1), click the Downloads link on the left side of the page, and download the appropriate version for your operating system. Once downloaded, the installation and setup process will differ depending on your operating system, so make sure to follow the appropriate instructions.

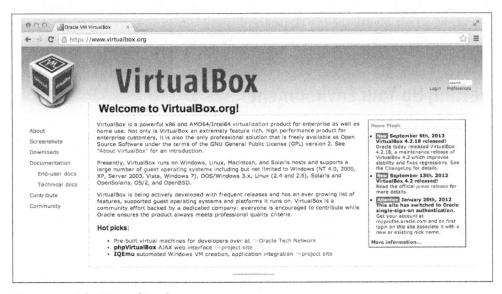

Figure 6-1. The VirtualBox home page

Next, you'll need to install the latest version of Vagrant. The latest version at the time of this writing is 1.4. To get the latest version, you can go to *http://www.vagrant up.com* (see Figure 6-2), click the Downloads link in the upper-right corner, and grab the latest installer for your platform. After downloading it, double-click the package and install it in the same way you installed VirtualBox.

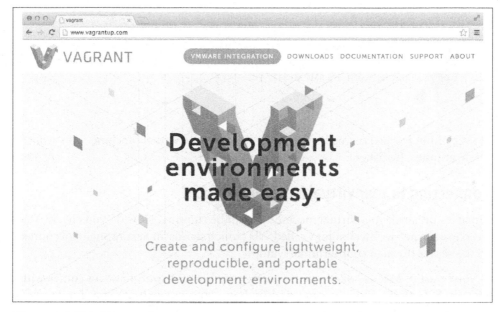

Figure 6-2. The Vagrant home page

If you're running Windows, you may have to reboot your machine after the installation to make sure your file path is set up correctly. You can test this out by opening a command window (click your Start menu, and type **cmd** into the search box) and typing **vagrant --version** at the prompt:

```
C:\Users\semmy>vagrant --version
Vagrant version 1.4.0
```

If that works, you're ready to go. If it does not, reboot your machine and try typing the **vagrant** command again.

Building Your Virtual Machine

If all is well, you're ready to clone the Git repository called node-dev-bootstrap from my GitHub page. This basically means you'll be downloading an entire Git repository that I've created and putting it on your computer. If you're using Windows this will require you to open your git-bash prompt. In either case, go into your *Projects* directory and clone the node-dev-bootstrap repository using the following command:

```
hostname $ git clone https://github.com/semmypurewal/node-dev-bootstrap Chapter6
```

This will create a directory called *Chapter6* and clone the node-dev-bootstrap repository into it. Next you can enter the project directory and type the **vagrant up** command:

```
hostname $ cd Chapter6
hostname $ vagrant up
```

 If you're running Windows, you may get a warning from the firewall asking if the program "vboxheadless" should allowed to access the network. It's safe to say "yes."

If everything worked correctly, Vagrant will build your virtual machine. This will take a few minutes. Be patient.

Connecting to Your Virtual Machine with SSH

Once it's finished, your virtual machine should be running. How do you check? You'll need to use a network technology called SSH (which stands for Secure Shell) to "connect" to the server through your terminal window.

If you're using Mac OS or Linux, it's pretty easy because your platform comes with a built-in SSH client. If you're running Windows, however, you may need to manually install an SSH client.

Either way, go ahead and type:

```
hostname $ vagrant ssh
```

If you're running Mac OS, it will connect you to your virtual machine. If you're running Windows, it may or may not work depending on the version. If it doesn't work, Vagrant will give you login credentials (most likely the host will be 127.0.0.1 and the port will be 2222). You'll need to download an SSH client to connect—I recommend PuTTY, which is available at the PuTTY downloads page (*http://www.chiark.greenend.org.uk/ ~sgtatham/putty/download.html*). The PuTTY home page is shown in Figure 6-3.

When you open up PuTTY, you'll type in the Host Name and the Port that Vagrant specified into the appropriate input boxes, as shown in Figure 6-4.

Then click Open. PuTTY will connect to your virtual server and ask you for a username and password. Both of these should be preset to "vagrant."

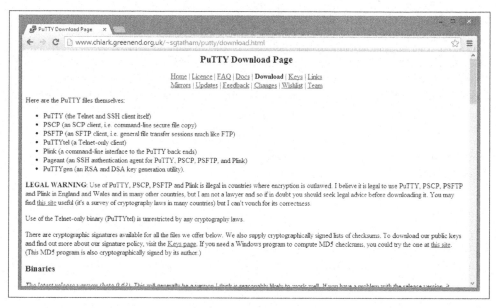

Figure 6-3. The PuTTY home/download page

Figure 6-4. Setting up PuTTY to connect to your virtual machine

Hello, Node.js!

Once you're logged in, you can navigate the terminal shell of your remote computer in the same way that you navigate the terminal shell of your local computer. For example, you can list the contents of your virtual machine directory in the same way that you examine the contents of a directory on your local machine—using the `ls` command:

```
vagrant $ ls
app postinstall.sh
```

You can ignore the *postinstall.sh* file for now. Using the command-line skills you learned in earlier chapters, navigate to the *app* directory of your virtual machine:

```
vagrant $ cd app
vagrant $ ls
server.js
```

You should see a file called *server.js* there. Let's make sure everything is working by starting it using the `node` command:

```
vagrant $ node server.js
Server listening on port 3000
```

You'll see a message that says "`Server listening on port 3000`" and should no longer get a terminal prompt. That's because your server is running. You can confirm that by opening Chrome and typing **localhost:3000** in your address bar. If everything worked correctly, you should see a "Hello World!" message. It should look something like Figure 6-5.

First things first: you can stop the program from the terminal window by hitting Ctrl-C. Once you're done working, you can exit out of your virtual server by typing **exit**:

```
vagrant $ exit
logout
Connection to 127.0.0.1 closed.
```

If you've logged in to your virtual machine via PuTTY on Windows, this will shut down the program. Then you can return to the terminal that you used to start your virtual machine. If you're in Mac OS, you'll immediately go back to your command line. Either way, you can stop the server by typing **vagrant halt**:

```
hostname $ vagrant halt
[default] Attempting graceful shutdown of VM...
```

You'll want to halt your VM whenever you're not using it because having a virtual machine running in the background will definitely be a drain on your computer's resources. Once halted, you can restart your box with `vagrant up`.

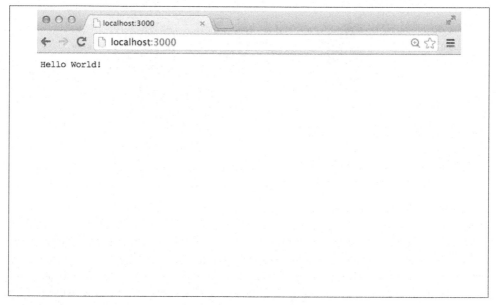

Figure 6-5. The default Node server viewed from Chrome

To completely remove the Vagrant-built virtual machine from your computer, you can type **vagrant destroy**. That will result in your VM being rebuilt next time you type **vagrant up** from that directory. So I would recommend sticking with vagrant halt for the time being.

Mental Models

In this section, we'll discuss some of the ways to think about clients, servers, hosts, and guests.

Clients and Servers

In the field of computer networking, we typically think of computer programs as being either *client* programs or *server* programs. Traditionally, a *server* program abstracts some resource over a network that multiple *client* programs want to access. For example, someone might want to transfer files from a remote computer to a local computer. An FTP server is a program that implements the *File Transfer Protocol*, which allows users to do exactly this. An FTP client is a program that can connect and transfer programs from an FTP server. The most general client-server model is illustrated in Figure 6-6.

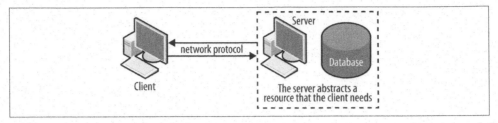

Figure 6-6. The client-server model

A lot of detail goes on in the world of computer networking that is ancillary to web application development, but a few important things are worth understanding.

The first is that (most of the time) the client is a web browser and the server is a remote machine that is abstracting resources via the *Hypertext Transfer Protocol*, or HTTP for short. Although it was originally designed to transfer HTML documents between computers, the HTTP protocol can now be used to abstract many different types of resources on a remote computer (for instance, documents, databases, or any other type of storage). We'll have a lot more to say about HTTP later on in the book, but for now we can think of it as the protocol that we're using to connect browsers to remote computers.

Our HTTP servers will be used to deliver the client-side part of the application that the web browser will interpret. In particular, all of the HTML, CSS, and JavaScript that we've learned up to this point will be delivered to the browser via the server. The client-side program running in the browser will be responsible for getting information from or sending information to our server, usually via AJAX.

Hosts and Guests

Typically, our HTTP server is running on a remote machine (in fact, later on in the book we'll make that happen). This causes problems for developers—if we're running our code on a remote server we have to actually either edit the code on the remote server and restart it, or we have to edit the code locally and push it every time we want to try it out. This can be highly inefficient.

We're working around this problem by running the server locally on our machine. In fact, we're taking it one step further. Instead of just running a server program and all of the software locally, we're creating a virtual machine inside our local computer that is running the server. To us, it almost looks like it's a remote machine (meaning we connect to it via SSH, which is the way we connect to real remote machines). But because it's running locally, we can easily share our development folder with our local machine so we can edit files.

Our local computer (that is running the virtual machine) is referred to as the *host* machine. The virtual machine is referred to as the *guest* machine. For the rest of this chapter, we'll have both running and I'll differentiate between them.

Practicalities

This abstraction can lead to some confusion—one that's worth overcoming early. First of all, it's good to list out the applications you have running in the development process, and the window that they are associated with:

The browser

You'll be using Chrome to test changes to your application.

The text editor

If you've been following along, this will most likely be Sublime. This will edit files living in a shared folder on both your host and guest machines.

Git

You'll have a Git terminal window open. You'll use Git from your host machine. If you're in Mac OS or Linux, this will be a terminal window. If you're in Windows, this will be the `git-bash` prompt.

Vagrant

You'll most likely interact with Vagrant in the same window that you use to interact with Git. That means you can type **vagrant up** and **vagrant halt** in the same place that you type `git commit`.

SSH

This will be running on your host machine, but you'll be using it to interact with your guest machine. If you're in Windows, this will be either PuTTY or an additional `git-bash` window depending on whether `vagrant ssh` connects you directly. If you're in Mac OS, it's a good idea to have an additional terminal open.

I typically have at least two terminal windows open in addition to the browser and my text editor. This is partially illustrated in Figure 6-7, although the text editor window isn't shown.

Hello, HTTP!

Now that we roughly understand the relationship between the guest virtual machine and our host machine, let's try to understand the actual code. Like I mentioned before, the great thing about running our code in virtual machine on our local computer (versus running it remotely) is that we can access and edit the code directly on our local computer using whatever text editor we choose.

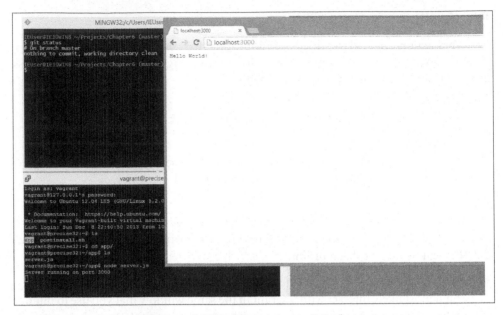

Figure 6-7. git-bash, PuTTY, and Chrome running in Windows

Using Sublime, open up the *app* directory inside the *Chapter6* directory. You should see a file called *server.js* that should look something like this:

```
var http = require("http"),
    server;

server = http.createServer(function (req, res) {
    res.writeHead(200, {"Content-Type": "text/plain"});
    res.end("Hello World!");
});

server.listen(3000);

console.log("Server listening on port 3000");
```

This code shouldn't look completely unfamiliar to you—you should be able to imme-diately identify some variable declarations, a `console.log` statement, an anonymous function, a JSON object, and the callback pattern that we used when we built UI elements in earlier chapters.

So what is this code doing? It turns out it's doing a lot—it's creating an HTTP server that is responding to web browser requests! As mentioned before, HTTP stands for *HyperText Transfer Protocol* and it's the basic technology that's behind the World Wide Web! You may have heard of programs like Apache or Nginx—these are industrial-strength, configurable HTTP server programs that are designed to host big websites.

Our HTTP server is much simpler than that: it's simply accepting a browser request and responding with a text response that says "Hello World."

We can think of the code as behaving exactly as our jQuery click handler behaves—the difference is that instead of the callback being called when a user clicks, it is called whenever a client (in this case, the browser) connects. The req parameter is an object that represents the HTTP request that is coming to our server from the client, and the res parameter is an object that represents the HTTP response that we'll send back to the client. The res.writeHead function creates the HTTP header that sets the attributes of the response, and the res.end function completes the response by adding "Hello World."

After we create the server, we make it *listen* on port 3000 (which is why we type **3000** after localhost in our web browser's address bar). The console.log statement prints out the statement to the server terminal when we run the program.

Modules and Express

Phew! That probably seems like a lot for such a little program! It's more than you likely realize—an HTTP server is a nontrivial piece of software that takes a good deal of skill to write correctly. Fortunately, we don't have to worry about the details because we imported the code via the Node.js http *module*. A module is simply a collection of code that we can use without completely understanding how it works internally—all we have to understand is the API that it exposes to us. The first line in our code is the require statement, which imports the http module and stores it in the http variable.

This HTTP server module is interesting if we need a bare-bones, stripped down HTTP server that simply accepts and responds to client requests. Once we want to start sending HTML or CSS files from the server, however, things become much more complicated. We can build a more complex server on top of the basic HTTP server that Node.js gives us but, lucky for us, somebody else already solved that problem, too! The Express module creates a layer on top of the core http module that handles a lot of complex things that we don't want to handle ourselves, like serving up static HTML, CSS, and client-side JavaScript files.

Indeed, one of the joys of programming in Node is that we can leverage numerous modules like Express, many of which do very useful things. The http module that we used earlier is part of the core distribution of Node.js, so we don't have to do anything special to use it. Express is not part of the core distribution of Node, so we need to do a little more work before we can access it as easily as we access the http module.

Fortunately, it turns out that every distribution of Node comes with another program called the *Node Package Manager* (or NPM for short). This tool allows us to easily install modules and then immediately leverage them in our code.

Installing Express with NPM

NPM is pretty easy to use. Let's start by creating a new directory inside the *app* directory and call it *Express*. You can do this in Sublime or in the terminal window. Either way, once you get the directory created, you'll want to SSH into your Vagrant box and navigate to the *Express* directory. Then you can type in **npm install express@3**:

```
vagrant $ ls
app postinstall.sh
vagrant $ cd app
vagrant $ ls
Express server.js
vagrant $ cd Express
vagrant $ npm install express@3
```

 Occasionally, NPM and VirtualBox will not work nicely together on a Windows machine. If you get errors when you attempt to install Express, try running the command npm install express@3 --no-bin-links and see if that helps.

NPM will respond by installing Express and a long list of its dependencies. Where do they get installed? It turns out that they get installed in your current directory, inside a subdirectory called *node_modules*. We can easily confirm this:

```
vagrant $ pwd
/home/vagrant/app/Express
vagrant $ ls
server.js node_modules
vagrant $ ls node_modules
express
```

Our First Express Server

Now that the Express module is installed, we can create a simple Express server. Let's create a file inside our *Express* directory called *server.js* and add the following content:

```
var express = require("express"),
    http = require("http"),
    app;

// Create our Express-powered HTTP server
// and have it listen on port 3000
app = express();
http.createServer(app).listen(3000);

// set up our routes
app.get("/hello", function (req, res) {
    res.send("Hello World!");
});
```

```
app.get("/goodbye", function (req, res) {
    res.send("Goodbye World!");
});
```

This may remind you of our previous example, but there are a few noticeable differences. First of all, we don't need to set up HTTP headers in the callbacks because Express does that for us. Also, we're simply using res.send instead of res.write or res.end. And last, but probably most important, we've set up two routes: hello and goodbye. We'll see what this does once we open our browser, but first let's start up the server.

Recall that we can do that by typing **node server.js** from the *Express* directory on our guest machine. Now when we go to our web browser, we can type *localhost:3000* like we did before. This time, however, we should see an error that says "Cannot GET /". But, if instead, we type in *localhost:3000/hello* or *localhost:3000/goodbye*, we should see the message that we specified in the callbacks. Try it now.

As you can see, the addition of hello and goodbye after the main URL of our app specifies which function gets fired. And you'll also see that Express doesn't set up a default route for us. If we want to make *localhost:3000/* work as it did before, we simply set up a root route by adding another three lines to *server.js*:

```
app.get("/", function (req, res) {
    res.send("This is the root route!");
});
```

If we stop our server (by pressing Ctrl-C) and start it again, we will be able to access *localhost:3000* as we did before! Express is handling the complexities of routing—we simply tell it what we want it to do when certain routes are requested.

Sending Your Client App

We've seen that we can send information to the web browser from the server. But what if we want to send something like a basic HTML page? Then things can get complicated relatively quickly. For example, we might try to do something like this:

```
app.get("/index.html", function (req, res) {
    res.send("<html><head></head><body><h1>Hello World!</h1></body></html>");
});
```

Although this will work, creating HTML that is bigger than this small example will become extremely cumbersome. Fortunately, Express solves this problem for us by allowing us to use it as a *static file server*. In doing so we can create HTML, CSS, and client-side JavaScript files as we've been doing throughout the rest of the book! And it turns out that it only takes one more line of code. We can modify the *server.js* file that looks like this:

```
var express = require("express"),
    http = require("http"),
    app = express();

// set up a static file directory to use for default routing
// also see the note below about Windows
app.use(express.static(__dirname + "/client"));

// Create our Express-powered HTTP server
http.createServer(app).listen(3000);

// set up our routes
app.get("/hello", function (req, res) {
    res.send("Hello World!");
});

app.get("/goodbye", function (req, res) {
    res.send("Goodbye World!");
});
```

If you try to run this example in Windows instead of your virtual machine, you'll most likely run into trouble because of the file-names. For simplicity of exposition, I've left out using the core `path` module that will make directory paths cross-platform compatible. On the other hand, I have used it in the code in our GitHub repository, so if you're having problems take a look at the examples there.

In the preceding example, we've used `app.use` to create a static file server directory. This means that any request sent to our server will initially be resolved by the static file directory (*client*) before it is handed off to our routes. This means that if we have a file called *index.html* in our *client* directory and we go to *localhost:3000/index.html*, it will return the contents of the file. If the file doesn't exist, it will then check to see if there's a match among our routes.

Here's where some confusion can arise—if you have a route with the same name as a file in your *client* directory, how does Express respond? It resolves to the client directory first, so if there's a match it doesn't even look at your routes. Be careful not to have routes and files that have the same name—that is almost certainly not what you intend to do.

Let's give this a try by copying one of our client-side apps into the *client* directory. Pick any of the apps that we've previously created (or, better yet, practice creating one from scratch) and copy it into the *client* directory of the *Express* directory.

We can now run our server from our guest machine using `node server.js`. Because the main HTML page is stored in the file *index.html*, when we open the page *localhost: 3000/index.html* in our browser, we should see it—including the CSS and the JavaScript!

Generalizations

In general, we'll build all of our web apps following this pattern. We'll have the browser code stored inside the *client* directory, and we'll have an Express server defined in a file called *server.js*. We'll also import and/or create modules to support the server-side part of our program.

The only thing we haven't seen yet is how to set up communication between the client and the server. As alluded to in the previous chapter, we'll use AJAX for communication and we'll use the JSON format to represent our messages. The next example will demonstrate this in addition to leveraging modules that do more interesting things—like connecting to the Twitter API.

Counting Tweets

In this example, we'll connect to the Twitter API and stream some data into our server. Let's start by firing up our virtual machine if it's not already running. So if you haven't already, type **vagrant up** from the *app* directory inside your *Chapter6* directory. Next, let's SSH into our guest machine. If we're in Windows, this may require us to use PuTTY, and if we're in Mac OS or Linux, we'll just type **vagrant ssh**.

Inside our *app* directory, we'll create a new directory called *Twitter*. Remember that even though we create this directory on our guest machine, the directory is mirrored on our host machine, so we can also open that directory (the *app* directory inside the *Projects* directory) in Sublime.

Getting Your Twitter Credentials

To access the Twitter streaming API, you'll need to first set up an application (*http:// dev.twitter.com*) and log in with your Twitter credentials. Of course, if you don't already have an account on Twitter, you'll need to create one—but don't worry! I'm not going to make you tweet anything!

After you log in to the Twitter developer page, you'll need to click the "Create a new application" button in the upper-right corner. Once you do that, you'll be presented with a form that looks something like Figure 6-8. Fill out all of the fields and submit your request.

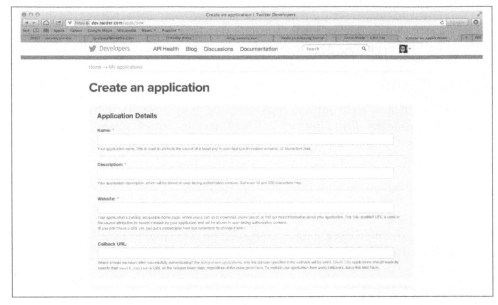

Figure 6-8. The form you use to create your first Twitter application!

There's a starred field in the form that requires you to add a website for your application. You probably don't have one just yet, so feel free to put a placeholder (I like to use *www.example.com*). You won't need to worry about a Callback URL for this example.

If your request is successful, you'll be presented with a page that includes all of your app's information including the *API key* and *API secret*. To access the streaming API, you'll also need to create an *Access token* for your app. You can get one by clicking the button at the bottom that says "Create my access token." When the page reloads, you should have all the credentials necessary to get the next example working.

Now we'll set up a simple file called *credentials.json* that we'll access from our program. This file will contain a single JSON object that includes your Twitter credentials. You'll replace the following strings with your actual credentials from the application home page on Twitter (don't forget to leave the quotes around them, because they are stored as strings):

```
{
    "consumer_key": "your app's API key here",
    "consumer_secret": "your app's API secret here",
    "access_token_key": "your app's Access token here",
    "access_token_secret": "your app's Access token secret here"
}
```

Whenever you build apps that require credentials, it's a good idea to leave them out of your Git repository just in case you want to share your code with someone else. That's why it's advantageous to store your credentials in a separate file. Git allows you to have a special *.gitignore* file that specifies local files that should be left out of your repository.

Connecting to the Twitter API

We'll start by installing the `ntwitter` module via NPM:

```
vagrant $ mkdir Twitter
vagrant $ cd Twitter
vagrant $ npm install ntwitter
```

Now we'll create another file called *tweet_counter.js* that will include the code that actually accesses the Twitter API. Note that we `require` the `ntwitter` module in the same way we `required` the `http` module in the server example. When we `require` the *credentials.json* file, we need to tell Node where to find it because, unlike `express` and `ntwitter`, we didn't install it with NPM. That's why we prepend it with `./`—that tells Node to look in the current directory:

```
var ntwitter = require("ntwitter"),
    credentials = require("./credentials.json"),
    twitter;

// set up our twitter object
twitter = ntwitter(credentials);

// set up our twitter stream with three parameters,
// separated by commas
twitter.stream(
    // the first parameter is a string
    "statuses/filter",

    // second parameter, an object containing an array
    { "track": ["awesome", "cool", "rad", "gnarly", "groovy"] },

    // the third parameter is our callback for when the stream is created
    function(stream) {
        stream.on("data", function(tweet) {
            console.log(tweet.text);
        });
    }
);
```

If we've set up everything properly, we can now type **node tweet_counter** from our virtual machine and we should see our terminal window fill up with tweets that have those words in them! If you're scared that your computer is going crazy, calm down and hit Ctrl-C to stop the stream.

What's Happening Here?

Let's take a look at the code again. We'll see several familiar things. First, we're declaring three variables and importing the `ntwitter` module along with our *credentials.json* file. Next we're creating a variable called `twitter` and storing the result of calling the `ntwitter` function with our credentials as an argument. This initializes the `twitter` object so we can start streaming.

After that, we define the stream by calling the `twitter` object's `stream` function. This function takes three arguments. The first is a string representing the type of stream— we'll filter the tweets by a list of words. The second is an object that contains information about our filter rules (in this case we're only watching for the occurrence of certain words—we can also filter by location, among other things). And last but not least, we send in a callback that is called when the stream is created.

The `stream` argument is itself an object on which we can listen for events (like a DOM element in jQuery). The event we're listening for is "data" and that event is fired whenever a new tweet comes through the stream. What do we do when we get a new tweet? We simply print it to the console! That's all it takes to stream Twitter to our terminal window!

Storing Counts

Instead of just printing the tweets to the console, let's keep a count of the number of times we've seen certain words. This means we'll need a separate variable for each word. Because we're keeping multiple variables all representing something similar, it probably makes sense to use an object representing the counts. The attribute associated with each count is the word, and the value of the attribute is the number of times that word has appeared.

We can modify the beginning of our code to declare and create such an object:

```
var ntwitter = require("ntwitter"),
    credentials = require("./credentials.json"),
    twitter,
    counts = {};

counts.awesome = 0;
counts.cool = 0;
counts.rad = 0;
counts.gnarly = 0;
counts.groovy = 0;
```

This initializes all the values to 0, meaning we haven't seen any of the words yet.

Using the indexOf function to find words

When we get data through our Twitter stream, we'll need to see if the `text` property of the `tweet` object has the word we're looking for. In the previous chapter, we saw that arrays have a method called `indexOf` that checks an array to see if it contains an object. It turns out strings have exactly the same functionality! A string object's `indexOf` function will return the index of the first appearance of a substring within a string, or –1 if the substring does not appear. For example, try typing the following into the Chrome JavaScript console:

```
var tweetText = "This is a tweet! It has lots of words but less than 140 characters."

// We use indexOf to see if it contains certain words
tweetText.indexOf("tweet");
//=> 10

tweetText.indexOf("This");
//=> 0

tweetText.indexOf("words");
//=> 32

tweetText.indexOf("char");
//=> 56

tweetText.indexOf("hello");
//=> -1

// note that indexOf is case-sensitive!
tweetText.indexOf("Tweet");
//=> -1
```

So you'll see that `indexOf` will search the tweet for a given word, and if the word appears as a substring the result will be bigger than –1. This allows us to remove the `console.log` statement and modify our code to do something like this:

```
function(stream) {
    stream.on("data", function(tweet) {
        if (tweet.text.indexOf("awesome") > -1) {
            // increment the awesome counter
            counts.awesome = counts.awesome + 1;
        }
    });
}
```

Using the setInterval function to schedule tasks

Without the `console.log` statement, how do we know if our code is working? One approach is to print out the counts every few seconds. That's a bit more manageable than printing out every tweet that we see. To do this, we can add a call to the `setInterval` function at the bottom of our streaming code:

```
// print the awesome count every 3 seconds
setInterval(function () {
    console.log("awesome: " + counts.awesome);
}, 3000);
```

Like the `setTimeout` function that we've used before, the `setInterval` function schedules a function to be called in the future. The difference is that it repeats the function call every time the number of milliseconds specified passes. So, in this case, the program logs the `awesome` count every three seconds.

If we're just interested in counting the number of times the word `awesome` appears, our entire *twitter.js* file would look something like this:

```
var ntwitter = require("ntwitter"),
    credentials = require("./credentials.json"),
    twitter,
    counts = {};

// set up our twitter object
twitter = ntwitter(credentials);

// initialize our counters
counts.awesome = 0;

twitter.stream(
    "statuses/filter",
    { "track": ["awesome", "cool", "rad", "gnarly", "groovy"] },
    function(stream) {
        stream.on("data", function(tweet) {
            if (tweet.text.indexOf("awesome") > -1) {
                // increment the awesome counter
                counts.awesome = counts.awesome + 1;
            }
        });
    }
);

// print the awesome count every 3 seconds
setInterval(function () {
    console.log("awesome: " + counts.awesome);
}, 3000);
```

Run this in your virtual machine by typing **node tweet_counter.js** to see it in action.

Modularizing Our Tweet Counter

Even though it's great that we can see tweets appearing in the terminal window, it would be better if we could somehow connect our tweet counter with an HTTP server so we can display the counts in our web browser. There are two possible ways to do this. The first possibility involves creating a server inside our tweet counter code that generates the page. This is a perfectly reasonable solution for a beginner.

The second solution is to convert the tweet counter code into a module, and then import the module into a program that has an HTTP server (like our original server example). In this case, the second solution is better because it allows us to make the tweet counter code reusable in other projects. In fact, I would say this solution follows what is emerging as one of the core tenets of the Node.js philosophy: create small modules that do one thing and do it well.

How can we convert our tweet counter code into a module? It turns out it's pretty easy. Every module has a special variable called `module.exports` that stores everything that we want to expose to the outside world. So in this case, we'd want to expose the `counts` object, which will be updated by the `tweet_counter` module as long as our program is running. At the bottom of the code in our *tweet_counter.js* we can simply add the following line to export the object:

```
module.exports = counts;
```

Here, we've exported an object that contains several integers, but you can export any type of JavaScript object, including functions. In the practice section at the end of this chapter, I'll give you a chance to make this module more usable by generalizing it so that it exports a function instead of an object.

Importing Our Module Into Express

Recall that our simple Express server looked something like this:

```
var express = require("express"),
    http = require("http"),
    app = express();

// configure the app to use the client directory for static files
app.use(express.static(__dirname + "/client"));

// create the server and have it listen
http.createServer(app).listen(3000);

// set up routes
app.get("/", function (req, res) {
    res.send("Hello World!");
});
```

We can copy this file (*server.js*) into our *Twitter* directory (the same one that contains *tweet_counter.js*) and then modify it so that it imports our tweet counter module and uses the counts that we've exported. We'll also return the counts to the browser as JSON:

```
var express = require("express"),
    http = require("http"),
    tweetCounts = require("./tweet_counter.js"),
    app = express();

// configure the app to use the client directory for static files
app.use(express.static(__dirname + "/client"));

// create the server and have it listen
http.createServer(app).listen(3000);

// set up routes
app.get("/counts.json", function (req, res) {
    // res.json returns the entire object as a JSON file
    res.json(tweetCounts);
});
```

If we log in to our guest machine, we can enter the *app/Twitter* directory and run the server with `node server.js`. When we do that, we'll see the terminal print out the counts every three seconds, but now we can open up our browser and connect to *localhost:3000/counts.json* and we should see the JSON object returned to us!

 Keep in mind that the *counts.json* route isn't an actual file. You can think of it as a virtual file created by your application server while it's running. When you set up the route using the `app.get` function, you're telling the server that when a client requests that particular file, build it using the internally stored `tweetCounts` object.

How can we leverage the JSON object in our client code? With AJAX, of course!

Setting Up a Client

Inside our *Twitter* directory, let's create a skeleton client that includes our usual *index.html*, *styles/style.css*, and *javascripts/app.js* files that we've become accustomed to programming on the client side. As before, we'll put them in the *client* directory of our *Twitter* directory. You can still run the server from your guest machine's *app/Twitter* directory:

```
vagrant $ node server.js
```

If you set up your *javascripts/app.js* file to print out `hello world` and go to *localhost: 3000/index.html* in your browser, you should see the `hello world` message printed to the JavaScript console as we have before.

If that works, let's modify our client-side *app.js* file to get the `counts.json` object with a call to jQuery's `getJSON` function:

```
var main = function () {
    "use strict";

    $.getJSON("/counts.json", function (wordCounts) {
        // Now "wordCounts" will be the object that
        // is returned by the counts.json route we
        // set up in Express
        console.log(wordCounts);
    });
}

$(document).ready(main);
```

Now our call to getJSON is connecting to the counts.json route we set up in Express, which is returning the counts. If everything is wired up correctly, this should print out the counts object to the console. We can explore the object in the console by drilling down with the drop-down arrows. And if we reload the page, we'll be able to see the updated values!

We can now modify our code to insert the counts into the DOM using jQuery's DOM manipulation capabilities. Here's a simple way to set this up:

```
var main = function () {
    "use strict";

    var insertCountsIntoDOM = function (counts) {
        // your DOM manipulation code here
    };

    // notice that insertCountsIntoDOM gets called with
    // the counts parameter when getJSON returns
    $.getJSON("counts.json", insertCountsIntoDOM);
}

$(document).ready(main);
```

Why set it up this way? Because, this actually allows us to do something we did with the server-side code—we can use the setInterval function to dynamically update the page!

```
var main = function () {
    "use strict";

    var insertCountsIntoDOM = function (counts) {
        // your DOM manipulation code here
    };


    // check the counts value every 5 seconds,
    // and insert the updated version into the DOM
    setInterval(function () {
        $.getJSON("counts.json", insertCountsIntoDOM);
    }, 5000);
```

```
    }

    $(document).ready(main);
```

I challenge you to play around with this code and really try to customize it and understand how it's working. This is our first example of a full web application that has both a client and server component, where both are communicating via AJAX.

Creating a Server for Amazeriffic

If you worked through the last example in the previous chapter, you managed to get Amazeriffic handling a to-do list served by a JSON file instead of having it hardcoded into your program. We can take that code and, with a few minor modifications, keep the to-do list stored on the server. For this example, I'll also get you started with Git so you can track your changes as you're working through it.

Setting Up Our Directories

We'll start by creating a directory inside our *Chapter6/app* directory that we'll call *Amazeriffic*. Remember that it doesn't matter if we do this on the host or the guest machine. Inside that directory, we'll create a directory to store our client code. We'll call it *client* and let's copy the contents of our last Amazeriffic example from Chapter 5.

One important difference between this example and the example from Chapter 5 is that we'll be storing our to-do list on the server. This means we will no longer need the *todo.json* file that stores the initial state of the to-do list. But because we'll want to eventually copy the contents of that file into our server, it would be helpful to keep the file around with a different name. To rename a file from the command line we simply use the mv command, which stands for "move":

```
hostname $ mv client/todos.json client/todos.OLD.json
```

Initializing a Git Repository

Next, we'll initialize our Git repository to include the copied files. Remember, we interact with Git from our host machine. From here, I'll let you decide the appropriate times to make commits:

```
hostname $ git init
Initialized empty Git repository ...
```

After that we can check the status of our repository and commit the client-side files as we've done in previous chapters. Now we can switch to our guest machine to install the Express module. Navigate to the Amazeriffic directory and type the following npm command:

```
vagrant $ pwd
/home/vagrant/app/Amazeriffic
vagrant $ npm install express@3
```

Building the Server

As it stands now, our app works perfectly fine under the assumption that the user never switches to another browser or another computer, and never reloads the page. Unfortunately, if the user does either of those things, she'll lose all the to-do items that she's created and will be back at square one.

We'll solve this problem by storing our to-do list on the server, and initializing our client with the data stored on the server. To get started, we'll create a to-do list in a variable on the server, and set up a JSON route that will return it:

```
var express = require("express"),
    http = require("http"),
    app = express(),
    toDos = {
        // set up todo list here by copying
        // the content from todos.OLD.json
    };

app.use(express.static(__dirname + "/client"));

http.createServer(app).listen(3000);

// This route takes the place of our
// todos.json file in our example from
// Chapter 5
app.get("/todos.json", function (req, res) {
    res.json(toDos);
});
```

Running the Server

Make sure you're in your guest machine terminal and run *server.js* with Node:

```
vagrant $ node server.js
```

Once the app is running, we should be able to visit our app by opening Chrome and entering *localhost:3000/index.html* in the address bar! In fact, we should be able to simply type *localhost:3000* into the address bar and the server will automatically route itself to *index.html*, which is typically considered the default page.

At this point, everything should work exactly as it did before, but we haven't really solved either of our problems yet. That's because our to-do list is being delivered by the server, but our client isn't sending any updates yet. And we haven't yet learned how to send information to the server when things get updated on the client.

Posting Information to the Server

Up until now, we've only had our client programs getting data from the server. This means our apps are only supporting one-way communication between the client and the server. To do this, we've relied on the getJSON function in jQuery. It turns out that jQuery has a function that allows us to just as easily send JSON to the server, but our server has to be prepared to accept it and do something with it.

The process of sending data from the client to the server over the HTTP protocol is called a *post*. We can start by setting up a post route in our Express server. The following example will set up a post route that simply prints a string out to the server terminal:

```
app.post("/todos", function (req, res) {
    console.log("data has been posted to the server!");

    // send back a simple object
    res.json({"message":"You posted to the server!"});
});
```

It looks just like our get routes, except we've replaced the get function call with a post function call. In practice, the difference is that we can't simply visit the route using our browser as we've done with the get routes. Instead, we need to modify our client-side JavaScript to post to the route to see the message. We'll do that when the user clicks the Add button. Modify your client code so it looks like this:

```
// this is inside a main function
// where toDoObjects has been
// previously defined

$button.on("click", function () {
    var description = $input.val(),
        tags = $tagInput.val().split(",");

    toDoObjects.push({"description":description, "tags":tags});

    //here' we'll do a quick post to our todos route
    $.post("todos", {}, function (response) {
        // this callback is called with the server responds
        console.log("We posted and the server responded!");
        console.log(response);
    });

    // update toDos
    toDos = toDoObjects.map(function (toDo) {
        return toDo.description;
    });

    $input.val("");
    $tagInput.val("");
});
```

The first argument to the $.post function is the route that we want to post to, the second is the data (represented as an object) that we want to send, and the third is the callback for the server response. At this point, our code should work exactly as it did before, only when we click the Add button, we'll see the server print out a message on its console and the client will print out the server's response.

So we're part of the way there, but we haven't actually sent a to-do item to the server yet. As I mentioned, the second argument to the post function is the object that gets sent to the server. It turns out that it's pretty easy to change the empty object to our new to-do object, but we have to do a little more work on the server to make it usable.

The easiest way to do this is to use Express's *urlencoded* plug-in, which will turn JSON sent by jQuery into a JavaScript object that the server can use:

```
var express = require("express"),
    http = require("http"),
    app = express()
    toDos = {
        // ...
    };;

app.use(express.static(__dirname + "/client"));

// tell Express to parse incoming
// JSON objects
app.use(express.urlencoded());

app.post("/todos", function (req, res) {
    // the object is now stored in req.body
    var newToDo = req.body;

    console.log(newToDo);

    toDos.push(newToDo);

    // send back a simple object
    res.json({"message":"You posted to the server!"});
});
```

This iteration of the server will print the object to the server's console when it is sent. After that, it will actually add the new to-do item to its list. Now a minor modification to our client app will actually send over the new to-do item:

```
$button.on("click", function () {
    var description = $input.val(),
        tags = $tagInput.val().split(","),
        // create the new to-do item
        newToDo = {"description":description, "tags":tags};

    $.post("todos", newToDo, function (result) {
        console.log(result);
```

```
            // we'll wait to push the new object
            // on the client until after the server
            // returns
            toDoObjects.push(newToDo);

            // update toDos
            toDos = toDoObjects.map(function (toDo) {
                return toDo.description;
            });

            $input.val("");
            $tagInput.val("");
        });
    });
```

This will send the new to-do item to the server and then print the server's response message to the JavaScript console. After it does that, it will add the new toDo object to the client's to-do list.

At this point, we can actually open up our app in two different browser windows, add to-do items in one of the browser windows, and reload it in the other to see the updated content!

Summary

In this chapter, we learned the basics of server-side programming using Node.js. Node.js is a platform that allows us to write servers in the JavaScript language. We commonly use it to write HTTP servers that communicate with our client applications that run in the browser.

Node.js programs are typically made up of many individual modules. We can create our own modules by writing some code and then attaching the parts we want to expose to the module.exports object. Afterward, we can import it into another program using the require function.

NPM is the *Node.js Package Manager*, which allows us to install Node.js modules that we didn't write ourselves and aren't included with the Node.js distribution. For example, we installed the Express module using NPM. Express is a wrapper around the Node.js http module that meets a lot of our common expectations of an HTTP server. Specifically, it allows us to easily serve our client-side HTML, CSS, and JavaScript files. It also lets us set up custom routes to server behaviors.

We used VirtualBox and Vagrant to set up a basic environment. These tools aren't essential to understanding how web applications work, but they help bootstrap the development process. Additionally, they create a clear separation between the client (the browser running on our host machine) and the server (the Node.js program running on our guest machine).

Last but not least, we learned how to set up an HTTP post request using jQuery, and how to have our server respond to HTTP post requests through `Express`.

More Practice and Further Reading

Installing Node.js Locally

In this chapter, we installed Node on a virtual machine via Vagrant. One primary reason for doing this is that the Vagrant scripts also set up software that we'll use in Chapter 7 and Chapter 8. It turns out, however, that installing Node.js on your local computer is very, very easy, and all of the examples in this chapter should work on your local machine with minimal changes. If you go to *http://nodejs.org/download*, you should be able to find installation packages for your platform.

It's a good idea to give this a try. If you can get it set up on your host machine, you can globally install a few other tools that might be useful, including JSHint, CSS Lint, and an HTML5 validator.

JSHint and CSS Lint via NPM

In Chapter 4, we learned about JSLint, a code quality-control tool that tells us when our code is violating certain JavaScript best practices. We used the online tool available at *http://jslint.com*, which required us to cut and paste our code into the browser. If this hasn't already become a problem for you, it definitely will as your code base grows.

It turns out that when we have Node.js installed on our local machine, we can use NPM to install other command-line tools that might come in handy, such as JSHint (*http://www.jshint.com/*). JSHint is very similar to JSLint, and can be used to check your code. You'll want to drop to the command line and install it with NPM. We use the `-g` option to tell NPM that we want to install this package globally. This makes `jshint` available as a standard command-line application, instead of installing it as a library in the local *node_modules* directory:

```
hostname $ sudo npm install jshint -g
```

In Mac OS and Linux, we have to use `sudo` to install packages globally. This is not necessary in Windows.

Once we do that, we can run JSHint directly on our files. Consider the following file called *test.js*:

```
var main = function () {
    console.log("hello world");
}

$(document).ready(main);
```

This code will, of course, run perfectly in the browser, but it's missing a semicolon after the definition of the `main` function. JSHint will tell us that:

```
hostname $ jshint test.js
test.js: line 3, col 2, Missing semicolon.

1 error
```

If our code is in good shape, JSHint will not output anything. If we add the missing semicolon and run JSHint, we won't see any response:

```
hostname $ jshint test.js
hostname $
```

Having JSHint installed on our machine makes it much easier to check our code quality for both server- and client-side code, so there's no excuse not to do it! You'll also find that JSHint is much more flexible, allowing you to easily set options from the command line. See the documentation at *http://jshint.com/docs*.

Similarly, NPM allows us to install and run CSS Lint from the command line, which makes it much easier to check our CSS for errors and bad practices:

```
hostname $ sudo npm install csslint -g
```

There are several options for HTML validators and linters as well. If you find yourself doing a lot more HTML, you may want to find one that suits your needs.

Generalizing Our Tweet Counter Code

Our tweet counter tracks an array of words on Twitter. In our code, however, we had to list out the words in several different places. For example, at the top of our *tweet_counter.js* file, we see the following:

```
counts.awesome = 0;
counts.cool = 0;
counts.rad = 0;
counts.gnarly = 0;
counts.groovy = 0;
```

And then, later, we see that we've told the `ntwitter` module to track those words:

```
{ "track": ["awesome", "cool", "rad", "gnarly", "groovy"] },
```

If you've already generalized the code, it's possible that you did something similar to increment your counters:

```
if (tweet.text.indexOf("awesome") > -1) {
    // increment the awesome counter
    counts.awesome = counts.awesome + 1;
}

if (tweet.text.indexOf("cool") > -1) {
    // increment the cool counter
    counts.cool = counts.cool + 1;
}
```

Why is this a problem? If we want to add or remove words from our code, we have to modify the code in three places! How can we improve this? First, we can define the array in exactly one place: at the top of our tweet_counter module:

```
var trackedWords = ["awesome", "cool", "rad", "gnarly", "groovy"];
```

This allows us to use the variable when we create the Twitter counter:

```
{ "track": trackedWords };
```

To improve the rest of the code, we'll use an awesome feature of JavaScript objects: the ability to use an object as a *map* data structure where the attributes are strings. It turns out that the following two approaches to indexing into an object are equivalent:

```
// this accesses the awesome counter
// using the dot operator
counts.awesome = 0;
counts.awesome = counts.awesome + 1;


// this accesses the awesome counter
// using a string
counts["awesome"] = 0;
counts["awesome"] = counts["awesome"] + 1;
```

Generally, it's a good idea to stick with the dot operator, because JavaScript programmers tend to find that more readable (and JSLint will complain when you don't). But the string-with-square-brackets approach has the advantage that we can use variables to access the values:

```
var word = "awesome";

counts[word] = 0;
counts[word] = counts[word] + 1;
```

Do you see where I'm going with this? Here's an approach to initializing our counter object that only depends on the array:

```
// create an empty object
var counts = {};
```

```
trackedWords.forEach(function (word) {
    counts[word] = 0;
});
```

This cycles through each word and initializes the count to 0. Similarly, we can update our code that checks to see if the tweet contains that word with a `forEach` loop! Once we do that, we can simply add or remove a word from our initial array and our entire app will be updated!

This makes our module a little more maintainable overall, but we can improve it even more. Imagine if instead of exporting the counts for specific tracked words, we allow the consumer of our module to decide which words should be tracked. For example, a consumer of our module might prefer to use it like this:

```
var tweetCounter = require("./tweet_counter.js"),
    counts;

// this starts our tweetCounter with the specified
// words instead of the built-in word list
counts = tweetCounter(["hello", "world"]);
```

We can achieve this by exporting a function instead of the `counts` object:

```
var setUpTweetCounter = function (words) {
    // set up the counts object
    // and the ntwitter stream
    // using the words array

    // ...

    // at the end, return the counts
    return counts;
}

module.exports = setUpTweetCounter;
```

This makes our module way more flexible from the consumer's perspective. A program that uses our module can decide which words should be tracked without ever looking at our code. Setting this up is a great exercise, so give it a try!

Poker API

Here's a straightforward project that will give you practice creating an API using Express. Create an Express app that responds to a single post route: */hand*. The route should accept an object that represents a poker hand, and then respond with a JSON object that specifies the best hand that it has. For example, if the following object gets posted:

```
[
    { "rank":"two", "suit":"spades" },
    { "rank":"four", "suit":"hearts" },
```

```
      { "rank":"two", "suit":"clubs" },
      { "rank":"king", "suit":"spades" },
      { "rank":"eight", "suit":"diamonds" }
    ]
```

Our API might respond like this, where we use the `null` reference (introduced in Chapter 5) to represent "no object":

```
{
    "handString":"Pair",
    "error": null
}
```

In other words, in this example we've sent a valid hand (five cards) and the highest rank of the hand is a pair. We set the `error` property to `null` to signify that there is no error. Alternatively, if someone posts an invalid hand (for example, if it has invalid ranks or too many cards), we'll set the `handString` to `null` and send back an error string:

```
{
    "handString": null,
    "error": "Invalid Card Hand!"
}
```

To facilitate this, we'll want to package the functions we wrote in Chapter 5 as a Node.js module. To use it in our app, we'll want to import it into our Express server like this:

```
var poker = require("./poker.js");
```

And then utilize functions like this:

```
var hand = [
    { "rank":"two", "suit":"spades" },
    { "rank":"four", "suit":"hearts" },
    { "rank":"two", "suit":"clubs" },
    { "rank":"king", "suit":"spades" },
    { "rank":"eight", "suit":"diamonds" }
]

var hasPair = poker.containsPair(hand);
//hasPair will be true now
```

How can we do this? We'll create a `poker` object in our module definition with several functions:

```
var poker = {};

poker.containsPair = function (hand) {
    // ... define the function
}

poker.containsThreeOfAKind = function (hand) {
    // ... define the function
}
```

```
module.exports = poker;
```

Our poker module will have several internal functions that we won't include in our exported object. For example, we'll include the `containsNTimes` function inside our module, but we won't export it:

```
var poker = {},
    containsNTimes;  // declare the function

// here we define our 'private' functions
// we don't add them to the poker object
containsNTimes = function (array, item, n) {
    // ... define the function
};

poker.containsPair = function (hand) {
    // ... use containsNTimes here
}

poker.containsThreeOfAKind = function (hand) {
    // ... use containsNTimes here
}

// only export the poker-related functions
module.exports = poker;
```

We'll want to include a few more functions that validate that the hand is actually a poker hand, and we may even want to include a function that returns an object as specified by the API. Then our route callback will essentially be a single line:

```
app.post("/hand", function (req, res) {
    var result = poker.getHand(req.body.hand);
    res.json(result);
});
```

To get this to work, you'll need to write a client app that creates some hands and posts them to your server with jQuery. If you can make all of this happen, you're really starting to get it!

## CHAPTER 7

The Data Store

In the previous few chapters, we learned how to create basic servers using Node.js and how to communicate between our client and server using AJAX. One of the more interesting applications involved keeping track of the number of mentions of certain words on Twitter and displaying counts on the client.

One of the major problems with this application is that it stores all of its information in the Node.js program's memory. That means that if we shut down our server process the word counts disappear with it. This is not the behavior that we want because we'll often need to shut down our server to update it or, more commonly, our server may shut itself down due to a bug. When either of these things happen, we would like all of the counts that we've taken so far to remain intact.

To solve this problem, we'll need to use some sort of data storage application that runs independently of our program. In this chapter, we'll learn two different approaches to solving this problem using NoSQL data stores. Specifically, we'll study Redis and MongoDB, and we'll learn how to integrate them into our Node.js applications.

NoSQL Versus SQL

If you've studied databases, you've probably seen the acronym SQL (sometimes pronounced *sequel*), which stands for *Structured Query Language*. It's a language that is used to ask questions of a database stored in a *relational* format. Relational databases store data as cells in tables, where the rows of the tables can easily be cross-referenced with other tables. For instance, a relational database might store a table of actors and actresses and a separate table of movies. A relational table can be used to map actors and actresses to the movies in which they star.

This approach has several advantages, but the primary reason that they are so widely used is because storing information in this way minimizes redundancy and, therefore, typically requires less space than alternative approaches. In the past this was an important feature, because storing large amounts of data was relatively expensive. In recent years, however, the price of storage has dropped dramatically and minimizing redundancy isn't as important as it had been.

This shift has led researchers and engineers to rethink their assumptions about storing data and begin experimenting with storage in nonrelational formats. These new data storage solutions, sometimes referred to as *NoSQL* data stores, make a trade-off: sometimes they store redundant information in exchange for increased ease-of-use from a programming perspective. Furthermore, some of these data stores are designed with specific use cases in mind, such as applications where reading data needs to be more efficient than writing data.

Redis

Redis is a perfect example of a NoSQL data store. It is designed for fast access to data that is used regularly. It offers this speedup at the expense of reliability by storing data in memory instead of on disk. (Technically, Redis does flush data to disk periodically, but for the most part you can think of it as an in-memory data store.)

Redis stores information in a *key-value* format—you can think of this as being similar to the way JavaScript stores object properties. Because of this, it allows a developer to organize information into traditional data structures (hashes, lists, sets, etc.), which makes it feel like a natural extension to storing data in our programs. It is perfect for data that needs to be accessed quickly or for temporarily storing frequently accessed data (referred to as *caching*) to improve the response time of our applications.

We won't explore these use cases in this book, but it's a good idea to keep them in mind as you continue on your journey. Our use of Redis will be relatively straightforward— we simply want to store our Twitter count data independently of our Node.js server. To do this, we'll use a key for each of the words, and each value will be an integer representing the number of times the word appears. Before we learn to do that programmatically, we'll learn to interact with Redis on the command line.

Interacting with the Redis Command-Line Client

To keep a clean separation from our previous work, let's start by re-cloning the node-dev-bootstrap project into our *Projects* directory as *Chapter7*. If you need a refresher on how to do this, you can look back at Chapter 6.

Once that's done, enter the directory, fire up your virtual machine, and SSH into your guest. Because you're rebuilding the machine from scratch, it will take some time:

```
hostname $ cd Projects/Chapter7
hostname $ vagrant up
...vagrant build stuff...
hostname $ vagrant ssh
```

Now we should be logged in to our virtual machine where Redis is already installed and configured. We can use the redis-cli command to start up the interactive Redis client:

```
vagrant $ redis-cli
redis 127.0.0.1:6379>
```

Storing data in Redis is as easy as using the set command. Here, we create a key for awesome and set its value to 0:

```
redis 127.0.0.1:6379> set awesome 0
OK
```

If all goes well, Redis should respond with "OK." We can check the value of the key by using the get command:

```
redis 127.0.0.1:6379> get awesome
"0"
```

Once we have the value stored, we can manipulate it in numerous ways. Of course, we're probably most interested in incrementing it by 1 when we see the word used in a tweet. Fortunately, it turns out that Redis has an incr command that does just that:

```
redis 127.0.0.1:6379> incr awesome
(integer) 1
redis 127.0.0.1:6379> incr awesome
(integer) 2
redis 127.0.0.1:6379> get awesome
"2"
```

The incr command is adding 1 to the value that is currently associated with the specified key (in this case, the key is awesome). To exit out of the interactive Redis client, we can type **exit**.

These three commands (set, get, and incr) are all we need to know to start storing our counts, but Redis offers a lot more than what I've shown you here. To get a taste of some of its other features, try out the outstanding interactive Redis tutorial (*http://try.redis.io*), as shown in Figure 7-1.

Installing the Redis Module via a package.json File

At this point, we know how to create a key for each word and then increment the value interactively, but we'd like to be able to do it programmatically from our Node.js programs.

We'll be working from our Twitter project from the last chapter, so copy our *Twitter* directory from our *Chapter6/app* directory into our *Chapter7/app* directory. You can use the cp command to do that from the command line, or you can do it through your normal GUI interface.

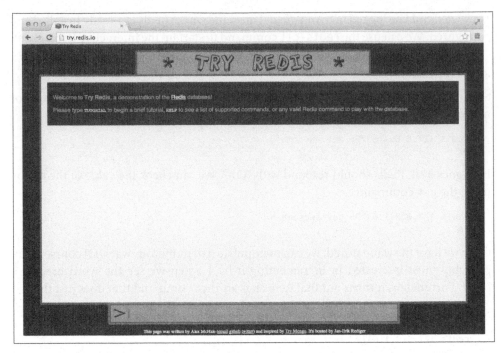

Figure 7-1. The home page of the interactive Redis tutorial

To get our Node.js program communicating with Redis, we'll need to install the node-redis module. Previously, we used the npm command from the command line to install the ntwitter module. This makes sense when we're just starting out, but as we move forward it's going to be important to track our dependencies in a more formal way. To do this, we use a special file called *package.json*, which keeps track of several different aspects of our project, including its dependencies.

In your *app* directory, create a file called *package.json*, and copy the following content:

```
{
    "name": "tutorial",
    "description": "a tutorial on using node, twitter, redis, and express",
    "version": "0.0.1",
    "dependencies": {
        "ntwitter": "0.5.x",
        "redis": "0.8.x"
    }
}
```

NPM offers an interactive approach to build a *package.json* file, but it will ask you for a lot more information than this. If you want to give it a try, type `npm init` in your project's directory.

As you can see, this specifies a few things about our project, including its dependencies (since `node-redis` is the recommended client for Node.js, it's simply referred to as `redis` in NPM). We'll use this in Chapter 8 to get our application and all of its dependencies deployed on Cloud Foundry. For now, however, using a *package.json* file simply has the advantage that it simplifies installation. Specifically, we can now install all dependencies by typing the following command on our guest machine:

```
vagrant $ cd app
vagrant $ npm install
```

Interacting with Redis in Our Code

On your host machine, use your text editor to open the *tweet_counter.js* file that we created in the previous chapter. It should be contained in the *Twitter* directory of your *app* folder. If you worked through the examples and the problems, your code is probably a little more in-depth than mine. Either way, you'll want to follow my lead and modify your code so it imports and uses the `redis` module:

```
var ntwitter = require("ntwitter"),
    redis = require("redis"), // require the redis module
    credentials = require("./credentials.json"),
    redisClient,
    twitter,
    // declare a counts objects to store the counts
    counts = {};

twitter = ntwitter(credentials);

// create a client to connect to Redis
redisClient = redis.createClient();

// initialize our counters
counts.awesome = 0;

twitter.stream(
    "statuses/filter",
    { track: ["awesome", "cool", "rad", "gnarly", "groovy"] },
    function(stream) {
        stream.on("data", function(tweet) {
            if (tweet.text.indexOf("awesome") > -1) {
                // increment the key on the client
                redisClient.incr("awesome");
```

```
                    counts.awesome = counts.awesome + 1;
                }
            });
        }
    );

    module.exports = counts;
```

We use the incr function just like we did with the interactive Redis client. In fact, we can use any of the Redis commands in exactly the same way—the client exposes a function with the same name as the command.

We can run this code in the usual way. Let it run for a bit—it should be keeping track of the number of tweets containing the word "awesome" in Redis, and if we kept our setInterval code in there, we should see it printing out the values periodically. Once we're satisfied that it has seen some tweets, we can verify that the counts are stored in Redis by stopping the program (with Ctrl-C) and then reconnecting with the redis-cli program. Once there, we can use the get command to see the stored value of the awesome key:

```
vagrant $ redis-cli
redis 127.0.0.1:6379> get awesome
(integer) "349"
```

 If, at any time, you want to clear out the Redis data store, you can type **flushall** at the redis-cli prompt.

Initializing the Counts from the Redis Store

At this point, we're storing the data while the program is running, but when we restart our server, we're still reinitializing the counts object with 0. To completely solve our problem, we want to make it so our tweet counter gets initialized with the data that we've stored in Redis. We can use the get command to get the values before we start the stream. Like most things in Node, however, the get function is asynchronous, so we have to handle it a little carefully:

```
var ntwitter = require("ntwitter"),
    redis = require("redis"), // require the redis module
    credentials = require("./credentials.json"),
    redisClient,
    counts = {},
    twitter;

twitter = ntwitter(credentials);
```

```
redisClient = redis.createClient();

// the callback gets two arguments
redisClient.get("awesome", function (err, awesomeCount) {
    // check to make sure there's no error
    if (err !== null) {
        console.log("ERROR: " + err);

        // exit the function
        return;
    }

    // initialize our counter to the integer version
    // of the value stored in Redis, or 0 if it's not
    // set
    counts.awesome = parseInt(awesomeCount,10) || 0;

    twitter.stream(
        "statuses/filter",
        { track: ["awesome", "cool", "rad", "gnarly", "groovy"] },
        function(stream) {
            stream.on("data", function(tweet) {
                if (tweet.text.indexOf("awesome") > -1) {
                    // increment the key on the client
                    redisClient.incr("awesome");
                    counts.awesome = counts.awesome + 1;
                }
            });
        }
    );
});

module.exports = counts;
```

You'll notice that the callback for get accepts two parameters: err and awesomeCount. The err parameter represents an error condition and will be set to an error object if there's any kind of problem with the request. If there is no problem with the request, it will be set to null. Typically when we make a request to our data store, the first thing that we'll do on the response is check for the error and handle it in some way. In the preceding case, we just print it out to let us know that there's some sort of problem, but you'll definitely want to handle errors more gracefully if your apps end up in production.

Next, you'll see that we have to do some processing of the awesomeCount value. That's because Redis stores all values as strings, so we have to convert the value to a number to do arithmetic operations on it in JavaScript. In this case, we use the global parseInt function, which extracts the number value from the string that Redis returns. The second parameter to parseInt is called the *radix*, and it means that we want the base-10 value of the number. If the value is not a number, parseInt returns the value NaN, which stands for—you guessed it—*Not a Number*.

Remember that || refers to JavaScript's *or* operator. This operator will return the first value in a list of values that are not *falsy*, which refers to values like `false` or 0 or `NaN`. If all the values are falsy, this operator will return the last one.

Essentially this line of code translates to "use the `awesomeCount` value if it is defined, otherwise use 0." This lets us initialize our code to 0 when awesome is not defined with a single line of code. At this point, you will probably want to generalize the code for all of the words that we're tracking, but it's helpful to learn one more Redis command first.

Using mget to Get Multiple Values

The `get` command is great for a single key-value pair, but what happens if we want to request the value associated with multiple keys? That's almost as easy using the `mget` function. We can generalize our code as follows:

```
redisClient.mget(["awesome", "cool"], function (err, results) {
    if (err !== null) {
        console.log("ERROR: " + err);
        return;
    }

    counts.awesome = parseInt(results[0], 10) || 0;
    counts.cool = parseInt(results[1], 10) || 0;
}
```

Using `mget`, we should be able to generalize this code to work for all of the words that we're tracking.

Redis is great for simple data that can be stored as strings. This includes data that is stored as JSON objects. But if we want a little more control over our JSON data it's better to use a data store that is designed with JSON in mind. MongoDB is a perfect example of such a data store.

MongoDB

MongoDB (or Mongo, for short) is a database that allows us to store data on disk, but not in a relational format. Instead, Mongo is a document-oriented database that conceptually allows us to store objects organized as *collections* in the JSON format. (Technically, MongoDB stores its data in the BSON format, but from our perspective we can think of it as JSON.) In addition, it allows us to interact with it completely in JavaScript!

Mongo can be used for more complex data storage needs, such as storing user accounts or comments in blog posts. It can even be used to store binary data like images! In our case, Mongo is perfect for storing Amazerrific to-do objects independently of our server.

Interacting with the MongoDB Command-Line Client

Like Redis, Mongo offers a command-line client that allows us to directly interact with the data store. You can fire up the Mongo client by typing **mongo** at the command line of your guest machine:

```
vagrant $ mongo
MongoDB shell version: 2.4.7
connecting to: test
>
```

 You may see some start-up warnings when Mongo first launches, but that's totally normal.

One immediate difference between Redis and Mongo is that we can interact with it using using JavaScript! For example, here we create a variable called `card` and store an object in it:

```
> var card = { "rank":"ace", "suit":"clubs" };
> card
{ "rank" : "ace", "suit" : "clubs" }
>
```

Likewise, we can create and manipulate arrays. Notice that in this example, we don't complete our JavaScript statement before the end of each line. When we press Enter, Mongo responds with three dots letting us know that the previous statement was incomplete. Mongo will automatically execute the first full JavaScript statement:

```
> var clubs = [];
> ["two", "three", "four", "five"].forEach(
... function (rank) {
...     clubs.push( { "rank":rank, "suit":"clubs" } )
... });
> clubs
[
    {
        "rank" : "two",
        "suit" : "clubs"
    },
    {
        "rank" : "three",
        "suit" : "clubs"
    },
    {
        "rank" : "four",
        "suit" : "clubs"
    },
```

```
    {
        "rank" : "five",
        "suit" : "clubs"
    }
]
```

In other words, the Mongo command-line client works a little bit like the JavaScript console in Chrome. But those similarities end when we want to start storing data. Mongo organizes data as *documents*, which we can think of as JSON objects. It stores *collections* of documents in *databases*. We can see the databases in our MongoDB by using the show dbs command:

```
> show dbs
local     0.03125GB
```

The local db is always there. We can switch to a different database with the use command:

```
> use test
switched to db test
```

Once we've selected a database to use, we can access it through the db object. We can save objects to a collection by calling the save function on the collection. If the collection doesn't already exist, Mongo will create it for us. Here, we save the card that we created earlier in our collection:

```
> show collections;
> db.cards.save(card);
> show collections;
cards
system.indexes
```

You'll see that the cards collection doesn't exist before we save an object to it. We can use the collection's find function with no arguments to see what documents are stored:

```
> db.cards.find();
{ "_id" : ObjectId("526ddeea7ba2be67c95558d8"),"rank":"ace","suit":"clubs" }
```

In addition to rank and suit properties, a card also has an _id associated with it. For the most part, every document in a MongoDB collection has one of these associated with it.

In addition to saving a single item, we can also add multiple documents to the collection in one call to save. Here we do that with the clubs array that we created previously:

```
> db.cards.save(clubs);
> db.cards.find();
{ "_id" : ObjectId("526ddeea7ba2be67c95558d8"),"rank":"ace","suit":"clubs" }
{ "_id" : ObjectId("526ddeea7ba2be67c95558d9"),"rank":"two","suit":"clubs" }
{ "_id" : ObjectId("526ddeea7ba2be67c95558da"),"rank":"three","suit":"clubs" }
{ "_id" : ObjectId("526ddeea7ba2be67c95558db"),"rank":"four","suit":"clubs" }
{ "_id" : ObjectId("526ddeea7ba2be67c95558dc"),"rank":"five","suit":"clubs" }
```

We can also add more objects to the db:

```
>hearts = [];
> ["two", "three", "four", "five"].
... forEach(function (rank)
... { hearts.push( { "rank":rank, "suit":"hearts" } )
... });
> db.cards.save(hearts);
> db.cards.find();
{ "_id" : ObjectId("526ddeea7ba2be67c95558d8"),"rank":"ace","suit":"clubs" }
{ "_id" : ObjectId("526ddeea7ba2be67c95558d9"),"rank":"two","suit":"clubs" }
{ "_id" : ObjectId("526ddeea7ba2be67c95558da"),"rank":"three","suit":"clubs" }
{ "_id" : ObjectId("526ddeea7ba2be67c95558db"),"rank":"four","suit":"clubs" }
{ "_id" : ObjectId("526ddeea7ba2be67c95558dc"),"rank":"five","suit":"clubs" }
{ "_id" : ObjectId("526ddf0f7ba2be67c95558de"),"rank":"two","suit":"hearts" }
{ "_id" : ObjectId("526ddf0f7ba2be67c95558df"),"rank":"three","suit":"hearts" }
{ "_id" : ObjectId("526ddf0f7ba2be67c95558e0"),"rank":"four","suit":"hearts" }
{ "_id" : ObjectId("526ddf0f7ba2be67c95558e1"),"rank":"five","suit":"hearts" }
```

Once we have enough varying documents in our collection, we can retrieve them by creating *queries* from JSON objects that represent the properties of the documents we want to retrieve. For example, we can retrieve all card documents with a rank of two and store them in a variable called twos:

```
> var twos = db.cards.find({"rank":"two"});
> twos
{ "_id" : ObjectId("526ddeea7ba2be67c95558d9"),"rank":"two","suit":"clubs" }
{ "_id" : ObjectId("526ddf0f7ba2be67c95558de"),"rank":"two","suit":"hearts" }
```

Or we can select all the aces:

```
> var aces = db.cards.find({"rank":"ace"});
> aces
{ "_id" : ObjectId("526ddeea7ba2be67c95558d8"),"rank":"ace","suit":"clubs" }
```

We can also remove the elements from the collection by calling the remove method and sending in a query:

```
> db.cards.remove({"rank":"two"});
> db.cards.find();
{ "_id" : ObjectId("526ddeea7ba2be67c95558da"),"rank":"three","suit":"clubs" }
{ "_id" : ObjectId("526ddeea7ba2be67c95558db"),"rank":"four","suit":"clubs" }
{ "_id" : ObjectId("526ddeea7ba2be67c95558dc"),"rank":"five","suit":"clubs" }
{ "_id" : ObjectId("526ddf0f7ba2be67c95558df"),"rank":"three","suit":"hearts" }
{ "_id" : ObjectId("526ddf0f7ba2be67c95558e0"),"rank":"four","suit":"hearts" }
{ "_id" : ObjectId("526ddf0f7ba2be67c95558e1"),"rank":"five","suit":"hearts" }
```

Or we can remove all of the documents from the collection by calling remove with an empty query:

```
> db.cards.remove();
> db.cards.find();
>
```

Similar to Redis, MongoDB offers an interactive MongoDB tutorial (*http://try.mongodb.org*), as shown in Figure 7-2, that you can try out in your web browser. I encourage you to work your way through this tutorial to learn a little more about Mongo's functionality and types of queries that are available.

Figure 7-2. The home page of the interactive MongoDB tutorial

In the end, however, we won't use many of the default Mongo commands in Node.js. Instead, we'll model our data as objects using a Node.js module called Mongoose.

Modeling Data with Mongoose

Mongoose is a Node.js module that serves two primary purposes. First of all, it works as a client for MongoDB in the same way that the node-redis module works as a client for Redis. But Mongoose also serves as a *data modeling* tool, which allows us to represent documents as objects in our programs. In this section, we'll learn the basics of data modeling and use Mongoose to create a data model for our Amazeriffic ToDos.

Models

A *data model* is simply an object representation of a collection of documents in a data store. In addition to specifying the fields that are in every document of a collection, it adds MongoDB database operations like *save* and *find* to the associated objects.

In Mongoose, a data model consists of a *schema*, which describes the structure of all of the objects that are of that type. For instance, suppose we wanted to create a data model for a collection of playing cards. We'd start by specifying the schema for a card—namely, explicitly declaring that every card has a rank and a suit. In our JavaScript file, this looks something like the following:

```
var CardSchema = mongoose.Schema({
    "rank" : String,
    "suit" : String
});
```

Once we create the schema, building a model is very easy. By convention, we use a capital letter for data model objects:

```
var Card = mongoose.model("Card", CardSchema);
```

Schemas can get more complicated. For example, we might build a schema for blog posts that contain dates and comments. In this example, the comments attribute represents an array of strings instead of a single one:

```
var BlogPostSchema = mongoose.Schema({
    title: String,
    body : String,
    date : Date,
    comments : [ String ]
});
```

What does a model do for us? Once we have a model, we can create an object of the model type very easily using JavaScript's new operator. For example, this line of code creates the ace of spades and stores it in a variable called c1:

```
var c1 = new Card({"rank":"ace", "suit":"spades"});
```

Great, but couldn't we have just as easily done that with this code?

```
var c2 = { "rank":"ace", "suit":"spades" };
```

The difference is that the Mongoose object allows us to interact with the database through some built-in functions!

```
// save this card to our data store
c1.save(function (err) {
    if (err !== null) {
        // object was not saved!
        console.log(err);
    } else {
        console.log("the object was saved!");
    }
});
```

We can also interact directly with the model to pull items out of the database using the find function that's part of the data model. Like the find function in the interactive

MongoDB client, this function takes in an arbitrary MongoDB query. The difference is that it restricts itself to the types that are defined by the model:

```
Card.find({}, function (err, cards) {
    if (err !== null) {
        console.log("ERROR: " + err);
        // return from the function
        return;
    }

    // if we get here, there was no error
    cards.forEach(function (card) {
        // this will print all of the cards in the database
        console.log (card.rank + " of " + card.suit);
    });
});
```

We can also update elements by finding the appropriate one (via its _id or another query) and saving it again. For instance, suppose we wanted to change all of the cards that have the suit hearts to the suit spades:

```
Card.find({"suit" : " hearts"}, function (err, cards) {
    cards.forEach(function (card) {
        // update the card to spades
        card.suit = "spades";

        // save the updated card
        card.save(function (err) {
            if (err) {
                // object was not saved
                console.log(err);
            }
        });
    });
});
```

Last but not least, we can remove elements from the database by calling the remove function on the data model:

```
Card.remove({ "rank":"ace", "suit":"spades" }, function (err) {
    if (err !== null) {
        // object was not successfully removed!
        console.log(err);
    }
});
```

At this point, we've seen examples of the four major data store operations using Mongoose: create, read, update, and delete. But at this point, we haven't actually seen Mongoose in an app yet! We'll see that now.

Storing Amazeriffic ToDos

To start, we can copy our current version of Amazeriffic with the client and the server to our *Chapter7* directory. We'll need to set up a *package.json* file that includes Mongoose as a dependency:

```
{
    "name": "amazeriffic",
    "description": "The best to-do list app in the history of the world",
    "version": "0.0.1",
    "dependencies": {
        "mongoose": "3.6.x"
    }
}
```

Once we do that, we can run npm install to install the mongoose module. We can then add code to *server.js* to import the module:

```
var express = require("express"),
    http = require("http"),
    // import the mongoose library
    mongoose = require("mongoose"),
    app = express();

app.use(express.static(__dirname + "/client"));
app.use(express.urlencoded());

// connect to the amazeriffic data store in mongo
mongoose.connect('mongodb://localhost/amazeriffic');
```

Next, we'll define our schema and subsequently our model for our to-do list items in our server code:

```
// This is our mongoose model for todos
var ToDoSchema = mongoose.Schema({
    description: String,
    tags: [ String ]
});

var ToDo = mongoose.model("ToDo", ToDoSchema);

// now we listen for requests
http.createServer(app).listen(3000);
```

We can update our todo get route to get the to-do items out of the database and return them:

```
app.get("/todos.json", function (req, res) {
    ToDo.find({}, function (err, toDos) {
        // don't forget to check for errors!
        res.json(toDos);
    });
});
```

Last but not least, we'll update our post route to add an element to the database. This is a little interesting, because in order to maintain compatibility with the client we modified in Chapter 2, we'll want to return an entire list of to-do items:

```
app.post("/todos", function (req, res) {
    console.log(req.body);
    var newToDo = new ToDo({"description":req.body.description,
                            "tags":req.body.tags});
    newToDo.save(function (err, result) {
        if (err !== null) {
            console.log(err);
            res.send("ERROR");
        } else {
            // our client expects *all* of the todo items to be returned,
            //   so we do an additional request to maintain compatibility
            ToDo.find({}, function (err, result) {
                if (err !== null) {
                    // the element did not get saved!
                    res.send("ERROR");
                }
                res.json(result);
            });
        }
    });
});
```

Now we can run our server and connect through our browser. Keep in mind that we didn't initialize our collection with any ToDos, so we'll need to add elements before we see any to-do items show up in our app.

Summary

In this chapter, we learned how to store data independently of our application. We saw two data storage solutions that can be considered examples of NoSQL databases—Redis and MongoDB.

Redis is a key-value store. It offers a fast, flexible solution for storing simple data. The node-redis module allows us to interact with Redis in almost the same way we interact with Redis from the command line.

MongoDB is a more robust data storage solution that organizes databases into collections. As users of the database, we can think of it as storing data as JavaScript objects. Additionally, the command-line interface for Mongo can be used as a basic JavaScript interpreter that allows us to interact with our collections.

Mongoose is a Node.js module that allows us to interact with MongoDB, but it also allows us to build data models. In addition to specifying what all elements in a collection of data must look like, data models allow us to interact with the database through objects in our program.

More Practice and Further Reading

Poker API

If you followed along with the practice sections in the previous chapters, you've built a poker API that will accept poker hands and return the type of hand (e.g., a pair, a full house). It would be interesting to add code to your Express server that stores the result of every hand and their type in Redis or Mongo. In other words, make it so your app keeps track of every valid hand that is posted to your API along with the result. Don't track the items that result in an error.

If you do that, you can set up a `get` route that responds with a JSON object that includes all of the posted hands. You may even want to make it so the `get` route returns only the five most recent hands.

If you want to make this example *really* interesting, try to find a library of playing card images, and have your client show images of the cards in the posted hand instead of the JSON objects or a text description. To do this, you can create an *images* subdirectory in the client part of your application and store the images there.

Other Database References

Database is a huge topic, worthy of several books' worth of material. If you want to learn more about web app development and programming in general, it's pretty essential that you eventually try to obtain a background in relational databases and SQL.

Coursera (*http://www.coursera.org*) is a great place to take free, online classes in topics such as databases. In fact, it has a self-study course in databases taught by Jennifer Widom of Stanford University!

If you prefer books, Jennifer Widom is a coauthor (along with Hector Garcia-Molina and Jeffrey Ullman) of *Database Systems: The Complete Book* (Prentice Hall, 2008). It definitely follows a more academic approach to the topic, but I think it's an excellent, readable introduction.

Another great book that covers different types of databases (including NoSQL databases) is *Seven Databases in Seven Weeks* by Eric Redmond and Jim Wilson (Pragmatic Bookshelf, 2012). In addition to covering Mongo and Redis, it also describes popular options such as PostgreSQL and Riak. It does a great job of describing the pros and cons of each database, along with various use cases.

## CHAPTER 8

The Platform

At this point, we roughly know how to build a web application using client- and server-side technologies, but our application is not going to see much use if it's only running on our computer. The next piece of the puzzle is sharing our application by getting it up and running on the Web.

In the past, making this happen required a tremendous amount of work—we'd have to purchase server space with a fixed IP address, install and configure the required software, purchase a domain name, and then point the domain name to our application. Fortunately, times have changed and these days there is a category of hosting services called *Platforms-as-a-Service* (PaaS) that takes care of the hard work for us.

You may have heard the term *cloud computing*; this related concept is based around the idea that low-level details of software maintenance and computation can and should be moved off of local computers and onto the Web. With a PaaS, we don't need to know any of the details of web-server management and configuration, and can focus more on just getting our applications to work correctly. In other words, a PaaS is the type of technology that the cloud computing model enables.

In this chapter, we'll learn how to deploy our web applications on an open source PaaS called Cloud Foundry. Although we'll focus on Cloud Foundry, most of the concepts that we'll learn can be generalized to other PaaS services like Heroku or Nodejitsu.

Cloud Foundry

Cloud Foundry is an open source PaaS originally developed by VMware. You can read more about the service on its home page, located at *http://run.pivotal.io* and shown in Figure 8-1. It offers a free 60-day trial that you can use to get some of the sample apps in this book deployed.

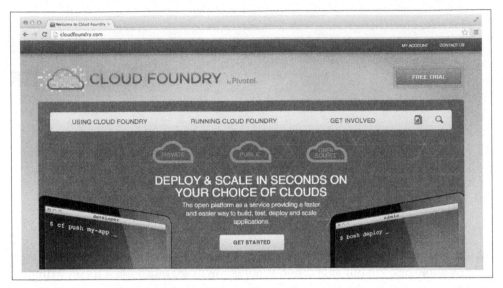

Figure 8-1. The Cloud Foundry (run.pivotal.io) home page

Creating an Account

To start, you'll need to create an account on *http://run.pivotal.io*. You can access the 60-day free trial by clicking the link in the upper-right corner and typing in your email address. You will get a response with information on how to set up your account.

Getting Your App Ready for Deployment

To deploy applications, you'll need a tool appropriately called `cf`. Installing that on your local machine requires you to first set up the Ruby language and the RubyGems package manager. I've also included the `cf` app as part of the `node-dev-bootstrap` project, so you'll be able to deploy directly from your guest machine without any additional setup!

To get started, set up a *Chapter8* directory by recloning the `node-dev-bootstrap` project as you did in the previous two chapters. Once you do that, start your guest machine and SSH into it.

We'll start by deploying the basic *server.js* program that comes with `node-dev-bootstrap`, but before we can do that we'll need to do two things. First, we'll need to add a *package.json* file because Cloud Foundry expects that file in all apps that we're going to deploy. Because our default server app doesn't depend on any external Node.js modules, it's very short:

```
{
    "name":"sp_example",
    "description": "My first Cloud Foundry app!"
}
```

Next, we'll need to make a minor modification to the default *server.js* file that's included with the node-dev-bootstrap project. This change involves the port number on which our server listens: for technical reasons, Cloud Foundry has to assign us a port number for our code to listen on, but we often won't know that port until our code is running. Fortunately, Cloud Foundry delivers the port number to us via an *environment variable* called PORT. We can access it through the process.env.PORT variable in our Node.js program:

```
var http = require("http"),
    // if the environment PORT is set up,
    // listen on that one, otherwise listen
    // on port 3000
    port = process.env.PORT || 3000;

var server = http.createServer(function (req, res) {
    res.writeHead(200, {"Content-Type": "text/plain"});
    res.end("Hello from Cloud Foundry!");
});

server.listen(port);
console.log("Server listening on port " + port);
```

Once again, we see the || idiom that was introduced in Chapter 7. Basically, this code says the following: if process.env.PORT is defined, use it; otherwise, use 3000. This lets us set up our port number so that our application works correctly on both our guest machine and when we get it deployed on Cloud Foundry.

Deploying Our App

At this point, we should be able to run it on our virtual machine and access it from our browser as we have in the past. And now that we've created a *package.json* file and set up our app to listen on the correct port, we are also ready to deploy it to Cloud Foundry.

As I mentioned before, that requires us to use the cf program, which is already installed on our guest machine. So to start, enter the directory that contains the *server.js* file on your guest machine.

The Cloud Foundry platform API is located at *api.run.pivotal.io*. So we start by telling cf where our target Cloud Foundry platform is located using the target subcommand:

```
vagrant $ cf target api.run.pivotal.io
Setting target to https://api.run.pivotal.io... OK
```

Next, we'll log in with the `login` subcommand and type in our credentials as we set them up when we created our Cloud Foundry account. Upon logging in, `cf` will ask which deployment space we want to use. I typically use the *development* space when I'm experimenting:

```
vagrant $ cf login
target: https://api.run.pivotal.io

Email> me@semmy.me

Password> ************

Authenticating... OK
1: development
2: production
3: staging
Space> 1

Switching to space development... OK
```

If everything has gone smoothly, our next step is to push our app to Cloud Foundry! How can we do that? It's as easy as using the `push` subcommand. Along with the push subcommand, we'll need to include the command that launches our app:

```
vagrant $ cf push --command "node server.js"
```

The push subcommand enters us into a dialogue with Cloud Foundry. It will ask us a few questions about our application and the environment we'll use. Here is the dialogue I had with Cloud Foundry—yours should look similar for this example:

```
Name> sp_example

Instances> 1

1: 128M
2: 256M
3: 512M
4: 1G
Memory Limit> 256M

Creating sp_example... OK

1: sp_example
2: none
Subdomain> sp_example

1: cfapps.io
2: none
Domain> cfapps.io

Creating route sp_example.cfapps.io... OK
Binding sp_example.cfapps.io to sp_example... OK
```

```
Create services for application?> n

Save configuration?> n

Uploading sp_example... OK
Preparing to start sp_example... OK
-----> Downloaded app package (4.0K)
-----> Resolving engine versions

       WARNING: No version of Node.js specified in package.json, see:
       https://devcenter.heroku.com/articles/nodejs-versions

       Using Node.js version: 0.10.21
       Using npm version: 1.2.30
-----> Fetching Node.js binaries
-----> Vendoring node into slug
-----> Installing dependencies with npm
       npm WARN package.json sp_example@ No repository field.
       npm WARN package.json sp_example@ No readme data.
       Dependencies installed
-----> Building runtime environment
-----> Uploading droplet (15M)
Checking status of app 'sp_example'...
  1 of 1 instances running (1 running)
Push successful! App 'sp_example' available at sp_example.cfapps.io
```

 The name of your app has to be unique among all names on that
domain. That means if you name your app something like *example*, it's likely that you'll get a failure when you try to deploy. I attempt to avoid that issue by adding my initials and an underscore to
the beginning of my name. This doesn't always work, so you may
have to find other approaches to generating unique app names.

If everything went smoothly, your app is actually running on the Web now! We can
confirm this by opening up a web browser and navigating to the URL that cf gave us
(in my case, it's *http://sp_example.cfapps.io*). Once you do that, you should see a response
from your app.

Getting Information About Your Apps

Now that your app is up and running, you can use other subcommands of cf to get
information about the status of your applications. For example, you use the apps subcommand to get a list of all of your applications on Cloud Foundry and their statuses:

```
vagrant $ cf apps
name          status    usage      url
sp_example    running   1 x 256M   sp_example.cfapps.io
```

One major issue with running your application on a PaaS is that you can't see the results of your `console.log` statements as easily as you can when running your application locally. This can be a major problem if your program crashes and you need to determine why. Fortunately, Cloud Foundry offers the `logs` subcommand that you can use on your running apps to view your program's logs:

```
vagrant $ cf logs sp_example
Getting logs for sp_example #0... OK

Reading logs/env.log... OK
TMPDIR=/home/vcap/tmp
VCAP_APP_PORT=61749
USER=vcap
VCAP_APPLICATION= { ... }
PATH=/home/vcap/app/bin:/home/vcap/app/node_modules/.bin:/bin:/usr/bin
PWD=/home/vcap
VCAP_SERVICES={}
SHLVL=1
HOME=/home/vcap/app
PORT=61749
VCAP_APP_HOST=0.0.0.0
MEMORY_LIMIT=256m
_=/usr/bin/env

Reading logs/staging_task.log... OK
-----> Downloaded app package (4.0K)
-----> Resolving engine versions

       WARNING: No version of Node.js specified in package.json, see:
       https://devcenter.heroku.com/articles/nodejs-versions

       Using Node.js version: 0.10.21
       Using npm version: 1.2.30
-----> Fetching Node.js binaries
-----> Vendoring node into slug
-----> Installing dependencies with npm
       npm WARN package.json sp_example@ No repository field.
       npm WARN package.json sp_example@ No readme data.
       Dependencies installed
-----> Building runtime environment

Reading logs/stderr.log... OK

Reading logs/stdout.log... OK
Server listening on port 61749
```

You'll see that Cloud Foundry prints the contents of four logs that are stored. The first is *env.log*, which has all of your environment variables that you can access via the `process.env` variable in your program. The second is *staging_task.log*, which logs everything that happens when your program first starts (you'll note that this is the same content that is printed out when you first run `cf push`. The last two are *stderr.log* and *stdout.log.* You'll see that *stdout.log* includes the `console.log` statement that you used in your program. If you use `console.err` instead, your message will appear in *stderr.log.*

Updating Your App

You can easily send a newer version of your app to Cloud Foundry by pushing it again. Modify your *server.json* so that it returns a little more information:

```
var http = require("http"),
    port = process.env.PORT || 3000;

var server = http.createServer(function (req, res) {
    res.writeHead(200, {"Content-Type": "text/plain"});
    res.write("The server is running on port " + port);
    res.end("Hello from Cloud Foundry!");
});

server.listen(port);
console.log("Server listening on port " + port);
```

Once you make that change, you can run the `push` subcommand again along with the name of the app you'd like to update. This will push the new changes without requiring you to answer all of the questions again:

```
vagrant $ cf push sp_example
Save configuration?> n

Uploading sp_example... OK
Stopping sp_example... OK

Preparing to start sp_example... OK
-----> Downloaded app package (4.0K)
-----> Downloaded app buildpack cache (4.0K)
-----> Resolving engine versions

       WARNING: No version of Node.js specified in package.json, see:
       https://devcenter.heroku.com/articles/nodejs-versions

       Using Node.js version: 0.10.21
       Using npm version: 1.2.30
-----> Fetching Node.js binaries
-----> Vendoring node into slug
-----> Installing dependencies with npm
       npm WARN package.json sp_example@ No repository field.
       npm WARN package.json sp_example@ No readme data.
       Dependencies installed
-----> Building runtime environment
-----> Uploading droplet (15M)
Checking status of app 'sp_example'...
  1 of 1 instances running (1 running)
Push successful! App 'sp_example' available at sp_example.cfapps.io
```

Deleting Apps from Cloud Foundry

Occasionally, we'll want to delete apps from Cloud Foundry, particularly when we're just experimenting. To do that, we can use the `delete` subcommand:

```
vagrant $ cf delete sp_example
Really delete sp_example?> y

Deleting sp_example... OK
```

Dependencies and package.json

In previous examples, our apps have had external dependencies like the `express`, `redis`, `mongoose`, and `ntwitter` modules. Using basic modules that don't connect to external services (like `express` and `ntwitter`) is pretty straightforward. Because we typically don't push our *node_modules* directory, we simply need to make sure that all of our dependencies are listed in our *package.json* file.

For example, consider one of our first Express apps. After some minor modifications that get it listening on the correct Cloud Foundry port, it looks like this:

```
var express = require("express"),
    http = require("http"),
    app = express(),
    port = process.env.PORT || 3000;;


http.createServer(app).listen(port);
console.log("Express is listening on port " + port);

app.get("/hello", function (req, res) {
    res.send("Hello World!");
});

app.get("/goodbye", function (req, res) {
    res.send("Goodbye World!");
});
```

We'll need to include our Express module dependency in our *package.json* file, which we can do exactly as we did in our previous *package.json* example:

```
{
    "name": "sp_express",
    "description": "a sample Express app",
    "dependencies": {
        "express": "3.4.x"
    }
}
```

You'll see that I specified that our app depends on the Express module, specifically any version number that starts with 3.4 (the x is a wildcard). This tells Cloud Foundry which version to install to make our app run correctly. Once we've included dependencies in our *package.json* file, we can push this to Cloud Foundry using the same command we used before:

```
vagrant $ ~/app$ cf push --command "node server.js"
Name> sp_expressexample
```

Once we do that, we can go to *http://sp_expressexample.cfapps.io/hello* or *http://sp_expressexample.cfapps.io/goodbye* to see our app respond!

Getting our Twitter app or our Amazeriffic app working is a little more challenging because they are dependent on other data storage services—specifically Redis and MongoDB. That means we'll need to create the services and then set up our app to use them.

Binding Redis to Your App

When we run our app on our virtual machine, services like Redis and MongoDB are running locally. That changes a little when we run our app on a PaaS. Sometimes the services run on the same host, but other times they are run on another hosting service.

Either way, you'll need to start by setting up the service that you want to run in your interactions with cf. In this section, we'll set up Redis on Cloud Foundry and then get our tweet counter app connecting to it.

We'll start by copying our Twitter app from Chapter 7 to our *Chapter8/app* directory. Make sure your *package.json* file exists and includes the redis and ntwitter dependencies. Mine looks like this:

```
{
    "name": "tweet_counter",
    "description": "tweet counter example for learning web app development",
    "dependencies": {
        "ntwitter":"0.5.x",
        "redis":"0.9.x"
    }
}
```

We'll also want to update *server.js* so that it listens on the port specified in process.env.PORT. Once we do that, we can try to push our app! I'll go ahead and mention ahead of time that this will fail, but it'll give us the opportunity to set up our Redis service:

```
vagrant $ cf push --command "node server.js"
Name> sp_tweetcounter

Instances> 1
```

```
1: 128M
2: 256M
3: 512M
4: 1G
Memory Limit> 256M

Creating sp_tweetcounter... OK

1: sp_tweetcounter
2: none
Subdomain> sp_tweetcounter

1: cfapps.io
2: none
Domain> cfapps.io

Binding sp_tweetcounter.cfapps.io to sp_tweetcounter... OK

Create services for application?> y

1: blazemeter n/a, via blazemeter
2: cleardb n/a, via cleardb
3: cloudamqp n/a, via cloudamqp
4: elephantsql n/a, via elephantsql
5: loadimpact n/a, via loadimpact
6: mongolab n/a, via mongolab
7: newrelic n/a, via newrelic
8: rediscloud n/a, via garantiadata
9: sendgrid n/a, via sendgrid
10: treasuredata n/a, via treasuredata
11: user-provided , via
```

Notice that here we have told Cloud Foundry that we'd like to create a service for our application:

```
What kind?> 8
Name?> rediscloud-dfc38

1: 20mb: Lifetime Free Tier
Which plan?> 1

Creating service rediscloud-dfc38... OK
Binding rediscloud-dfc38 to sp_tweetcounter... OK
Create another service?> n

Bind other services to application?> n

Save configuration?> n
```

Finish out the dialog and you'll find that your push will fail. That's because we haven't told our app how to connect to the external Redis service yet. The logs should clue us in to that. In fact, when running cf logs sp_tweetcounter, I should see something like the following in my *logs/stderr.log*:

```
Reading logs/stderr.log... OK

events.js:72
        throw er; // Unhandled 'error' event
        ^
Error: Redis connection to 127.0.0.1:6379 failed - connect ECONNREFUSED
    at RedisClient.on_error (/home/vcap/app/node_modules/redis/index.js:189:24)
    at Socket.<anonymous> (/home/vcap/app/node_modules/redis/index.js:95:14)
    at Socket.EventEmitter.emit (events.js:95:17)
    at net.js:441:14
    at process._tickCallback (node.js:415:13)
```

In our app, we don't send any arguments to Redis, so it attempts to connect on the local server (127.0.0.1), along with the default port number (6379). We need to tell it to connect to the Redis cloud service on the host and port that Cloud Foundry provides for us. Where does Cloud Foundry give us that information? Just like the port number, it gives us information about our bound services in the process.env variable!

If you've already typed cf logs sp_tweetcounter, you can scroll up to see the environment variables and look at the contents of the VCAP_SERVICES variable. In the logs, it's one long JSON string, so I've formatted it here to look a little more readable:

```
VCAP_SERVICES = {
    "rediscloud-n/a": [{
        "name": "rediscloud-dfc38",
        "label": "rediscloud-n/a",
        "tags": ["redis", "key-value"],
        "plan": "20mb",
        "credentials": {
            "port": "18496",
            "hostname": "pub-redis-18496.us-east-1-4.2.ec2.garantiadata.com",
            "password": "REDACTED"
        }
    }]
}
```

It includes all of the information that we need to connect to a remote Redis service, including a URL, a port, and a password. If we were so inclined, we could easily code these Redis credentials directly into our program. But it's probably better to do it programmatically in the same way that we set up the port number.

 One minor gotcha is that the VCAP_SERVICES environment variable is stored as a string, so we have to use the JSON.parse command in the same way that we did in Chapter 5 to convert it into an object that we can access like any other JavaScript object.

In short, we can get Redis working by modifying the first part of our *tweet_counter.js* module to look like this:

```
var ntwitter = require("ntwitter"),
    redis = require("redis"), // require the redis module
    credentials = require("./credentials.json"),
    redisClient,
    counts = {},
    twitter,
    services,
    redisCredentials;


// create our twitter client
twitter = ntwitter(credentials);

// set up our services if the environment variable exists
if (process.env.VCAP_SERVICES) {
    // parse the JSON string
    services = JSON.parse(process.env.VCAP_SERVICES);
    redisCredentials = services["rediscloud-n/a"][0].credentials;
} else {
    // otherwise we'll set up default values
    redisCredentials = {
        "hostname": "127.0.0.1",
        "port": "6379",
        "password": null
    };
}

// create a client to connect to Redis
client = redis.createClient(redisCredentials.port, redisCredentials.hostname);

// authenticate
client.auth(redisCredentials.password);
```

In this code snippet, we're checking to see if the VCAP_SERVICES environment variable exists, and if it does we're parsing the string associated with it to produce a JavaScript object from the JSON representation. Next, we're pulling out the credentials associated with the rediscloud-n/a property of the services object. That object is itself an array (because our app could be associated with multiple Redis instances) so we're getting the first element out of the array.

If the VCAP_SERVICES environment variable is not defined, we're setting up a redisCredentials object that has the default values. After that, we're connecting to Redis by specifying the port and hostname, and then we're sending along the password. If we're connected to the local Redis instance on our virtual machine, we send null for the password because it doesn't require us to authenticate.

If we've already pushed the app once and it failed, we can simply push it again to update it. This time, I'll push it using the name that I gave it previously. If I've forgotten it, I can always use cf apps to see a list of my apps.

```
vagrant $ cf apps
Getting applications in development... OK

name                    status    usage       url
sp_example              running   1 x 256M    sp_example.cfapps.io
sp_express              running   1 x 256M    sp_express.cfapps.io
sp_tweetcounter         running   1 x 256M    sp_tweetcounter.cfapps.io
vagrant $ cf push sp_tweetcounter
```

If everything is set up properly, you'll see the app successfully pushed and you should be able to access it at the URL that Cloud Foundry gives you!

Binding MongoDB to Your App

Getting MongoDB up and running in Cloud Foundry is almost as easy as getting Redis running. Let's start by copying our Amazeriffic app from *Chapter7* into our current directory. We'll have to make a few modifications that follow the same pattern as before.

First, we'll change it so it listens on process.env.PORT if that value exists. The code for that is identical to the examples in the preceding section.

After that, we'll need to get our MongoDB credentials out of process.env.VCAP_SERV ICES. That code will look very similar to the Redis code. The main difference is that our MongoDB credentials are all contained in a single string—the uri:

```
// don't forget to declare mongoUrl somewhere above

// set up our services
if (process.env.VCAP_SERVICES) {
    services = JSON.parse(process.env.VCAP_SERVICES);
    mongoUrl = services["mongolab-n/a"][0].credentials.uri;
} else {
    // we use this when we're not running on Cloud Foundry
    mongoUrl = "mongodb://localhost/amazeriffic"
}
```

Once we get that working, we can push our app to Cloud Foundry as we have before. One minor change is that we'll need to set up the MongoLab service:

```
Create services for application?> y

1: blazemeter n/a, via blazemeter
2: cleardb n/a, via cleardb
3: cloudamqp n/a, via cloudamqp
4: elephantsql n/a, via elephantsql
5: loadimpact n/a, via loadimpact
6: mongolab n/a, via mongolab
```

```
 7: newrelic n/a, via newrelic
 8: rediscloud n/a, via garantiadata
 9: sendgrid n/a, via sendgrid
10: treasuredata n/a, via treasuredata
11: user-provided , via
What kind?> 6

Name?> mongolab-8a0f4

1: sandbox: 0.5 GB
Which plan?> 1

Creating service mongolab-8a0f4... OK
```

Once the Mongo service is created, we simply bind it to our application like we did with Redis. As long as our code is ready to connect to the remote service via the URL that is provided to us by the VCAP_SERVICES environment variable, our program should launch exactly as we'd expect.

Summary

In this chapter, we learned how to use Cloud Foundry to get our applications on the Web. Cloud Foundry is an example of a *Platform as a Service*. A PaaS is a cloud computing technology that abstracts server setup, administration, and hosting, usually through a command-line program or a web interface.

To get our applications running on Cloud Foundry (or any other PaaS), we typically have to make some minor modifications to the code so that it behaves differently depending on whether we're running it locally in our development environment or in production on Cloud Foundry's servers.

Cloud Foundry provides external services like Redis and MongoDB as well. To get our applications running with these services, it is necessary for us to both *create* the service with the cf program, and then *bind* our application to it.

More Practice and Further Reading

Poker API

In the practice sections of the previous chapters, we created a simple poker API that would determine poker hands. In the last chapter, we added a database component to that application. If you have that working, try modifying it and getting it deployed on Cloud Foundry.

Other Platforms

There is no shortage of cloud platforms these days. One of the most popular ones is Heroku (*http://heroku.com*). It allows you to sign up for free without a credit card. If you want to add Redis or Mongo, however, you'll be required to provide one even though they have free tiers for both of these services.

If you want more practice, try reading Heroku's Node.js deployment documentation and getting one or more of our apps deployed on its service. I would also encourage you to try others, including Nodejitsu (*http://nodejitsu.com*) and Microsoft's Windows Azure (*http://windowsazure.com*). They are all a little different, so comparing and contrasting the features of each is a great learning exercise.

## CHAPTER 9

The Application

If you've made it this far in our journey, you should be able to make things happen on both the client and the server using HTML, CSS, and JavaScript. And if you have an idea for a web application, you can most likely use what you've learned to cobble some code together to do what you need it to do.

This chapter is mostly about why you shouldn't do that, at least not yet. David Parnas once said that "one bad programmer can easily create two new jobs a year." While I think this is true, in my experience "bad" programmers aren't inherently bad, but rather they just lack the experience and wisdom to think about the organization and maintainability of their codebase. Code (especially JavaScript) can quickly become an unmaintainable mess in the hands of an inexperienced programmer.

As I mentioned in the preface, as a beginner it's completely acceptable to hack code together while you're learning, but as you continue on you'll quickly find that it's not the best way to handle larger, more complex engineering problems. In other words, there is still (and will always be) much to learn.

On the other hand, software engineers have been building database-driven web applications for many years now so it's probably inevitable that some basic patterns have emerged that inform better code design. In fact, entire development frameworks, such as Ruby on Rails, have been engineered to *force* (or at least *strongly encourage*) developers to build applications using some of these patterns. As we end our journey through the basics, we'll revisit Amazeriffic and attempt to understand how we can make our current code more maintainable. We'll also see how some of our code can be modified to fit these patterns.

Refactoring Our Client

We'll start with our client code. In my experience, the client is one of the easier places for our code to become unmaintainable. I think that this can be attributed to the fact that client-side code is often associated with seemingly simple visual actions, and therefore it *feels* like it should be very easy to implement. For example, executing a specific behavior when a user performs a trivial action such as clicking a button seems like it *should* be a trivial coding task. But that's not always the case.

In our example, creating a tabbed user interface seems like it should be relatively straightforward. And for our use case it was. But we can make it much more maintainable by doing a tiny bit of refactoring and following some basic advice.

Generalizing Meaningful Concepts

You should always try to generalize meaningfully related concepts as much as possible. As I have mentioned a few times in this book, when entities in our program are related, it's best if they are concretely related through real programming constructs. Our tabs don't follow this advice: they have a lot in common, but the logic and structure is spread out in several places. For example, we define the name of the tab in the HTML:

```
<div class="tabs">
  <a href=""><span class="active">Newest</span></a>
  <a href=""><span>Oldest</span></a>
  <a href=""><span>Tags</span></a>
  <a href=""><span>Add</span></a>
</div>
```

And in the JavaScript, we use the tab's location in the DOM to determine what action to take:

```
if ($element.parent().is(":nth-child(1)")) {
    // generate the 'Newest' tab content
} else if ($element.parent().is(":nth-child(2)")) {
    // generate the 'Oldest' tab content
} else if ($element.parent().is(":nth-child(3)")) {
    // generate the 'Tags' tab content
} else if ($element.parent().is(":nth-child(4)")) {
    // generate the 'Add' tab content
}
```

Notice that we never actually associate a tab name with an action. This is an example of two programming entities that are related, but only in the programmer's mind—not through any code construct. A very basic symptom of this is that every time we add a tab to our user interface, we have to modify both the HTML and JavaScript. In Chapter 5, I pointed out that this makes our code error prone.

How can we improve this? One course of action is to generalize a tab as an object, just as we did with the card example in Chapter 5. The difference is that the tab object will have a string value associated with the name of the tab, and a function value associated with the action that creates the tab's content. For example, we can generalize our "Newest" tab as an object like this:

```
var newestTab = {
    // the name of this tab
    "name":"Newest",

    // the function that generates this tab's content
    "content": function () {
        var $content;

        // generate the "Newest" tab's content and return it
        $content = $("<ul>");
        for (i = toDos.length-1; i >= 0; i--) {
            $content.append($("<li>").text(toDos[i]));
        }

        return $content;
    }
}
```

It turns out that once we have this structure, we've actually solved most of the problem. Our user interface consists of a set of tabs, so instead of having our tab name and the corresponding action stored in separate places in our code, we can create an array of tab objects that keeps them together:

```
var main = function (toDoObjects) {
    "use strict";

    var toDos,
        tabs;

    toDos = toDoObjects.map(function (toDo) {
        return toDo.description;
    });

    // create an empty array of tabs
    tabs = [];

    // add the 'Newest' tab
    tabs.push({
        "name":"Newest",
        "content":function () {
            // create 'Newest' $content
            return $content;
        }
    });

    // add the 'Oldest' tab
    tabs.push({
        "name":"Oldest",
        "content":function () {
            // create 'Oldest' $content
            return $content;
        }
```

```
    });

    // add the 'Tags' tab
    tabs.push({
        "name":"Tags",
        "content":function () {
            // create 'Tags' $content
            return $content;
        }
    });

    // add the 'Add' tab
    tabs.push({
        "name":"Add",
        "content":function () {
            // create 'Add' $content
            return $content;
        }
    });
};
```

Once we have the array that stores the tab objects, we can greatly simplify our approach to building the UI. We'll start by removing the tabs from the HTML altogether (but leaving the div):

```
<div class="tabs">
  <!-- this is where our tabs used to be defined      -->
  <!-- we'll dynamically build them in the JavaScript -->
</div>
```

Next, we can loop over our tabs array. For each one we'll set up our click handler and add the tab to the DOM:

```
tabs.forEach(function (tab) {
    var $aElement = $("<a>").attr("href",""),
        $spanElement = $("<span>").text(tab.name);

    $aElement.append($spanElement);

    $spanElement.on("click", function () {
        var $content;

        $(".tabs a span").removeClass("active");
        $spanElement.addClass("active");
        $("main .content").empty();

        // here we get the content from the
        // function we defined in the tab object
        $content = tab.content();

        $("main .content").append($content);
        return false;
    });
```

```
    // add aElement to the tabs
    $("main .tabs").append($aElement);
});
```

AJAXifying Our Tabs

Another issue that our application has right now is that if someone visits it from another browser and adds a to-do item to our list, we won't see that new to-do item if we click a different tab. Instead, we actually need to reload the entire page to see the update.

This is because our application is storing and loading the to-do items when the page is first loaded and not changing them until the page is loaded again. To solve this problem, we'll make it so that each tab does an AJAX request when it is loaded. We can do that by wrapping our action in calls to jQuery's get function:

```
tabs.push({
    "name":"Newest",
    "content":function () {
        $.get("todos.json", function (toDoObjects) {
            // create 'Newest' $content

            // we can no longer 'return' $content
        });
    }
});
```

 Another solution is to make our program issue real-time updates to the client, meaning that when another user updates the page we're looking at, the server pushes the new data to us. That's a bit beyond the scope of this book, but it is possible with a Node.js module called *socket.io*.

Note that this changes the way our functions behave because now we'll be doing an asynchronous request inside our function call. This means that this code will no longer correctly return the content to the caller because we'll have to wait until the AJAX call completes:

```
$content = tab.content();
$("main .content").append($content);
```

We have a couple of options that will fix this. The easiest is to move the DOM update into the content function itself:

```
tabs.push({
    "name":"Newest",
    "content":function () {
        $.get("todos.json", function (toDoObjects) {
            // create 'Newest' $content
```

```
        // update the DOM here
        $("main .content").append($content);
    });
  }
});
```

I don't like this approach for two reasons. The first is more of an aesthetic reason: the content function should create and return the content of the tab—it shouldn't affect the DOM. Otherwise we should call it `getContentAndUpdateTheDOM`.

The second reason is probably a little more important: if we want to do more than just update the DOM at the end, we'll need to add that logic to every `content` function for every tab.

One solution to both of these problems is to implement the continuation approach that we've used in the past for asynchronous operations. To achieve this, we'll let the calling function include a callback as a parameter, and call that function inside our `content` function:

```
// we create our content function
// so that it accepts a callback
tabs.push({
    "name":"Newest",
    "content":function (callback) {
        $.get("todos.json", function (toDoObjects) {
            // create 'Newest' $content

            // call the callback with the $content
            callback($content);
        });
    }
});

// ...

// now inside our calling function, we send a callback
tab.content(function ($content) {
    $("main .content").append($content);
});
```

This solution is probably the most common approach that you'll find in the Node.js community, but other approaches are becoming popular, including Promises and Reactive JavaScript. If your asynchronous operations start getting complicated and you find yourself in (what's commonly referred to as) *callback hell*, you may want to explore these options.

Ridding Ourselves of Hacks

Now that we have each tab *AJAXified*, we can get rid of a compatibility hack that's been hanging around. Previously, we made our server return the entire list of ToDo objects because that's what our client expected whenever an add was done. Now, instead of doing that, we'll jump back to the Newest tab whenever a ToDo object gets added.

Our add tab button handler code currently looks something like this:

```
$button.on("click", function () {
    var description = $input.val(),
        tags = $tagInput.val().split(","),
        newToDo = {"description":description, "tags":tags};

    $.post("todos", newToDo, function (result) {
        // here is some leftover cruft from when we were
        // maintaining all the ToDo items on the client
        toDoObjects = result;

        // update client toDos
        toDos = toDoObjects.map(function (toDo) {
            return toDo.description;
        });

        $input.val("");
        $tagInput.val("");
    });
});
```

In actuality, we don't need to maintain the ToDos on the client anymore, so we can get rid of the majority of this. In fact, all we really need to do once the new ToDo is successfully posted is to clear out the input boxes and then *redirect* to the Newest tab. This will do our AJAX request and will order the result by the newest item.

We can use the `trigger` jQuery function to trigger the click event on the Newest tab, and our code ends up looking something like this:

```
$button.on("click", function () {
    var description = $input.val(),
        tags = $tagInput.val().split(","),
        newToDo = {"description":description, "tags":tags};

    $.post("todos", newToDo, function (result) {
        // clear out our input boxes
        $input.val("");
        $tagInput.val("");

        // 'click' on the Newest tab
        $(".tabs a:first span").trigger("click");
    });
});
```

This little change also allows us to greatly simplify the server-side code that creates a new ToDo object on a post:

```
app.post("/todos", function (req, res) {
    var newToDo = new ToDo({"description":req.body.description,
                            "tags":req.body.tags});
    newToDo.save(function (err, result) {
        console.log(result);
        if (err !== null) {
            // the element did not get saved!
            console.log(err);
            res.json(err);
        } else {
            res.json(result);
        }
    });
};
```

Handling AJAX Errors

We've largely ignored the problem of error handling in all of our code so far, but once you start writing larger-scale apps, you'll find that thinking about errors is essential. There are times when your client code will be loaded, but the server will become unavailable (or crash inadvertently). What happens then?

In a lot of cases our error conditions will mean that our callbacks won't be called correctly. When this happens it will look like the application is not responding. Worse, our code might respond by adding ToDos on the client but they won't get added to the data store correctly. This can cause our users to lose data they think is successfully added.

Fortunately, jQuery allows us to account for this scenario pretty easily using the `fail` function, which can be chained from an AJAX call. This is an example of a promise-type API that was alluded to in the previous section, but we're not going to go into much detail about what that means. I think that the best way to handle this situation is to follow the pattern we've seen in both the Mongoose and Redis modules for Node.js. We'll let our calling code send in a callback that accepts an error and the actual data, and let the callback handle the error if it's not set to `null`:

```
// we create our content function
// so that it accepts a callback
tabs.push({
    "name":"Newest",
    "content":function (callback) {
        $.get("todos.json", function (toDoObjects) {
            // create 'Newest' $content

            // call the callback with the error
            // set to null and the $content as
            // the second argument
```

```
            callback(null, $content);
    }).fail(function (jqXHR, textStatus, error) {
        // in this case, we'll send the error along
        // with null for the $content
        callback(error, null);
    });
    }
});
```

The `fail` function's callback accepts three arguments. The error is the one that we're most interested in and is the one that we'll pass to the calling function's callback.

Now in our calling function's callback, we'll handle the error just like we did in our Redis and Mongoose examples:

```
tab.content(function (err, $content) {
    if (err !== null) {
        alert("Whoops, there was a problem with your request: " + err);
    } else {
        $("main .content").append($content);
    }
});
```

We can test this behavior by changing the route in our call to `get` into a nonexistent one (other than *todos.json*). The error message in that case should be "Not Found."

Refactoring Our Server

We've seen a few tips on refactoring our client code. We can easily apply these same tips, but there are additional considerations on the server. In this section, we'll learn to organize our server code using the *Model-View-Controller* design pattern.

Code Organization

Right now, our server-side code is all in one file, *server.js*. That's not too complex for a small application such as ours, but as our application grows and includes other entities other than ToDo objects, this can get overwhelming quickly. So let's break things up a little.

Separating concerns: models

We'll start by moving the Mongoose model definition out of *server.js* and organizing it into an independent Node.js module. I like to put the model definitions in their own directory, because as my app grows, the number of models that I'm creating will grow as well. So we'll create a file called *todo.js* in a directory called *models* that lives inside our *Amazeriffic* directory. Inside that file, we'll define my model just as we did before and we'll export it:

```
var mongoose = require("mongoose");

// This is our mongoose model for todos
var ToDoSchema = mongoose.Schema({
    description: String,
    tags: [ String ]
});

var ToDo = mongoose.model("ToDo", ToDoSchema);

module.exports = ToDo;
```

Now we can `require` the module in *server.js* and remove the `ToDo` code contained in the file:

```
var express = require("express"),
    http = require("http"),
    mongoose = require("mongoose"),
    // import our ToDo model
    ToDo  = require("./models/todo.js"),
    app = express();
```

If we run our server now, everything should work exactly like it did before.

Separating concerns: controllers

Moving the models into their own directory allows us to more easily keep a clean separation of responsibility in our program. We know that when we need to change the way our `ToDo` data is stored in our database, we can edit the *todo.js* file in our *models* directory. Similarly, when we need to change the way our program responds to requests from the client, we'll edit an associated *controller* file.

Currently, when our `get` and `post` requests come into our Express server, we're responding with anonymous functions. Let's give those anonymous functions names and move them into a separate module. This module will consist of a single controller object that has a set of *actions* that get triggered via our Express routes. In the case of our `ToDo` objects, we'll create two actions: `index` and `create`.

To this end, we'll create a directory called *controllers* that lives next to our *models* directory, and in that directory, we'll create a file called *todos_controller.js*. Inside that module, we'll import our `ToDo` model and create a `ToDosController` object. We'll attach functions that do the same things the anonymous functions were doing in our *server.js* file:

```
// note that this needs to start up one
// directory to find our models directory
var ToDo = require("../models/todo.js"),
    ToDosController = {};

ToDosController.index = function (req, res) {
```

```
        ToDo.find({}, function (err, toDos) {
            res.json(toDos);
        });
    };

    ToDosController.create =  function (req, res) {
        var newToDo = new ToDo({"description":req.body.description,
                                "tags":req.body.tags});
        newToDo.save(function (err, result) {
            console.log(result);
            if (err !== null) {
                // the element did not get saved!
                console.log(err);
                res.json(500, err);
            } else {
                res.json(200, result);
            }
        });
    };

    module.exports = ToDosController;
```

Like we did with our model, we'll import it into our *server.js* code using `require`. Once we do that, we'll update our route actions to point to these functions instead of having anonymous functions. Note that because we no longer have to access the ToDo model in *server.js*, we've removed the `require` statement for the model:

```
var express = require("express"),
    http = require("http"),
    mongoose = require("mongoose"),
    // import our ToDo controller
    ToDosController = require("./controllers/todos_controller.js"),
    app = express();

    // other setup/Cloud Foundry/mongoose code here ...

    // routes
    app.get("/todos.json", ToDosController.index);
    app.post("/todos", ToDosController.create);
```

Now our code is a little more organized and more maintainable because we've separated our concerns. Our *server.js* file mostly handles setting up the basics of the server and routing, our controller handles actions that need to happen when a request arrives, and our model handles the issues involved with the database. This separation of concerns makes it much easier to maintain our code as it grows, and it also makes it very easy to map HTTP requests from our client to actions on our server.

HTTP Verbs, CRUD, and REST

In Chapter 6 we briefly discussed the HTTP protocol. In subsequent sections we learned that we can make two types of HTTP requests: GET requests and POST requests. Those correspond to `get` and `post` routes in our Express server, which, in turn, correspond to actions that we've set up in our controller. It turns out that HTTP also has two other verbs that we haven't used yet: PUT and DELETE. These four verbs map pretty nicely to the CRUD data-store operations we learned about in Chapter 7 (see Table 9-1)!

Table 9-1. HTTP/CRUD/controller mappings

HTTP	CRUD	Action	Behavior
POST	Create	`create`	Create a new object and return its ID
GET	Read	`show`	Return an object with a given ID
PUT	Update	`update`	Update an object with a given ID
DELETE	Delete	`destroy`	Delete an object with a given ID

This mapping allows us to create APIs that create a clean and simple interface to resources that are available on our server. APIs that behave in this way are typically referred to as *RESTful* web APIs. REST stands for *Representational State Transfer*, and—roughly speaking—it's an idea that describes how resources on web servers should be exposed via the HTTP protocol.

Setting Up Routes by ID

One nice feature that Express offers us is the ability to create variables in our routes. This allows us to create a single rule that responds to an entire set of requests. For instance, suppose we wanted to be able to get a single to-do item by its associated MongoDB ID:

```
// routes
app.get("/todos.json", ToDosController.index);

// basic CRUD routes
app.get("/todos/:id", ToDosController.show);
app.post("/todos", ToDosController.create);
```

Here, we've created our `get` route that maps to a single to-do item. It maps to the `show` function in our controller. Notice that the route uses a colon (:) to create a variable. This will allow the route to respond to *any* route that starts off with */todos/*. So if we set our browser to */todos/helloworld*, this will send the request to our controller's `show` action. It's the controller's action that is responsible for finding the element with an ID of `helloworld`.

How can we access the variable that gets sent to the controller? It turns out that the request object keeps track of these in its `params` property. Our code for the action might look something like this, where we query the model and return the response. If we don't find the ID, we return a string that says "Not Found":

```
ToDosController.show = function (req, res) {
    // this is the id that gets sent to the URL
    var id = req.params.id;

    // find the ToDo item with the associated id
    ToDo.find({"_id":id}, function (err, todo) {
        if (err !== null) {
            res.json(err);
        } else {
            if (todo.length > 0) {
                res.json(todo[0]);
            } else {
                res.send("Not Found");
            }
        }
    });
};
```

Assuming we've already inserted some to-do items in our database, we can check to see if this is working by firing up the MongoDB client from the command line and getting out an ID:

```
vagrant $ mongo
MongoDB shell version: 2.4.7
connecting to: test
> show dbs
amazeriffic      0.0625GB
local            0.03125GB
> use amazeriffic
switched to db amazeriffic
> show collections
system.indexes
todos
> db.todos.find()
{ "description" : "first", "_id" : ObjectId("5275643e0cff128714000001"), ... }
{ "description" : "second", "_id" : ObjectId("52756de289f2f5f014000001"), ... }
{ "description" : "test", "_id" : ObjectId("5275722a8d735d0015000001"), ... }
{ "description" : "hello", "_id" : ObjectId("5275cbdcd408d04c15000001"), ... }
```

Now that we can see the _id field, we can run our server, open up Chrome, and try typing something like *http://localhost:3000/5275643e0cff128714000001* into the address bar. If everything works out, we should see the JSON returned from our server!

 If you type in an invalid Object ID (meaning a string that doesn't consist of 24 numbers or letters a through f), the preceding code will throw an error that says you've used an invalid ID. That's okay for now—we'll fix it in "More Practice and Further Reading" on page 271.

Using jQuery for put and delete Requests

In addition to making get and post requests, jQuery has the ability to perform put and delete requests via the general $.ajax function. In fact, we can also make get and post requests this way as well:

```
// PUT example with jQuery
// Here, we update the description of the ToDo
// object which has id 1234
$.ajax({
    "url" : "todos/1234",
    "type": "PUT",
    "data": {"description":"this is the new description"},
}).done(function (response) {
    // success!
}).fail(function (err) {
    // error!
});

// DELETE example with jQuery
// We delete the ToDo object which has id 1234
$.ajax({
    "url" : "todos/1234",
    "type": "DELETE",
}).done(function (response) {
    // success!
}).fail(function (err) {
    // error!
});
```

We can easily associate these actions with button-click events to update or delete objects in our database from the client. This is assuming we have the associated routes exposed on the server.

HTTP Response Codes

In addition to HTTP including a series of verbs that map nicely to our CRUD operations, it also defines a set of standard response codes that represent possible responses to an HTTP request. You may have tried to visit a nonexistent website or a page and received the infamous *404* error, which means the page is not found. It turns out that 404 is one of the response codes defined by the HTTP protocol.

Other HTTP response codes include 200, meaning that the request was successful, and 500, which represents a generic internal server error. Express lets us send these values back to a client along with the response value. So to make our show route a little more robust, we can include the appropriate HTTP response codes along with the data we're sending:

```
ToDosController.show = function (req, res) {
    // this is the id that gets sent to the URL
```

```
var id = req.params.id;

ToDo.find({"_id":id}, function (err, todo) {
    if (err !== null) {
        // we'll return an internal server error
        res.json(500, err);
    } else {
        if (todo.length > 0) {
            // we'll return success!
            res.json(200, todo[0]);
        } else {
            // we didn't find the todo with that id!
            res.send(404);
        }
    }
});
};
```

If you run your server now, and you type in an invalid Object ID, you should see that the Chrome browser automatically knows to respond with a "Not Found" message when it receives a 404 response code via HTTP.

Model-View-Controller

This brings us to one of the most important concepts in all of web application development—the Model-View-Controller (MVC) design pattern. This is an approach to application architecture that mostly dictates the design of a database-driven application, and it has become the de facto standard for writing web apps. The pattern is so widely accepted as the best way to write web applications that it has become entrenched in most popular web application frameworks.

We've already refactored our Amazeriffic code to fit this pattern, but it's a good idea to take a step back and understand the responsibility of each of the components and how the application fits together.

The *controller* is typically the simplest part of the three. When a web browser makes an HTTP request to the server, the router hands off the request to an associated controller action. The controller translates the request into an action, which usually coordinates a database action through the model and then sends (or renders) the response through a view. You can see this in the show action—the controller finds the to-do item with the requested ID (if one exists) and it generates the view (in this case the JSON) object to send in the response.

The *model* is the object abstraction of elements in our database. Fortunately, most frameworks include an object modeler like Mongoose. In Rails, the default one is called *Active Record* and behaves roughly the same way Mongoose does. In our case, the ToDo model consists entirely of a schema definition, but typically our model definition can include much more than that. For example, it may define relationships with other models, and specify functions that get fired when certain aspects of the model changes.

Last but not least is the *view* component. In our case, the view can be thought of as our client-side HTML and CSS. Our controller simply sends the data as JSON to the client and the client decides where to put it. Views can easily be much more interesting, however. For example, most MVC frameworks include server-side templates that allow the controller to construct the HTML at the time of the request. In the JavaScript/Node.js world, *Jade* and *EJS* are two commonly used HTML templating engines.

More generally speaking, the application works roughly like this: the client requests a resource via an HTTP verb and route. The *router* (in our case, *server.js*) decides which controller and action to send the request to. The controller then uses the request to interact with the model in some way and then decides how the view should be constructed. Once it does that, it responds to the request. Figure 9-1 sums it all up!

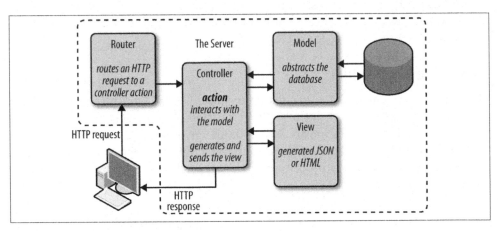

Figure 9-1. The Model-View-Controller pattern

Let's see this in action. We'll add users to our application so that each user can have their own set of ToDos.

Adding Users to Amazeriffic

At this point, Amazeriffic has exactly one entity: ToDo objects. That's fine if we're the only ones who want to keep track of ToDo objects, but we'll never build a billion dollar business that way. So what can we do if we want to let an arbitrary number of people use our app to keep track of their to-do list? It turns out that we'll need to add another entity to our application: users.

Building the User Model

We'll start by building a model for our users. The User model will consist of a string representing the username and the default MongoDB Object ID. We'll attach a user ID to the ToDo objects that are owned by that user, and we'll set up routes that only return the ToDo objects associated with the given user.

When using Mongoose, setting up a simple model like this is actually pretty easy. We'll create a file called *user.js* in our *models* directory. In that file, we'll build a schema and Mongoose model. And, as before, we'll export the Mongoose model to the Node.js program that uses it via a require statement:

```
var mongoose = require("mongoose");

// This is our mongoose model for users
var UserSchema = mongoose.Schema({
    username: String,
});

var User = mongoose.model("User", UserSchema);

module.exports = User;
```

It might make sense to include an array of ToDo objects as well, but we'll keep things simple for now. A bit later, we'll set up a relationship between the ToDo objects and the User objects.

Building the User Controller

Next, we can *stub out* our user controller. This means we create empty placeholder functions that we'll fill out later as we need them. We'll set up an action for each of the CRUD operations, along with an index action to return a list of all of the User objects:

```
var User = require("../models/user.js"),
    mongoose = require("mongoose");

var UsersController = {};

UsersController.index = function (req, res) {
    console.log("index action called");
    res.send(200);
};

// Show a User
UsersController.show = function (req, res) {
    console.log("show action called");
    res.send(200);
};

// Create a new user
```

```
UsersController.create = function (req, res) {
    console.log("create action called");
    res.send(200);
};

// Update an existing user
UsersController.update = function (req, res) {
    console.log("update action called");
    res.send(200);
};

// Delete an existing user
UsersController.destroy = function (req, res) {
    console.log("destroy action called");
    res.send(200);
};

module.exports = UsersController;
```

Hopefully, you can generalize these actions from the ToDosController example. In "More Practice and Further Reading" on page 271, you'll create a user interface that allows you to interact with the User model in the same way that we previously interacted with the ToDo model.

For now, however, we'll create an example user to work with in the following sections by adding the following code to the top of our user controller:

```
// This checks to see if a User already exists
User.find({}, function (err, result) {
    if (err !== null) {
        console.log("SOMETHING WENT HORRIBLY WRONG");
        console.log(err);
    } else if (result.length === 0) {
        console.log("Creating Example User...");
        var exampleUser = new User({"username":"semmy"});
        exampleUser.save(function (err, result) {
            if (err) {
                console.log(err);
            } else {
                console.log("Saved Example User");
            }
        });
    }
});
```

We'll use this sample user to test our routes. You can create other test or default users by following the same basic format.

Setting Up Routes

In this example, the routes are where things are going to get interesting. First of all, we can set up our basic HTTP/action mapping for our User model as we did before. Open up *server.js* and add the following basic routes that map HTTP requests to controller actions:

```
app.get("/users.json", usersController.index);
app.post("/users", usersController.create);
app.get("/users/:username", usersController.show);
app.put("/users/:username", usersController.update);
app.del("/users/:username", usersController.destroy);
```

 Notice that Express uses del instead of delete for HTTP DELETE requests. This is because delete has a different meaning in JavaScript.

Now we'd like to set up our app so we can have the routes and behaviors shown in Table 9-2.

Table 9-2. Routes/behaviors

Verb	Route	Behavior
GET	/users/semmy/	Show my Amazeriffic page
GET	/users/semmy/todos.json	Get all of my ToDos as an array
POST	/users/semmy/todos	Create a new ToDo for me
PUT	/users/semmy/todos/[id]	Update my ToDo with the given ID
DELETE	/users/semmy/todos/[id]	Delete my ToDo with the given ID

You'll see that the routes behave almost exactly the way our existing ToDo routes behave, with the exception that they are associated with a particular username. How can we make this happen with our existing code? We'll simply set up another set of routes that include the users/:username prefix, and we'll point those to our ToDosController actions:

```
app.get("/users/:username/todos.json", toDosController.index);
app.post("/users/:username/todos", toDosController.create);
app.put("/users/:username/todos/:id", toDosController.update);
app.del("/users/:username/todos/:id", toDosController.destroy);
```

Now that we have some basic routing set up we can start integrating our changes. First, we're going to want to send along our existing client-side *index.html* file when we request the user page instead of creating a different one. We can easily make this happen by modifying our show action. We want our show action to send a view for that user. Fortunately, the user's view will be the same as the default view, so we can simply send along our *index.html* file using the Express response's `sendfile` function:

```
UsersController.show = function (req, res) {
    console.log("show action called");
    // send the basic HTML file representing the view
    res.sendfile("./client/index.html");
};
```

If we run our server now and go to *localhost:3000/users/semmy/*, we should see the same interface that we saw previously, including whatever ToDo objects are currently in our data store. That's because we haven't gotten restricted to the subset of ToDos owned by a user yet.

But there's a problem. Open your browser and go to *localhost:3000/users/hello/*. We'll see the same thing, and *hello* is not actually a user! Instead, we want to return a 404 when the route points to an invalid user. We can do that by querying the user model against the username sent in as a parameter. So our show action will change to this:

```
UsersController.show = function (req, res) {
    console.log("show action called");
    User.find({"username":req.params.username}, function (err, result) {
        if (err) {
            console.log(err);
            res.send(500, err);
        } else if (result.length !== 0) {
            // we've found a user
            res.sendfile("./client/index.html");
        } else {
            // there is no user with that name,
            // so we send a 404
            res.send(404);
        }
    });
};
```

Now we should only get responses to this route when a valid user is requested.

Improving Our ToDo Controller Actions

Before we go any further, we need a way to tie our User model and our ToDo model together. To do this, we'll modify our ToDo model so that each ToDo object has an owner. The owner will be represented by an ObjectID in the ToDos collection, which will reference a user element in the Users collection. In classical database terms, this is roughly the same thing as adding a *foreign key* that relates a given table to a different table.

To set this up, we'll modify our ToDo model and schema to include the reference to the User model:

```
var mongoose = require("mongoose"),
    ToDoSchema,
    ObjectId = mongoose.Schema.Types.ObjectId;

ToDoSchema = mongoose.Schema({
    description: String,
    tags: [ String ],
    owner : { type: ObjectId, ref: "User" }
});

module.exports.ToDo = mongoose.model("ToDo", ToDoSchema);
```

When we create a ToDo object, we'll also include an owner or the value null if the owner doesn't exist (in the case that we add a ToDo from the default route, for example).

Next, we can start working on our ToDo controller actions so that they take into account the possibility that they can be called via a route associated with a username. To start with, we'll modify our index action so that it responds with a user's ToDos if the user is defined:

```
ToDosController.index = function (req, res) {
    var username = req.params.username || null,
        respondWithToDos;

    // a helper function that gets ToDos
    // based on a query
    respondWithToDos = function (query) {
        ToDo.find(query, function (err, toDos) {
            if (err !== null) {
                res.json(500,err);
            } else {
                res.json(200,toDos);
            }
        });
    };

    if (username !== null) {
        // get the todos associated with the username
        User.find({"username":username}, function (err, result) {
            if (err !== null) {
                res.json(500, err);
            } else if (result.length === 0) {
                // no user with that id found!
                res.send(404);
            } else {
                // respond with this user's todo objects
                respondWithToDos({ "owner" : result[0].id });
            }
        });
    } else {
        // respond with all todos
        respondWithToDos({});
```

```
        }
    };
```

Finally, we'll modify our `create` action so that it adds the user to the new ToDo if the user is defined:

```
ToDosController.create =  function (req, res) {
    var username = req.params.username || null,
        newToDo = new ToDo({"description":req.body.description,
                            "tags":req.body.tags});

    User.find({"username":username}, function (err, result) {
        if (err) {
            res.send(500);
        } else {
            if (result.length === 0) {
                // the user was not found, so we
                // just create an ownerless todo
                newToDo.owner = null;
            } else {
                // a user was found, so
                // we set the owner of this todo
                // with the user's id
                newToDo.owner = result[0]._id;
            }
            newToDo.save(function (err, result) {
                if (err !== null) {
                    res.json(500, err);
                } else {
                    res.json(200, result);
                }
            });
        }
    });
};
```

Here, you'll see that we are setting the `owner` to `null` if the user doesn't exist and we'll set the `owner` to the user's associated `_id` if they do exist. Now when we run our server, we should be able to visit a route for each test user we created and create ToDos associated with that user under their route. And if we go to the main page *localhost:3000*, we should see all ToDos for all users.

Summary

Writing a web application is not hard once you know how all the parts work. On the other hand, writing a *maintainable* web application requires some forethought and planning. Code maintainability in web applications is closely related to the idea of the separation of concerns of certain aspects of the application. In other words, a program should be made up of many small parts that do one thing and do one thing well. The interaction between these parts should be minimized as much as possible.

In this chapter, we saw a few basic tips on how to keep our client-side code clean and straightforward. One of the most essential parts of this is that we learned how to generalize meaningful concepts. This is closely related to the idea of *object-oriented programming*.

On the server side, there's a *design pattern* that dictates the structure of the code. The *Model-View-Controller* design pattern is an accepted practice for organizing maintainable client/server applications. The practice is so widely accepted that entire frameworks have been built that force developers to write applications using it. These frameworks include Ruby on Rails.

In the MVC pattern, the *model* abstracts the database using some sort of data modeling tool. In our examples, the *view* is simply the client portion of our application (the HTML, CSS, and client-side JavaScript). The *controller* maps requests from the view to actions on the model and responds with data that can be used to update the view.

Another common practice is to organize the server-side part of a web application as a *RESTful* web service. A RESTful web service exposes program resources (such as data models) to the client-side portion of the application through straightforward URLs. The client makes a request with a specific URL, some data, and an HTTP verb, which the application *router* maps to a controller action.

More Practice and Further Reading

Removing ToDos

One thing that we haven't set up yet is the ability to remove ToDos from the app. Fill in the destroy action in the ToDo controller so that it removes the ToDo with the specified ID. Next, we'll want to add the ability to remove the ToDo from the UI.

How can we do that? If we've defined our routes and actions correctly, we're returning the entire ToDo object from the todos.json route. Then we are only using the descrip tion field of our object to create the UI. We'll also want to use the _id field to build a remove link.

For instance, suppose our tab that lists out our ToDos looks like this:

```
"content":function (callback) {
    $.get("todos.json", function (toDoObjects) {
        var $content = $("<ul>");

        // create 'Oldest' $content
        toDoObjects.forEach(function (toDo) {
            $content.append($("<li>").text(todo.description));
```

```
        });

        // call the callback with the $content
        callback($content);
    });
}
```

Here, we're adding an li element for each ToDo object. Instead of just adding the text to the li, we want to include an a element that removes the item. For example, we would want our resulting DOM element to have HTML that looks like this:

```
<li>This is a ToDo item <a href="todos/5275643e0cff128714000001">remove</a></li>
```

We can do this by manipulating our $content object a bit:

```
var $todoListItem = $("<li>").text(todo.description),
    $todoRemoveLink = $("<a>").attr("href", "todos/"+todo._id);

// append the remove anchor
$todoListItem.append($todoRemoveLink)

$content.append($todoListItem);
```

Next, we can modify this to attach a click handler to the remove link:

```
var $todoListItem = $("<li>").text(todo.description),
    $todoRemoveLink = $("<a>").attr("href", "todos/"+todo._id);

$todoRemoveLink.on("click", function () {
    $.ajax({
        // call the delete HTTP request on the object

    }).done(function () {
        // once we successfully remove the item from
        // our app, we can remove this list item from
        // the DOM
    });

    // return false so we don't follow the link
    return false;
});

// append the remove anchor
$todoListItem.append($todoRemoveLink)

$content.append($todoListItem);
```

This is tricky to get working correctly, so plan to spend some time on it!

Adding a User Admin Page

So far, we don't have any way to add or remove users from our app. We'll create a users admin page that lists all of the users along with an input field that allows us to add a user to the app. This will require adding an additional page to our client, along with an additional JavaScript file for handling the UI for that page. For example, you might create a *users.html* file that imports a *users.js* file stored in our *javascripts* directory. You will probably reuse the majority of the CSS from your existing app, so it's okay to just link the *style.css* file in your *stylesheets* directory. There, you'll probably add a few custom styling elements.

Once you get all of that working, it might be interesting to add a button to each user that allows you to remove them from the app. This will, of course, trigger the `destroy` action on the user model. In addition to removing the user from the user collection, you'll want to also remove all the to-do items associated with that user in the action.

This is a little trickier than the remove problem, so try to get that one working first!

Views Using EJS and Jade

One major topic that I've left out of this treatment of MVC and Node.js is templating engines. That's not because I don't think they are useful or important. Instead, I was making an effort to keep the content a little more manageable and to give you more of an opportunity to work with client-side AJAX calls.

That being said, I encourage you to take some time to read about both Jade (*http://jade-lang.com*) and EJS (*http://embeddedjs.com*). They take very different approaches to generating HTML dynamically on the server-side, and they both integrate very nicely with Express.

Build Another App

We built a simple to-do list app. Try building another one from scratch. Try generalizing the ideas that you've learned and build another application. If you look at other tutorials, you'll often see examples involving blogging platforms or Twitter clones. Those are straightforward, manageable projects that will help you solidify the knowledge that you've gained from this book.

Ruby on Rails

One of my major goals with this book was to give readers enough background to start learning Ruby on Rails, one of the most popular web frameworks. At this point, I hope you have enough of a background to undertake Michael Hartl's Rails Tutorial (*http://ruby.railstutorial.org*). In this tutorial, he walks you through using test-driven development to build a simple Rails application. Many of the concepts that I presented here should carry over to his tutorial.

Index

We'd like to hear your suggestions for improving our indexes. Send email to index@oreilly.com.

block-style, 57
child elements, 34
definition of, 33
dynamic manipulation of, 104
first-child elements, 64
inline display of, 57
parent elements, 34
prepending vs. appending, 116
removing from the DOM, 116
styling with pseudoclasses, 62
stylistic elements, 40
void elements, 46
else statements, 123
Emacs text editor, 22
Enter key action, 107
Enter vs. Shift-Enter keys, 121
environment variable, 235
errors
    during Express module installation, 192
    HTTP response codes, 262
    identifying pre-install, 170
    identifying with Chrome Developer Tools,
        80, 105
    identifying with CSS Lint, 78
    identifying with HTML validation, 35
    identifying with JSHint, 209
    identifying with JSLint, 128
    invalid ID, 261
    null value, 153
even value, 102
event listeners, 103, 107
event-driven programming, 116
exploratory coding, 6
Express module
    API creation with, 212
    converting JSON into JavaScript object, 207
    Express server creation, 192
    importing into, 201
    installation of, 192
    overview of, 208
    sending information, 193
    specifying in Cloud Foundry, 240

F

fadeIn method, 108
fadeOut method, 116
falsy values, 222
files
    accessing external JSON, 155

app.js file, 98
associating external, 98
creating new, 14, 43
defining JSON objects in external, 154
displaying hidden, 13
leaving out of GIT repository, 197
loading time required, 98
overcoming access restriction, 156
saving vs. committing, 18
style.css file, 54
transferring between computers, 187
filesystem
    filename requirements, 5, 194, 237
    tree diagram mental model, 11
    Unix commands for, 8, 20
find function, 228
first-child elements, 64
first-class functions, 122
500 response code, 262
fixed-width design, 86
FizzBuzz problem, 143
Flickr
    getting images from, 160
    slideshow, 176
float property, 66–72
fonts, 72
footer (<footer>) tag, 45
for loops, 125
forEach loops, 127
404 error code, 262
Frequently Asked Questions (FAQ) page, 51
FTP (File Transfer Protocol), 187
function calls, chaining of, 104
functions
    attached to jQuery objects, 153
    first class, 122
    inputs/outputs, 122
    scheduling of, 117, 200
    testing pre-install, 170

G

get command, 217, 220
getJSON function, 157
Git
    -m (message) flag, 16
    branching, 23
    commands, 20
    configuring, 12
    git add command, 16

ls (List the Contents of the Current Directory) command, 13

M

-m (message) flag, 16
Mac OS
    file access in Chrome, 156
MacOS
    built-in SSH client, 184
    Git installation, 7
    global package installation in, 209
    Terminal program, 9
main (<main>) tag, 45
main global function, 99
maintainable web applications, 271
map data structures, 211, 215
map function, 165
margins, 57
markup validation, 35
    (see also errors)
max-width property, 89
media queries, 95
memorization
    tasks for development workflow, 21
    tasks for JavaScript/jQuery, 141
    tasks for splash page creation, 50
    tasks for splash page styling, 93
mental models
    client-server model, 187
    DOM tree diagrams, 34
    filesystem tree diagrams, 11
    hosts and guests, 188
    HTML tree diagrams, 50
metadata, 26
mget function, 222
Microsoft's Windows Azure, 247
min-width (minimum-width) property, 87
mkdir (make directory) command, 11
Model-View-Controller design pattern, 257, 263, 271
modules, 191, 201
MongoDB
    accessing databases in, 224
    additional reading/practice, 226
    benefits of, 222
    command-line interaction, 223
    JSON storage format of, 222
    modeling data with Mongoose, 226, 230
    overview of, 230

removing elements from collections in, 225
retrieving documents in, 225
saving multiple documents, 224
saving objects to collections in, 224
storage organization in, 224
switching databases in, 224
using with Cloud Foundry, 245

N

NaN (Not a Number) value, 221
navigation (<nav>) tag, 45
Node.js
    benefits of, 191
    communicating with Redis, 218
    development environment for, 181–186
    Express module, 191–195
    further practice/reading, 209
    http module, 191
    NPM (Node Package Manager), 191, 208, 219
    overview of, 208
    socket.io module, 253
Nodejitsu, 247
nonrelational database format, 216
NoSQL data stores, 216
not (!) operator, 124
nth-child pseudoclass, 102
null value, 153
numeric bullets, 32

O

object-oriented programming, 149, 271
objects
    adding variables to, 152
    benefits of, 153
    changing variables in, 151
    creation of, 150
    empty objects, 151, 152
    further practice/reading, 177
    JSON arrays of, 158
    null value for, 153
    object literals, 152, 154
    placeholders for, 153
    representing documents as, 226
    with functions attached, 153
odd value, 102
on pattern processing, 116
or (||) operator, 124, 222

V

Vagrant
  benefits of, 181
  building virtual machines with, 183
  in development process, 189
  installation of, 182
  overview of, 209
val method, 107
validation programs, 35, 210
  (see also errors)
variables
  $ character for jQuery objects, 104
  adding to objects, 152
  collections of, 149
  declaring with var keyword, 130
  environment variable, 235
  function variables, 153
  out-of-scope variables, 159
  possible data types in, 121
  process.env variable, 243
vboxheadless warning, 184
version control systems
  definition of, 7
  exploratory coding, 6
  Git commits, 16
  Git configuration, 12
  Git installation, 7
  Git repository history, 17
  Git repository initialization, 13
  Git repository status, 14
  in development process, 189
  saving vs. committing changes, 18
  Unix command-line basics, 8
Vim text editor, 16, 22
virtual machines
  benefits of, 188

building, 183
  connecting to with SSH, 184
  definition of, 181
  exiting, 186
  hosting of, 188
  removing, 187
VirtualBox
  installation of, 182
  Node Package Manager and, 192
  overview of, 209
visited pseudoclass, 62
void elements, 46

W

web application development
  additional resources, xiv
  code repository for, xiv
  code used in, xv
  prerequisites to learning, xiii
  teaching, xiv
  technology choices, xii
web browsers
  as developer tools, 19, 189
  overcoming security restrictions in, 156
  removing inconsistencies in, 76
  top-down page display in, 98
web fonts, 72
Windows
  file access in Chrome, 156
  Git Bash terminal simulator, 8
  global package installation in, 209
  manual SSH installation, 184
Windows Azure, 247
workflow (see development workflow)

About the Author

Semmy Purewal spent about a decade teaching computer science and working as a freelance JavaScript consultant. During that time, he worked with a diverse group of clients that included startups, nonprofits, and research labs. These days, he primarily works as a software engineer in San Jose, CA.

Colophon

The animals on the cover of *Learning Web App Development* are German Grey Heath (*Graue Gehörnte Heidschnucke*): long-haired, short-tailed sheep native to the northern hemisphere from Scotland to Siberia, and specifically in north Germany in a special area called the Luneburg Heath. Some breeds are classed as domestic species threatened with extinction, so their preservation is subsidized within the European Union.

The German Grey Heath's hair is greyish and very long, but too coarse for most textile applications; the wool is suitable for only coarsely woven fabrics such as carpets. Both sexes have horns, which curl back on themselves, and their meat is said to have a gamey flavor, which makes it popular to consume.

Sheep numbers dropped off by the turn of the 20th century and have been in decline ever since. During the 1990s, however, many small farms throughout Germany started breeding the sheep and saved the German Grey Heath from extinction. In fact, these animals are so celebrated that "Moorland Sheep Day" takes place every year on the second Thursday in July in a small village in Germany. Young rams are presented to breeders and onlookers, and the best animals are awarded prizes.

The cover image is from *Meyers Kleines Lexicon*. The cover fonts are URW Typewriter and Guardian Sans. The text font is Adobe Minion Pro; the heading font is Adobe Myriad Condensed; and the code font is Dalton Maag's Ubuntu Mono.

Have it your way.

Get even more for your money.

Join the O'Reilly Community, and register the O'Reilly books you own. It's free, and you'll get:

- $4.99 ebook upgrade offer
- 40% upgrade offer on O'Reilly print books
- Membership discounts on books and events
- Free lifetime updates to ebooks and videos
- Multiple ebook formats, DRM FREE
- Participation in the O'Reilly community
- Newsletters
- Account management
- 100% Satisfaction Guarantee

Signing up is easy:

1. Go to: oreilly.com/go/register
2. Create an O'Reilly login.
3. Provide your address.
4. Register your books.

Note: English-language books only

To order books online:
oreilly.com/store

For questions about products or an order:
orders@oreilly.com

To sign up to get topic-specific email announcements and/or news about upcoming books, conferences, special offers, and new technologies:
elists@oreilly.com

For technical questions about book content:
booktech@oreilly.com

To submit new book proposals to our editors:
proposals@oreilly.com

O'Reilly books are available in multiple DRM-free ebook formats. For more information:
oreilly.com/ebooks

CPSIA information can be obtained at www.ICGtesting.com
Printed in the USA
BVOW09s1527150315

391765BV00014B/46/P